ROAD RESEARCH

new research
on the role of alcohol and drugs
in road accidents

**A REPORT PREPARED
BY AN OECD ROAD RESEARCH GROUP**

SEPTEMBER 1978

ORGANISATION FOR ECONOMIC CO-OPERATION AND DEVELOPMENT

The Organisation for Economic Co-operation and Development (OECD) was set up under a Convention signed in Paris on 14th December 1960, which provides that the OECD shall promote policies designed:

- to achieve the highest sustainable economic growth and employment and a rising standard of living in Member countries, while maintaining financial stability, and thus to contribute to the development of the world economy;
- to contribute to sound economic expansion in Member as well as non-member countries in the process of economic development;
- to contribute to the expansion of world trade on a multilateral, non-discriminatory basis in accordance with international obligations.

The Members of OECD are Australia, Austria, Belgium, Canada, Denmark, Finland, France, the Federal Republic of Germany, Greece, Iceland, Ireland, Italy, Japan, Luxembourg, the Netherlands, New Zealand, Norway, Portugal, Spain, Sweden, Switzerland, Turkey, the United Kingdom and the United States.

The Road Research Programme has two main fields of activity:
- promotion of international co-operation in the field of research on road transport, the co-ordination of research facilities available in Member countries and the scientific interpretation of the results of joint experiments;
- International Road Research Documentation, a co-operative scheme for the systematic exchange of information on scientific literature and of current research programmes in Member countries.

The present programme is primarily concerned with defining the scientific and technological basis needed to assist governments of Member countries in decision-making on the most urgent road problems:
- development and evaluation of integrated urban and suburban transport strategies, taking into account economic, social, energy and environmental requirements;
- traffic control systems, both in urban and rural areas to optimise traffic operation and to enhance quality of service provided to road users;
- formulation, planning and implementation of common overall strategies for road safety;
- planning, design and maintenance of the total road infrastructure, taking account of economic, social and technical developments and needs.

*

* *

The Research Group on "New Research on Alcohol and Drugs" was created as a follow-up of earlier OECD activities in this field. Its aim was to exchange information and analyse research results on the drinking/driving problem (including roadside surveys and alcohol measuring equipment) and to prepare a state-of-the art review of the drug problem. The report was finalised at the Group's four meetings held between July 1975 and March 1977 at OECD headquarters. It reviews the research findings on alcohol, drugs and traffic safety which have been published since 1968, date of an earlier OECD publication, and in particular examines countermeasure programmes. There is a need for continuous international co-operation on this subject.

ABSTRACT

An OECD Road Research Group has examined the effects of alcohol and drugs on traffic safety and reviewed the effectiveness of accident countermeasures. Firstly, the report examines the general methodological approaches that thave been taken in research on alcohol and drugs in relation to driving in order to descern the limitations in the current knowledge in these areas. It then contains a study of the alcohol problem, its extent and nature, as well as the identification of the road user population at risk and the determination of the specific effects of alcohol on behaviour; emphasis is laid on the most recent research findings especially as regards the application of countermeasures. The aim of the subsequent chapter on drugs is to examine the kinds of substances that probably are important to road safety in terms both of the extent of consumption and of their appropriate information, education and rehabilitation programmes. Finally the report ends by suggesting a number of recommendations regarding the implementation in OECD countries of an epidemiological research programme with the aim of evaluating and controlling the alcohol and drug/driving problem as well as the development of more sensitive and practical assay techniques.

Investigations reveal that 80 to 90% of all traffic accidents are a direct result of human error. The term "human error", however, is often a misnomer for it does not satisfactorily describe the large number of injuries and deaths that occur on our roads as a result of driving while abilities to do so are impaired by alcohol and/or drugs.

In spite of a number of safety measures taken alcohol continues to plan a detrimental role in increasing a driver or pedestrian's chances of being involved in a traffic accident. Drugs, on the other hand, are creating a new dimension to the problem of impaired driving; while the assessment of the drug-driving interface is less advanced than it is for alcohol, it is evident that there is an increasing consumption of central nervous system active drugs in OECD countries and in increasing public concern about the role of drugs in traffic accidents.

The present report contains a state-of-the-art review of alcohol and drugs in relation to traffic safety examining the research results obtained since the publication of an earlier OECD Road Research report on this subject in 1968. The objectives were as follows:

(a) review existing scientific literature and other available information on the role of alcohol and drugs in traffic accidents;

(b) examine information related to impaired driving countermeasures and evaluate their effectiveness;

(c) identify the research results obtained on current practices proven successful that can be recommended for general and immediate application in Member countries;

(d) indicate priority needs for research in the fields of alcohol, drugs and traffic safety and outline possible future international co-operative activities.

In addition, the Research Group, who prepared the report, established a revised methodology to conduct national roadside surveys of drinking-driving behaviour and prepared a list of available equipment for measuring alcohol level in drivers.

Based on the fact that existing evidence indicates that alcohol is a major contributor to the cause of traffic accidents, whereas such evidence is not yet available for drugs, and based on the fact that countries are progressively developing more effective drinking-driving countermeasure programmes, the principal recommendation specifies that the major countermeasure activities continue to be focussed on efforts to resolve the alcohol problem in traffic safety.

The major task related to drug and traffic safety is the design of valid research studies to establish the extent and nature of drug use among drivers and pedestrians. The most urgent need in this area is the development of more sensitive and practical assay techniques.

TABLE OF CONTENTS

I

INTRODUCTION

I.1 Statement of the Problem

I.1.1 Alcohol

Accident statistics from OECD countries indicate that traffic accidents are the major cause of death among people under the age of forty. In the years between 1965 and 1973, fatalities and injuries in Member countries as a whole increased by approximately 17 percent to the point where over 160,000 people were killed and over five million were injured in motor vehicle accidents. Since 1973, however, the trend has reversed with fatality rates indicating à 15 percent reduction.

Traffic accidents are generally the result of a multiplicity of factors, and it is often the interaction of two or more variables that lead to the occurrence of an accident. Statements attributing accident causation to a specific variable, therefore, are often tenuous and subject to criticism. The repeated appearance of the presence of alcohol in drivers involved in traffic accidents, however, has led to the hypothesis that impairment is a major factor in predicting an individual's potential for being involved in a traffic accident. For example, a comparison between Blood Alcohol Concentration (BAC) data from non-accident involved drivers and from fatally injured drivers in Canada, reveals that the probability of an impaired driver being fatally injured, as compared to the non-drinking driver, is 17 times greater for the 30-34 year old, 39 times greater for drivers over 50 years of age, and 165 times greater for the 16 and 17 year old(*). The magnitude of the problem, however, varies between countries. The percentage of dead drivers with BAC's equal to or greater than 80 mg%(**) is 20 percent in France, 34 percent in England and Wales and approximately 45 percent in North America (see Chapter III).

In addition to drivers, there are other road users who are posing a problem with respect to the impairing effects of alcohol. Pedestrian fatality data from England/Wales and North America indicate that 20 to 33 percent of all pedestrians killed in traffic accidents have BAC's in excess of 80 mg%.

Operators of two-wheeled vehicles represent another potential problem group of road users. Unfortunately, the epidemiological evidence needed to assess the seriousness of alcohol problems among cyclists is extremely sparse. An OECD report on two-wheeled vehicles(2) has suggested, however, that for countries in which adult riders of two-wheelers (i.e. motorcyclists, bicyclists and moped operators) comprise a large part of the road user population, the role of alcohol be considered similar to that for car drivers.

(*)   See list of references at the end of this Chapter.

(**) The standard unit of reporting the BAC is milligrammes of alcohol per 100 millilitres of blood. Using this system 0.10 percent BAC w/v or $1.00^{0}/00$ w/v is reported as 100 mg%.

I.1.2 Drugs

During the last decade there has been increasing concern that drugs other than alcohol may be making a substantial contribution as a causative factor in motor vehicle accidents throughout the world. The role of drugs in traffic accidents is not as clearcut as in the case of alcohol. Studies indicate, however, that large quantities of drugs are being consumed in OECD countries. In Sweden alone, it is estimated that the monthly drug consumption per one million of the population - based on numbers of normal doses - is 7.3 million analgesics, 2.1 million sedatives, 1.8 million barbiturates and other hypnotics, 1.3 million antispasmodics, 7 million anti-hypertensives and 0.4 million anti-depressants and central nervous system stimulants (see Chapter IV). Many of these and other drugs - which act primarily on the central nervous system, and affect the processes of vision, hearing, neuromuscular control or disposition of other substances within the body - have demonstrated potential for interfering with the operation of a motor vehicle.

The concern that drugs and alcohol are independently hazardous to driving safety is enhanced by the knowledge that they are often used in combination - and may interact with deleterious effect. Given the high incidence of alcohol and drug usage within our societies, it is therefore important to consider the intricate question of the combined use of alcohol and drugs in traffic situations.

I.2 Background

In recognition of the seriousness of the problem, the OECD published a state-of-the-art review in 1968 on the "effects of alcohol and drugs on driving behaviour and their importance as a cause of road accidents"(3). As a result of this publication, a series of follow-up activities on specific aspects of the problem of impaired driving were under-taken within the framework of the OECD Road Research Programme and of other international organisations. Included in the activities were the development of a methodology for conducting roadside surveys(4); a review of countermeasure activities in 28 countries(5); an examination of analytical methods for determining the presence of alcohol in body material(6); and the initiation of a reporting system designed to facilitate the exchange of information among countries on roadside survey data and on items related to alcohol and traffic safety in general(7).

It is evident that countries are expending a great deal of time and money in the quest for solutions to the problem of impaired driving. For all this effort, however, there are only a few examples where countermeasure programmes have been evaluated and proved effective. Many programmes have not been introduced in a manner which would allow evaluation, primarily because information which is essential for the design and evaluation of countermeasure programmes is not available.

The situation pertaining to alcohol is slowly changing - primarily as a result of the advent of breath-testing equipment. Through activities such as roadside surveys, these devices are now beginning to provide valuable data on the extent of the drinking-driving problem. In addition, the data obtained can be used to estimate the effective-ness of specific planned alcohol abuse countermeasure programmes.

The laws designed to control alcohol impaired driving have also changed as a result of breath-testing equipment. Both qualitative and quantitative devices are now being actively employed to detect alcohol impaired drivers in some OECD countries.

No comparable situation exists for drugs. Procedures for detecting the presence of drugs in body material are complex and costly. Until these problems are resolved by measures such as technical innovation, efforts to define the extent and nature of the drug-driving problem will be difficult.

I.3 Outline of the Report

The purpose of this report is to examine (i) the causative role of alcohol and drugs in traffic safety and (ii) the effectiveness of countermeasures designed to resolve the impaired driving problem. It is important to recognize that more is known about the problems of alcohol and driving than about those of drugs and driving. The contents of this report reflect this imbalance. The examination of the drug problem is limited almost entirely to a discussion of the epidemiological evidence. The alcohol problem, on the other hand, is followed through to an examination of the information related to drinking-driving countermeasures and their effectiveness. The major portion of the report consists of an examination of the research findings on alcohol, drugs and traffic safety which have been published since 1968.

The report is divided into five basic sections as follows:

(1) examination of statistical and design considerations necessary for an accurate assessment of the interaction between drugs, alcohol and traffic;

(2) evaluation of the extent and nature of the alcohol and drug problem with respect to traffic safety;

(3) identification of the driver at risk and the effects of alcohol and/or drugs on driving performance;

(4) examination of countermeasure programmes;

(5) conclusions and recommendations.

In establishing the guidelines for assessing the vast amount of information on drugs, the procedure adopted was to examine the kinds of drugs which were considered to be important in road safety, both with respect to the extent of consumption and to the effect of drugs in impairing driving performance. For this reason, the classification system used in this report is simpler than the one recommended by the World Health Organisation.

Two annexes are attached. Annex A contains a recommended methodology for roadside surveys which is a slightly modified version of that established by an OECD initiated group in 1972(4). Included among the amendments is a section outlining the procedure for reporting roadside survey data. A number of countries have completed surveys and the major results from these are presented in Section III.2 of this report. Further comparative evaluations of the results, however, are limited as there is no uniform method for reporting the data.

In order to achieve uniformity in the procedures employed in sampling drivers, a paper has been prepared by Wolfe entitled "Sampling and Nonresponse Weights in a Roadside Survey"(*). The size of this paper prevented it from being included in this report. Copies have been distributed among members of this Research Group, however, with the recommendation that it be given serious consideration during the planning and evaluation phase of roadside surveys.

Finally, Annex B is a summary report on the available equipment for measuring driver alcohol levels and the levels of performance of these devices. The task of summarising the material on equipment was essentially viewed as a follow-up of earlier OECD activities.

(*) This report can be obtained from OECD.

REFERENCES

1. Warren, R.A., Total Impairment Risk Factors. Traffic Injury Research Foundation of Canada. Ottawa, 1976.

2. OECD Road Research. Prevention of Accidents to Users of Two-Wheeled Vehicles. Paris, to be published in 1978.

3. Goldberg, L. and Harvard, J.D.J., Alcohol and Drugs. The Effects of Alcohol and Drugs on Driver Behaviour and Their Importance as a Cause of Road Accidents. OECD Road Safety Research. Paris, 1968.

4. Transport Canada. Alcohol and Highway Safety. A Review of the Literature and a Recommended Methodology. Traffic Safety, Ministry of Transport, Ottawa, Ontario, 1974.

5. Transport Canada. Alcohol and Highway Safety; Supporting Documentation. Traffic Safety, Ministry of Transport, Ottawa, Ontario, 1974.

6. U.S. Department of Transportation. Recently Published Analytical Methods for Determining Alcohol in Body Materials - Alcohol Countermeasure Literature Review. NHSTA, DOT HS-371-3-786, National Technical Information Service, Springfield, Va., 1974.

7. Transport Canada. Draft Report on an Initial Exchange of Information on Alcohol and Highway Safety. Traffic Safety, Ministry of Transport, Ottawa, Ontario, 1975.

II

METHODOLOGY

II.1 Introduction

The purpose of this Chapter is to examine the general methodological approaches that have been taken in research on alcohol and on drugs in relation to driving, in order that the reader may better understand the limitations in the current knowledge in these areas and the reasons why substantial additional effort in research is needed to deal with these problems.

Since this Chapter amounts to a critique of methodologies currently in use, it runs the risk of appearing over negative with regard to the current status of the alcohol/drugs and driving field. The reader should not be misled; there is a considerable body of knowledge, based on effective, well grounded research. It is important however, that programme administrators be well aware of the difficulties to be encountered in investigating this field; they can thus appreciate the considerable effort that will be required to obtain the knowledge on which to develop effective countermeasure programmes for this serious problem and have a basis for distinguishing adequate from inadequate research.

This Chapter is not intended to provide a description or catalogue of the methods used in this field. The reader who is interested in becoming acquainted in more detail with the analytical, behavioural or statistical methods discussed in this section is referred to several key references covering this methodology (1,2,3,4,5)*. Four major topics are covered: methods by which the role of alcohol or of drugs in driving is determined (epidemiology); problems in measuring alcohol and drug levels in the body; problems in measuring driving behaviour; and the problems which arise in evaluating the effectiveness of traffic safety programmes.

II.2 Epidemiology: Demonstrating the Role of Alcohol or a Drug in Crashes

The primary method by which an agent such as alcohol or a drug is demonstrated to have a role in a traffic accident is to contrast the frequency with which this agent is present in the bodies of crash-involved drivers with the frequency with which it is present in drivers using the road at the same times and places, but who are not involved in accidents. The mere presence of the agent in crash-involved drivers is not sufficient evidence of its effect, since some drugs (i.e. aspirin, alcohol, and amphetamines) are so widely used that they might be expected to turn up in any sample of normal human beings. It is the contrast in their use by the group exhibiting the behaviour of interest (crashes) with a group, similar in every other respect but not crash involved, that provides the evidence for causality. A method for calculating the additional risk associated with alcohol is described by Warren(6).

This technique has been used extensively in demonstrating the role of alcohol in highway crashes(6), (see Chapter III). The problems which arise with this procedure are

---

(*) See list of references at the end of this Chapter. Portions of Sections II.3 and II.4 are taken from Joscelyn and Maickel(2).

that, frequently, the specific accident and non-accident involved groups of interest are not available for study and the alcohol levels in these groups must be estimated from less valid sets of data.

In the case of crash-involved drivers, several problems may arise. First, since the interest is in crash causation, it is the driver responsible for the crash, not the innocent party, who is most of interest(7). However, for many accidents the responsible driver is not determined and, where such information is available, it is frequently based on a judgment made by a police officer who did not witness the accident. Further, data are often incomplete. It follows that the notion of "responsibility" for an accident cannot be accepted as having a really scientific strictness. Blood alcohol tests are generally conducted on only a portion of the crash-involved drivers. In most countries tests are limited to fatally injured drivers, and valid tests can be made only on those who die within four hours of the crash. Fatally injured drivers under age 16 and surviving drivers are generally not tested. This results in the data on alcohol in crash-involved drivers being very incomplete(8, 9). In many areas alcohol tests may be conducted on only a portion of the eligible fatally injured drivers, which may result in biased results through the selection of these cases in which drinking is believed to have occurred. The data on drugs in crash-involved drivers is even more fragmentary and unreliable(2).

There is also a lack of data on drivers using the road and not involved in crashes; this is needed in order to provide a comparison with the alcohol and drug levels in the crash-involved drivers. Several well controlled, voluntary roadside surveys of alcohol use by drivers have been conducted and are summarized in Chapter III.2. The number of roadside surveys which have collected blood or other fluid samples for the detection of drugs in drivers is very limited (Chapter IV). The validity of these roadside surveys depends upon the statistical adequacy of the sample of drivers from which chemical test data are obtained and the care with which the tests are made(10). With the assistance of the OECD a standardized procedure has been developed for conducting roadside surveys for alcohol, which permits comparisons between nations. This procedure is described in Annex A. If all countries would make provision for regular roadside surveys, and for the routine collection of blood samples from all fatally injured drivers, each nation would be able to assess the severity of the alcohol safety problem in relation to other countries, and would be able to evaluate the effectiveness of their own countermeasure programmes and those of other governments. Until such data are collected by all nations regularly, international comparisons will not be possible.

Methods which attempt to obtain data on the drivers at risk by less direct means are generally subject to significant errors. One typical procedure is to retrospectively examine the driving records of individuals known to be drug users or alcoholics and compare their records with other drivers. But since the exposure (amount of driving) of such groups is generally not known, interpretation of these data is difficult(2, 7).

Another problem may relate to the method of data collection. Studies that rely on self-reporting are usually invalid and under-reporting generally occurs. While this criticism is commonly made of questionnaire approaches, it has special importance in the impaired driving field. Many subjects are not aware of the nature of drugs they are taking and have no comprehension of dosage or potency. Illicit users can be expected to report incorrectly. Thus, the roadside survey procedure when combined with the regular chemical testing of crash involved drivers remains the method of preference in epidemiology.

II.3 Problems in the Measurement of Drug Levels in the Body

II.3.1 Design of clinical studies

An examination of the research literature reveals a diverse group of studies utilising

widely varying experimental designs to determine the effects of drugs on human behaviour
(or in some cases animal behaviour) (see Chapter IV). Studies may examine the effect of
a single drugs, or multiple drugs may be evaluated comparatively. Additive, synergistic
and antagonistic effects may be examined.

The drug or drugs can be administered in various dosage regimens. Acute dosage
studies (single administration or over a short time period) are more prevalent because
they are simpler and less costly, although chronic dosage studies (repetitive usage) have
also been conducted. In both types there are ethical constraints against administering
drugs to subjects for whom the drug is not therapeutically indicated. Of the two types,
chronic studies provide more useful data since they examine a population which is more
representative of the population at risk in traffic accidents related to alcohol and drugs.

The use of normal subjects for drug studies may produce questionable results. Legg,
Malpas and Scott(11) have suggested that the pharmacological effects of a drug on a
patient taking the drug for its therapeutic action are very likely to be reflected in
improved behavioural performance. In contrast, the same drug taken by a normal subject
may have no effect or may adversely affect behavioural performance.

A common type of drug study administers varying levels of acute dosages and measures
the magnitude of the response associated with each dose level. This procedure is known
as a dose-response study. The simplest form of a dose-response study involves a single
subject who is given varying dose levels. Another approach uses a number of subjects
each receiving a different dose level. This latter design suffers from a serious disadvantage in that individual variation may not be adequately controlled. In all dose-
response studies participant bias and observer bias must be minimised to the extent
possible.

A placebo which is the administration of a non active substance in the same mode as
the test drug is used for this purpose. This may be done as a blind study where the subject does not know whether the test drug or the inactive placebo is administered. This
is designed to reduce participant bias. Another method uses a double blind approach
where neither the subject nor the observer is aware of whether the drug or the placebo
has been administered. This is designed to control for both participant and observer
bias.

The problems of variation in research settings and subject state are addressed by
the use of a crossover design. Commonly, the subjects are divided randomly into two
groups. One group receives the placebo and then the test drug. The other, the test drug
and then the placebo. More complex cross over designs balance all variables (drugs,
order of administration, dosage, route of administration, etc.) in a systematic manner.

II.3.2 Methodological problems

A number of studies report effects observed after administration of a drug in a
dosage that was undetermined or cannot be determined from the report of the study.
Without knowledge of the dosage, little can be said about the responses, except in terms
of generalisations. When known dosages are administered, adequate understanding of the
drug's pharmacological action is also required. Valid conclusions cannot be obtained
from tests that run before or after the drug can be expected to have had maximum effect.

Placebo Contamination: The use of a placebo may present a problem rather than a
solution if it turns out not to be a placebo but rather an active agent. For example,
it is not totally agreed that delta-nine-tetrahydrocannabinol (9THC) is the sole active
component of marijuana. Yet many studies have reported the use of marijuana, has been
processed to be 9THC free, as a placebo. It is not clear that this results in a true placebo.

Thus, studies that report no differences must be examined with care.

Subject Selection: One of the major problems with existing studies lies in the method of subject selection. Many studies represent experiments of convenience. The negative aspects of the tendency to perform acute rather than chronic dosage studies are enhanced when one finds that most acute studies are done on samples of convenience, often a few healthy college students that were easily accessible for the researcher. It is unlikely that such a sample is representative of the drug using or driving population. Thus, the validity of the results of these studies must be questioned and generalisations avoided.

Subject Control: Few researchers report adequate measures to determine if the subjects were using other drugs. Objective testing measures involving analytical measurement of body fluids to determine the presence, if any, of drugs other than the test drug(s) are most desirable to ensure subject control. The use of paid subjects and/or subjects from a drug using population increases the probability that other drugs may be present. Studies of fatally injured drivers indicate that from 1/3 to 1/2 of those with a significant level of a drug in their body also had sufficient alcohol in their blood to seriously impair their performance(12).

Equal concern must be devoted to ascertaining variation in physiological or psychological state. Sleep deprivation, emotional strain or other alteration in subject state may significantly effect responses to some drugs. In the absence of any control or attempt to control for these variables, one must be concerned about the validity of the report results.

Sample Size: Most experimental studies utilise relatively few subjects. The limited sample size may not detect drug effects that will occur in the general population. An unusual sensitivity that may occur in 1 out of 200 people may go undetected. Such responses become significant when a drug is used widely. Even a low frequency of adverse reactions may result in a significant number of absolute cases when use is widespread.

It is an adage that no statistical method can turn bad data into good results. Unfortunately, the literature also contains examples of poor analysis of good data. These problems may stem from ignorance of quantitative methods or ethical concerns that require that the minimum number of subjects be exposed to a drug. Thus, careful statistical designs and analysis are required and sample sizes should be adequate.

II.4 Problems in the Measurement of Driving Performance

Earlier sections have focussed on the problems associated with the detection and measurement of alcohol or drugs in humans. Of equal concern are the problems associated with the detection and measurement of the effects of these agents on human behaviour, and more specifically, on driver behaviour.

A full understanding of an alcohol/drug/driving problem will require the ability to relate a drug level to behavioural effects. To do this, the behavioural tasks involved in driving must be adequately defined, and testing methods must be developed to reliably examine human performance in the driving situation, especially critical driving situations. Whereas considerable information already exists on the impairment of driving behaviour due to alcohol (ee section III.3), less is known about than due to other drugs(2, 12).

II.4.1 Development of test methods

The development of tests that measure human behaviour have been the subject of intense effort by experimental psychologists for many years. Researchers have tended to develop tests that relate directly to the particular subject matter of their research. One tends to find tests developed to assess specific aspects of human performance in a laboratory setting without reference to the real world activity. Moreover, the psychological literature tends to contain material on the development of tests rather than on their real world relevance.

A somewhat similar bias exists in the pharmacological literature. Pharmacologists have focused on the examination of alcohol and/or drug effects and have tended to develop tests that allow detection of the effects. While these tests may be quite adequate for detection of drug effects, it may not be possible to correlate the test results directly with the driving task.

A limited effort has been made to develop tests that are more directly related to the driving task or are believed to simulate subtasks involved in driving. These efforts are encouraging but the results are not conclusive. Some of the approaches in common use are briefly described in the following sections.

II.4.2 Observation of vehicle operation

A number of research studies have examined the driving task through observation of a subject operating a motor vehicle(16). In some cases the vehicle is operated on the highways while in others the operation is restricted to a driving range or quasi-laboratory situation. If the nature of the experiment involves the degradation or potential degradation of the subject's driving ability, the use of dual control vehicles as a safety measure is common.

The observation or "in-vehicle" approach provides some relief from the artificiality of the pure laboratory situation. However, operation on a driving range is still artificial as it is difficult if not impossible to create test situations that replicate the range of road, traffic and weather conditions encountered in driving. Such closed course systems do not correlate well with the totality of the driving task.

Actual highway operation, even with dual control vehicles, appears to present significant risks. This is particularly true if prior evidence indicates that the drug is likely to adversely affect the subject's driving behaviour. The risk may be legally unacceptable. Such studies cannot be undertaken without a rigorous examination of ethical and legal issues.

II.4.3 Driving simulators

Driving simulators are attractive measurement devices as they present the opportunity for exposing the subject to controlled conditions and facilitate the measurement of responses. An ideal simulator is one that would produce all the possible conditions, including inertia, that would be encountered in the real world driving situation. Unfortunately, no such simulator exists. A descriptive discussion of existing simulators is presented by Hulbert and Wojcik(13).

Simulators are generally viewed as having severe limitations as a valid measurement instrument. Perhaps, the major one of these is the inability to create in the artificial atmosphere of the laboratory the real life stresses of on-the-road driving. The questionable validity of simulators has been critically examined by Edwards, Hahn and Fleishman(14). They found almost no correlation between simulator performance and actual driving.

II.4.4 Laboratory performance tests

A multitude of procedures have been devised over the years to measure and evaluate human performance in the laboratory. These tests or modified versions of them have been used to collect data on human behaviour under relatively well controlled conditions, in the belief that a relationship exists between the skills covered by these tests and real life activities such as driving.

Some tests focus on the measurement of "decision making", others examine "vigilance", "attention" or "psychomotor performance". The basic problem with the utilisation of these tests is the lack of evidence that the tests, or the test results, are actually related to driver impairment and particularly to accident causation. Gross impairment, as in the case where the subject is totally unable to function, it is likely to be relevant, but such an effect is likely to be detected by simple observation without the need for sophisticated testing.

A major reason why the results of laboratory performance testing can fail to correspond to the role of alcohol or a drug in crash causation is the failure to reproduce or measure the attitudinal or motivational factors in the driving situation. Because of the artificiality of the situation, the subject is aware that a test is in process and is likely to react differently than in a non-test situation. The ability of individuals to compensate at least in part for alcohol or other drug effects is well demonstrated. Thus, it is likely that testing does not detect effects that might be observed in the real world.

It has been argued by a number of researchers that, if one accepts the artificiality of a testing situation and the ability of individuals to compensate, the deleterious effect is important because it is likely that the agents tested would produce more significant effects in the real world situations than those observed on tests. While the argument is not illogical, it is not supported by clear empirical evidence.

II.5 Evaluating Countermeasure Programmes

Once a relationship between a drug such as alcohol and driving behaviour has been established, an official countermeasure programme may be proposed. Several such programmes are discussed in Chapter V. Once implemented, the effectiveness of these programmes in reducing highway crashes must be evaluated since it is quite possible that, while there may be a true causal relationship between the drug and crash involvement, the countermeasure programme will not result in a measurable reduction in highway fatalities, injuries or property damage. This could occur 1) if the countermeasure programme is poorly conceived or 2) if it is badly managed or 3) because it is implemented in an area where the drug/driving problem does not exist to a significant extent. It can also fail to show impact because of a number of research problems which are discussed below.

As generally understood, the process of evaluation involves comparing highway accident rates before and after the institution of a special safety programme. To those not deeply involved in evaluation, this appears to be a straightforward, relatively simple process. The difficulty is that, on close examination, the actual requirements of evaluation are far more subtle and difficult than generally believed. At least six significant problems arise in demonstrating the impact of a safety programme on traffic accidents.

II.5.1 <u>Obtaining an appropriate criterion measure</u>

While accident record systems have been improving in most countries, even in the most highly industrialised nations considerable inaccuracies remain in accident files. Many crashes are not reported to the authorities, because they involve relatively minor damage, because of fear of prosecution, or concern that insurance rates will be increased. Moreover, in the records of the accidents which do appear in official files, there may be significant gaps or errors in the information presented which make it difficult to use the information for research purposes.

Many accident record systems do not identify the responsible driver. Since the interest is in alcohol and drugs as <u>causes</u> of accidents, the driver who is the victim of another driver's error is of relatively less interest. Even where the responsible driver is identified, or where causes are listed, such data must generally be based on police judgment and are therefore subject to error and bias.

Data on the role of alcohol and other drugs in accident record files are particularly subject to such bias. Chemical tests for alcohol are rarely made on other than the drivers who die in crashes. In most countries, even these data are incomplete, involving half or less of all fatally injured drivers. Living drivers involved in accidents are generally tested only if there is sufficient evidence to lead to an arrest for drunken driving, and this occurs in only a small portion of traffic accidents. Some accident data collection forms provide for an estimate by the police officer as to whether the driver had been drinking. However most studies suggest that working under operational conditions most police will fail to recognize about half of the drivers who are seriously impaired by alcohol, with whom they come in contact. Compared to alcohol, the data on other drugs available in traffic record systems are even more incomplete and unreliable.

In selecting a measure to use as a criterion for project effectiveness, the evaluator must be careful to be sure that it is appropriate to the programme he is investigating and will not be biased by the initiation of the project itself. Since most countermeasure programmes are applied to only one of many accident causes (a particular drug such as alcohol, or a particular behaviour such as speeding), they cannot be expected to have an impact on all accidents. Even if the programme is successful in reducing this one cause, the others are not impacted and the overall chance variability in the average number of accidents may mask the effect of the project. Therefore more specific measures of project impact than the total number of crashes are required. Lacking good data on the alcohol usage by drivers in accidents, researchers have turned to <u>surrogate</u> measures such as the time of day at which the crashes have occurred. For example nighttime as compared to daytime crashes are considered in order to take advantage of the normal drinking patterns which in many countries result in most alcohol being consumed at night(7).

Another type of criterion measure often selected is a <u>proxy</u> measure, such as the number of drivers with alcohol in their bodies, alcohol levels being determined through roadside surveys(6), (see Annex A). The use of this type of criterion involves taking one step back from the crash itself and <u>assuming</u> that since the relationship between blood alcohol concentration and crashes is well established, lower BACs in drivers using the roads will result in fewer crashes(7).

Frequently,the criterion cited for success of a project is not directly related to crashes at all. A large increase in traffic arrests is often cited as an indication of the success of a new enforcement programme. However, since the relationship between number of citations and crash reductions has not been demonstrated, this measure is not an adequate criterion of project effectiveness. For this reason, project evaluations are usually classified into two types: <u>administrative evaluations</u> where the money and effort expended are related to the amount of activity generated: (arrests, students trained, drivers contacted, etc.) and _scientific impact evaluations_ which attempt to relate the money and effort expended to the number of crashes forestalled(5).

II.5.2 Proving a change has occurred

The number of crashes in any given area varies as a function of time. These changes may be more or less random, or they may be responding to seasonal effects, economic conditions, and other factors. Thus, in determining the impact of a project, a measurement must be made against this moving background. Frequently, when reporting the impact of a safety programme, descriptive information is given. For example: "After implementing the special drunk driving patrol, nighttime crashes went down about 25 percent." This kind of descriptive data may appear to be important but may actually lack any significance at all because of random variation in crash data. If, after a special patrol is put in operation the number of crashes goes up, no one mentions this fact. It is only when they go in the expected direction that the results are reported. This failure to report the negative cases can result in an impression of success where none exists.

For this reason, purely descriptive statements are not acceptable as scientific evaluations. Steps must be taken to ensure that the results reported cannot be accounted for by random variation in the crash data. "Time-series analysis" provides one method of controlling these sources of error in studies of changes in crash data in relation to a past series of data(15).

II.5.3 Demonstrating causation

The fact that a decrease in accident rate occurred at approximately the same time as a safety programme was implemented does not necessarily prove that the change was due to that safety programme. Since, as noted above, the number of crashes is changing all the time, it is quite possible that the change was due to some other factor. Campbell and Stanley(4) have discussed these "threats to validity". In order to prove the change was caused by the project, it is necessary to disprove these potential causes which provide alternative hypotheses for explaining the observed reduction in crashes. This often requires data that are not easily available and may be costly to obtain.

One of the major ways in which causality is demonstrated is by the use of a control area or group for which no new or additional safety programme is conducted. If crashes in the experimental area go down while crashes in the control area remain the same or go up, there may be evidence that the project produced this effect. This, of course, assumes that the control area is experiencing the same extraneous conditions as the test area, and therefore, that any difference must be due to the experimental project. Unfortunately, in the area of road safety, it is very difficult to obtain a control group or area in which all other factors remain the same.

Another approach to the demonstration of causality is to evaluate the external factors which might be most likely to account for the change other than the programme itself and, if possible, demonstrate that they could not have produced the observed change. Thus, for example, a reduction in the number of accidents may be due to a reduction in total vehicle miles driven.

A third method of demonstrating that the change in crashes was produced by the safety programme is to create a "chain of action or effect" between the safety measures taken and the reduction in crashes. For example, if one can demonstrate that extra police placed on the road resulted in a significant increase in arrests, which was followed by a reduction in the number of drivers with high BACs which in turn was followed by reduction in alcohol related crashes, the argument is strengthened that it was the safety programme which produced the reduction. Time-series analysis technique provides a system for correlating change in project activities in both amount and timing with later changes in accident frequency.

II.5.4 <u>Requirement for a comprehensive programme</u>

At the community level, road safety is dependent upon the integrated efforts of many organisations. Road safety programmes frequently involve the driver licensing agency, the vehicle registration departments, schools, driver rehabilitation organisations, the police, courts and various private voluntary groups. As increased effort by one element almost always affects another, it is rarely possible to measure a change in crashes when only one element of the system is changed, since this element is dependent upon at least one or two of the other units in the total system.

Only when several different countermeasure programmes involving several agencies are integrated is an impact on crashes possible. However, when the several different countermeasure elements are put together, it is not possible to determine which one is having the major effect on crashes. Many of the current safety projects cannot be evaluated with clear relevance to a specific countermeasure.

II.5.5 <u>Requirement for ensuring sufficient effort to produce a positive result</u>

Because the number of crashes is constantly fluctuating, it is necessary to create an impact on this measure which is larger than its standard background variation. This usually requires an intensive effort. Small improvements in a local safety system are not likely to effect a significant impact upon accident rates. Yet, many safety projects are quite small efforts.

To a certain extent, a low total effort level can be compensated for by more sensitive and specifically relevant criterion measurements. Thus, for example, if one adds six police patrol officers to a sixty man department, we can expect no more than ten percent increase in overall effort. However, if these men are placed on duty between the hours of 22:00 hours and 04:00 hours, and if only the crashes that occur during these hours are considered, these six individuals may represent a much greater increase in patrol effort. In this case, the possibility of measuring an impact on crashes is much greater.

II.5.6 <u>Requirement for sensitivity in measurement</u>

The more sensitive the measurement technique, the more likely it is that a given programme will be shown to have had an impact on accident rates. In planning countermeasure projects, it is important to determine the sensitivity of the statistical procedures that will be used. This will permit a determination of how large a change will have to occur before a statistically significant result will be claimed.

There are two types of error that can be made in evaluating any programme. On the one hand, there may be no true impact but the scientist erroneously accepts the result of the evaluation as indicating that there is. This is "<u>type 1 error</u>". On the other hand, there may be a true difference but he comes to the conclusion that there is no impact. This is "<u>type 2 error</u>". Statistical convention sets the significance levels in favour of avoiding type 1 error by providing that only a result which can be produced by chance only five times in a hundred will be considered significant. Because the statistical convention is purposely "biased" in this way, there is a higher probability of a type 2 error, i.e. rejecting a true effect. The ability of a research design and statistical procedures to avoid a "type 2 error" and detect an effective programme defines the 'power' of a test. Many safety programme evaluations conducted to date have lacked designs of adequate power to ensure that positive effects were detected.

The issue for planning evaluation programmes is the sensitivity of the evaluation system for a given project. A decision must be made as to the amount of change required for a statistically significant result. If the sensitivity of the evaluation techniques or design is low, many programmes will appear to be inneffective. If the sensitivity requirements are set too high, unnecessary expenses may be incurred when treating large groups of subjects.

References

1. Brodie, B.B., and Gillette, J.R., eds., Handbook of Experimental Pharmacology, Springer-Verlag, New York, 1971.

2. Joscelyn, K.B. and Maickel, R.P., Drugs and Driving: A Research Review. National Highway Traffic Safety Administration; U.S. DOT Report N° DOT-HS-802-189. Washington, D.C., January, 1977.

3. Harger, R.N., Recently Published Analytical Methods for Determining Alcohol in Body Materials, National Highway Traffic Safety Administration, U.S. DOT, Washington, D.C., 1974.

4. Campbell, D.T. and Stanly, J.C., Experimental and Quasi-experimental Designs for Research, Chicago: Rand McNally & co., 1966.

5. NHTSA, Management and Evaluation Handbook for Demonstration Projects. In Traffic Safety 1976. National Highway Traffic Safety Administration, U.S. DOT, Washington, D.C.

6. Warren, R.A., Total Impairment Risk Factors. Traffic Injury Research Foundation of Canada, Ottawa, Canada, 1976.

7. Perrine, M.W., Alcohol and Highway Safety and Alcohol and Health; New Knowledge. A special report to the U.S. Congress by the Secretary of Health, Education and Welfare. U.S. Dept. HEW Washington, D.C., 1974.

8. NHTSA, Alcohol Safety Action Projects Evaluation of Operations. Vol. 2 and 3, U.S. DOT, Washington, D.C., 1972.

9. Havard, J.D.J., Cross National Comparisons of Drinking Driving Laws. In Isrealstam, S. and Lambert, S. Alcohol, Drugs and Traffic Safety, Research Foundation of Ontario, Toronto, 1974.

10. Wolfe, A.C., Sampling and Non-response Weights in a Roadside Survey. University of Michigan Highway Safety Research Institute, Ann Arbor, Michigan, U.S.A., December, 1977.

11. Legg, N.J., Malpas, A. and Scott, D.F., Effects of Tranquilizers and Hypnotics on Driving. British Medical Journal 1 (5850):417, 1973.

12. Nichols, J.L., Drug Use and Highway Safety: A Review of the Literature. National Highway Safety Administration, U.S. DOT Report N° DOT-HS-800-580. Washington, D.C., 1971.

13. Hulbert, S. and Wojcik, C., Driving Task Simulation. In T.W. Forbes, Ed., Human Factors in Highway Traffic Safety Research. Wiley-Interscience. New York, 1972.

14. Edwards, D.W., Hahn, C.P., and Fleishman, E.A., Evaluation of Laboratory Methods for the Study of Driving Behavior: The Relation Between Simulator and Street Performance. American Institutes for Research, Accident Research Center USPHS Grant 9501 UI 00695. Washington, D.C., 1969.

15. Box, G.E.P. and Tiao, G.C., A Change in Level of a Non-stationaly Time-series. Biometrika, 52 181-192, 1965.

16. OECD Road Research. Driver Behaviour, OECD, Paris, 1970.

III

ALCOHOL

III.1 Introduction

Since the time of the earlier OECD study published in 1968, much effort has been devoted to research on drinking and driving. The different fields of study include evaluation of the extent and nature of the problem, identification of the road user population at risk, and determination of the specific effects of alcohol on behaviour. It is not proposed to reiterate here the earlier findings, but to highlight the more recent conclusions, particularly those relevant to application of countermeasures.

At the outset it is important to stress that experience from different countries suggests that, whereas risks related to alcohol levels may be generally applicable, the extent and nature of the problem and the population at risk vary so greatly that it is essential for each country to undertake its own epidemiological research to quantify these aspects.

The research studies undertaken will be reviewed under the general headings of epidemiological evidence, from which target populations at risk may be identified, and behavioural studies related to impairment and driving ability.

III.2 Epidemiological Evidence

A major source of epidemiological evidence is the amount of alcohol actually found in the body, referred to as the blood alcohol concentration (BAC). But neither the presence of alcohol in the body nor the magnitude of the BAC can be taken alone as conclusive evidence that alcohol caused or even contributed to an accident. Rather, special methods of sampling and collecting data have had to be developed to determine the role of alcohol. The main method to provide a quantitative assessment of risk is the "case-control" study.

To investigate the contribution of alcohol (or any other factor) to crashes, requires determining the extent to which crash involved drivers with alcohol are representative of drivers with similar alcohol exposure but not involved in the crashes. Thus, it is necessary to compare the distribution of BACs of drivers involved in crashes to those of "control" or "comparison" drivers randomly selected while driving at equivalent places and times as the crashes occurred. Such sets of data make it possible to determine the similarities and differences between the two groups of drivers in terms of the proportions of each group with no alcohol and with different levels of BAC.

Despite differences in many methodological details, the general findings from a number of different studies are generally compellingly consistent: drivers with high BACs are grossly overrepresented in fatal and serious injury crashes in comparison with samples of uninvolved drivers. Furthermore, these findings were obtained in studies which range across the major types of driving experience in the United States, namely, in metropolitan areas in the Manhattan study[1](*), in urbanised areas in the Grand Rapids study[2],

(*) See list of references at the end of this Chapter.

23

and in rural areas in the Vermont study(3). Similar findings have also been reported more recently from those Department of Transportation Alcohol Safety Action Projects which were designed to gather relevant data(4) as well as from the case-control studies, conducted in other countries and reported by Stroh(5, 6).

Another approach to determining the role of alcohol in accidents has been adopted in the United Kingdom, where subjective assessments of impairment and blameworthiness based on detailed accident investigation including attendance at the scene and interviews with drivers have been successful in establishing the magnitude of the problem and identifying dominant features associated with drinking and driving(7).

III.2.1 Alcohol and the driving population

Estimates of the BAC distribution in the driving population come from both types of roadside research surveys: case-control studies in North America (.e. the Toronto, Manhattan, Grand Rapids, and Vermont surveys), are deliberately biased in favour of drivers who crashed at the sites and times which were used to determine the survey points. The non-case control studies involve survey points which do not necessarily correspond to previous crashes, but rather are selected for other reasons, such as an attempt to describe the driving population in a particular area on the basis of a 24-hour saturation sampling procedure(8), or simply to describe the nighttime driving population(9).

It is noteworthy that, for general descriptive purposes, the results from both type of studies are essentially the same; a high proportion of the driving population is found with no alcohol (less than 10 mg%), while a relatively low proportion is in excess of 100 mg%. Some of the distributions of BACs amongst the driving population in a number of surveys in different countries are given in Table 1.

The lower percentages observed in England and France - compared to the other countries - may be attributed to the time of day the surveys were conducted. The French survey examined periods during the day and night and the English survey was conducted between the hours of 6 p.m. and midnight. The Dutch, Canadian and U.S. studies, on the other hand, commenced later at night (e.g. 10 p.m.) and ran until either 3 or 4 a.m.

TABLE 1

PERCENTAGE DRIVING POPULATION WITH DIFFERENT LEVELS OF BAC

Country & Year	Blood alcohol concentration (BAC) - mg%				
	0 - 9	10 - 49	50 - 99	100 - 149	150 and +
England - 1964*	87.6	10.2	1.9	0.2	0.1
France - 1977	---------	92,4	5,3	1,6	0,7
Netherlands - 1973	73.0 ---	12.0**	9.0	---------6.0------	
Canada - 1974	79.6	9.2	7.1	---------4.1------	
United States - 1973	77.4	9.1	8.5	---------5.0------	

 * Pre-legislation

** Division at 19.

III.2.2 Alcohol and non-fatal crashes

From studies in United States and Canada it has been concluded that, despite probable

under-reporting due to selective sampling and to legal and logistic problems, it seems
safe to estimate that legally impaired drivers (100 mg% or higher) are involved in 5 to
10 percent of the run-of-the-mill crashes, and approximately 45 percent of the serious
injury crashes. Furthermore, injury to the driver is more likely after drinking, and
both the probability and the severity of injury appear to increase as the amount of alcohol rises, the likelihood of being responsible for the crash is also greater if the
driver has been drinking. Also, higher BACs are associated with higher proportions of
drivers responsible for the crashes.

In the United Kingdom experience of non fatal crashes (including non-injury crashes),
the at-the-scene investigations to which reference has already been made(7) indicate that
25 percent of accidents involve a drinking driver and in nearly 10 percent impairment by
alcohol is a major contributory factor. In the 'drinking hours' (10 p.m. - 4 a.m.) two-
thirds of accidents involve a drinking driver and in nearly one-third alcohol is a major
contributory factor in the occurrence of the accidents. Drinking drivers were found to
be $1\frac{1}{2}$ times more likely to be at fault in accidents than non-drinking drivers, and features
particularly associated with the drinking driver were driving too fast for the conditions,
and loss of control linked with a predominance of single vehicle accidents.

III.2.3 Alcohol and fatal crashes

More complete BAC data are available about fatal crashes than about other types.
Table 2 summarises some of the results for different countries.

TABLE 2

PERCENTAGE FATALLY INJURED DRIVERS WITH DIFFERENT LEVELS OF BAC

Country & Year	Blood alcohol concentration (BAC) - mg%					
	0 - 9	10 - 49	50 - 79	80 - 99	100 - 149	150 +
England & Wales - 1975	45	12	7	2	10	24
France - 1969	--------80.0--------			--------19.9--------		
Canada - 1973	55.8	3.2	------5.5-------		--------35.5---	
United States - 1972	38.9	3.6	------8.2-------		--------49.3---	

In those European countries where figures are available, the proportions exceeding
100 mg% tend to be lower than in the North American countries. However, comparisons in
Table 2 should be made with care as the distributions in different countries relate to
different years. The trends in the percentages of fatally injured drivers in England and
Wales over the years since the introduction of the 1967 legislation imposing a limit of
80 mg% are of particular interest (Fig. 1).

Fatal accidents also provide data on blood alcohol levels of other road users. A
study in the United Kingdom for England and Wales(10) has indicated trends over the years
in BACs for passengers, pedestrians and pedal cyclists. Although legislation does not
apply to any of these road users, it is interesting to note that the level of BAC for
passengers, which in pre-legislation was slightly higher than for drivers, decreased
dramatically after the introduction of the 1967 Act. Subsequently, the proportion with
BACs over 80 mg% has increased more slowly than for drivers, only reaching the pre-legis-

lation level (29 percent) in 1974. Figures for 1975 indicate the proportion has now increased to 34 percent, compared with 36 percent for drivers (see Table 2 and Fig. 1). Legislation has had no effect on the proportion of pedestrian fatalities in excess of 80 mg% and the figure has varied over the years between 20 and 25 percent. Very few pedal cyclists killed were found to have substantial levels of alcohol in their blood: about 20 percent exceeding 10 mg% and 5 percent exceeding 80 mg%.

In North American experience about one-third (ranging from 28 to 43 percent) of fatally injured adult pedestrians have BACs of 100 mg% or higher. There is a striking similarity between the BAC distributions for adult pedestrian fatalities and for drivers fatally injured in multiple-vehicle crashes.

III.2.4 Crash probability and blood alcohol concentration

The relative probability of being involved in a crash can be inferred by comparing the BAC distribution of the population at risk (as indicated by the sample of "Control" drivers obtained at corresponding times and places of crashes) with the BAC distribution of the drivers actually involved in these crashes for which the control drivers were sampled.

Hurst(11, 12), in his extensive review of five relevant studies (Evanston, Toronto, Manhattan, Grand Rapids, and Vermont) has calculated that the relative probability of crashing with no alcohol is equal to 1.0. The resulting relative hazard functions are shown in Figure 2. Hurst has offered several tentative inferences derived from the data: (1) relative hazard or probability of crash involvement is steeper for the more urban populations, and (2) the incidence of more serious crashes has a greater acceleration than run-of-the-mill crashes, as shown by the right-hand portions of the curves in Fig. 2 beginning in the region indicated by a BAC of 80 mg%.

Allsop(13), on the basis of a re-appraisal of the Grand Rapids study, has demonstrated (Fig. 3) the different risk curves for drivers of different ages and different drinking habits. The increase in accident risk with increasing alcohol levels is greater for young and elderly drivers than for middle-aged drivers, being especially marked for teenagers. The risk curve is also appreciably steeper for the less experienced drinkers than the heavy drinkers.

A crucial issue concerns responsibility for initiating a fatal crash as a function of alcohol. The Vermont data used in Figure 4 shows the relative probability of being responsible for initiating a fatal crash as a function of BAC. At BACs between 50 and 100 mg%, the relative probability of fatal crash responsibility begins to increase appreciably, such that at a BAC of 100 mg% a driver would be 7 times more likely to be responsible for having a fatal crash than he would with no alcohol. The relative hazard curve rises very sharply above this level, such that at a BAC of 150 mg% a driver would be 25 times more likely to be responsible for a fatal crash, at 180 mg% he would be 60 times more likely, and at 200 mg% (namely, at the average BAC found among convicted drivers and among fatally injured drivers who would have been eligible for a conviction) he would be at least 100 times more likely to be responsible for a fatal crash than if he had not been drinking at all.

It should be noted that similar results were obtained in the Grand Rapids study for drivers assumed responsible for all crashes, regardless of severity. A comparison of drivers assumed responsible for crashes in these three case-control studies (Grand Rapids, Manhattan, and Vermont) has been presented by Hurst. The implications of these studies are very clear: concentrations of 80 mg% or higher "are incompatible with safe driving, and the higher the concentration, the greater the incompatibility". Small increases in

Figure 2

RELATIVE PROBABILITY OF CRASH INVOLVEMENT AS
A FUNCTION OF BLOOD ALCOHOL CONCENTRATION

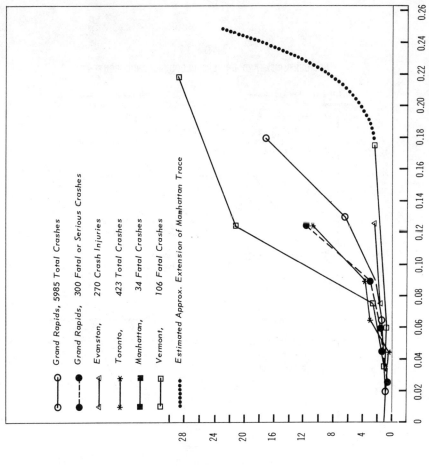

Relative probability of involvement[1]

Grand Rapids, 5985 Total Crashes
Grand Rapids, 300 Fatal or Serious Crashes
Evanston, 270 Crash Injuries
Toronto, 423 Total Crashes
Manhattan, 34 Fatal Crashes
Vermont, 106 Fatal Crashes
Estimated Approx. Extension of Manhattan Trace

Blood alcohol concentration, percent

1. 1.0 = Relative probability at zero alcohol.

Source : Hurst (1973).

Figure 1

DRIVERS KILLED IN ACCIDENTS OVER LEGAL LIMIT
(England and Wales) (TRRL)

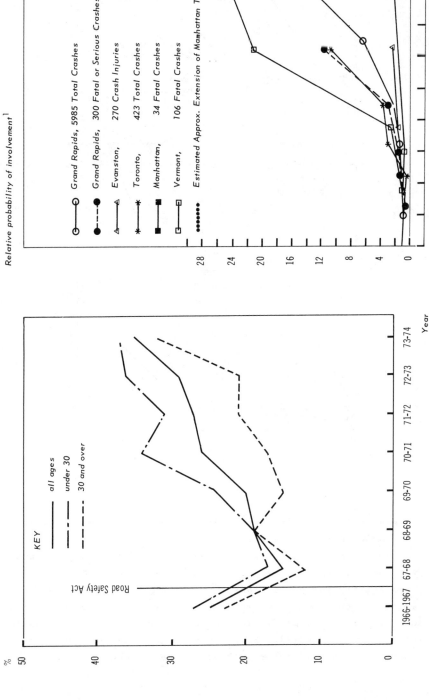

KEY
all ages
under 30
30 and over

Road Safety Act

Year

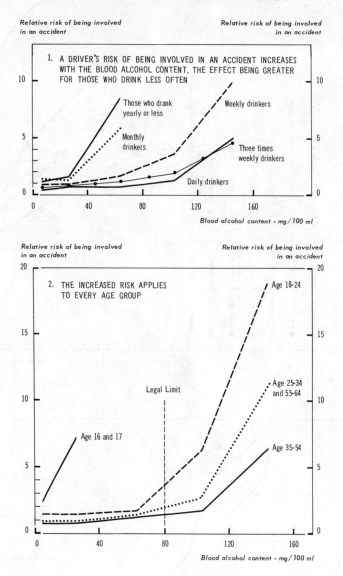

Figure 3

ACCIDENT RISK AND DRIVERS BLOOD ALCOHOL CONTENT

blood alcohol concentration above 80 mg% result in "disproportionately large increases in crash risk"(14). For example, among fatally injured drivers in the Vermont study who were assumed to have been at fault, 52 percent had BACs of 80 mg% or higher, whereas among those not at fault only 14 percent were at or above this same BAC.

The crash probability for pedestrians in relation to alcohol intake has also been studied to a limited extent. One investigator has attempted to evaluate the relationship between BAC and crash "responsibility" in a manner conceptually analogous to the scheme developed by McCarrol and Haddon(1). He found that adult pedestrians with BACs of 100 mg% or higher were usually responsible for initiating the crashes. Waller concluded that

28

"when the pedestrian has alcohol in his system, it is the driver of the striking vehicle who is innocent rather than the pedestrian". More recently Clayton et al.(15) have conducted a case-control study in Birmingham, England. The BAC distributions for both male accident and control groups were significantly higher than those for the females. For males 47.4 percent of the accident group had been drinking (BAC$\geq$ 10 mg%) and 28.9 percent had BACs in excess of 100 mg% compared with 14.7 percent and 7.3 percent respectively for females. In the male control group, 33.1 percent had been drinking and 6.9 percent had BACs in excess of 100 mg%. For the female group, the corresponding figures were 6.6 percent and 0.2 percent respectively.

Figure 4

RELATIVE PROBABILITY OF BEING RESPONSIBLE FOR A FATAL
CRASH AS A FUNCTION OF BLOOD ALCOHOL CONCENTRATION

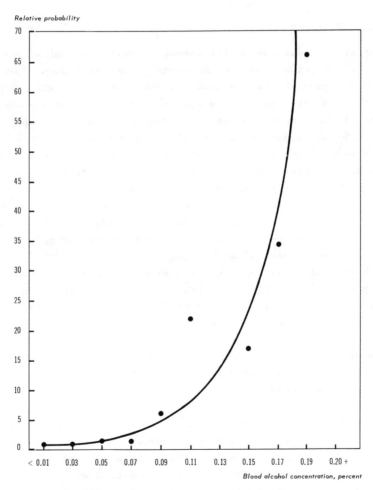

Source : Perrine et Coll. (1971).

Relative accident rates calculated after Allsop(13) showed that the relative risk
of accident involvement increased rapidly above 120 mg%. Impaired pedestrians comprised
27 percent of the male fatalities and 7 percent of the female fatalities who died within
12 hours of the accident. Amongst males, impairment appears to be over-represented
in the young and middle aged, semi-skilled and unskilled manual workers, and those
who are divorced or separated. For injured pedestrians with high BACs, treatment of their
drinking problems would appear to be as important as treatment of their physical injuries.
Alcohol related accidents, particularly those involving high BACs, tend to occur mainly
in the late evening. The highest incidence was in the 23:00 to 03:00 hours period, when
70.2 percent of the accident group had BACS 80 mg% and 50.9 percent had BACs> 150 mg%.
The time distributions for both accident and control groups at these levels are shown in
Figure 5.

III.3 Behavioural Studies

III.3.1 Physiological factors

Despite considerable research on the manner in which alcohol affects neurons and
possible sites of actions of alcohol in the central nervous system, there still appears
to be little firm data to link what is known of the behavioural effects of alcohol to the
effects of alcohol on the central nervous system or to biochemical processes. Of more
immediate relevance to driving safety is the variation of blood alcohol concentration
(BAC) as determined by the absorption, distribution, and elimination of alcohol in the
body. For a given alcohol dose, the peak BAC achieved and the duration of presence of
alcohol are affected by factors such as length of drinking time, contents of the stomach
and intestines, and the amount and concentration of alcohol consumed. While research on
agents which might significantly change the rate of alcohol metabolism has been unproduc-
tive as yet, it is clear that advising individuals to consume food during alcohol drinking
sessions will markedly reduce peak blood alcohol concentrations and, to some minor degree,
decrease the duration of presence of alcohol(16).

A greater behavioural impairment occurs during the period when the blood alcohol
curve is rising than when it is falling. (First noted by Mellanby in 1919.) This effect
has recently been investigated by Hurst and Bagley(17) and Moskowitz, Daily and
Henderson(18). Both studies described the phenomenon as an example of acute alcohol
tolerance developed in the initial phases of an acute experience. However, Moskowitz, et
al.(18) found the degree of this effect equivalent to only that of 10 or 20 mg% change in
BAC and of little importance with relevance to driving safety, although of interest as
a tool for investigations regarding the nature of tolerance effect.

While there has been frequent mention of a possible bi-phasic effect of alcohol
with small doses producing a stimulation, there appears to be little experimental fact
upon which to base such a proposal. The most frequently quoted evidence for a stimula-
tory effect of alcohol is that contained in the Borkenstein, et al. report(2), where
BACs in the neighbourhood of 20 to 30 mg% were associated with lower accident rates
than found in the zero BAC population. This curve, however, was shown to be a result of
the mingling of data from differing subject populations and to be an artifact of the data
handling process. In the monograph of Allsop(13), using the data from the Grand Rapids
study, it was clearly shown that, at any BAC departing from zero, accident probabilities
were always greater than that at zero blood alcohol level.

Figure 5

BAC DISTRIBUTIONS BY TIME OF DAY
FOR MALES AND FEMALES COMBINED

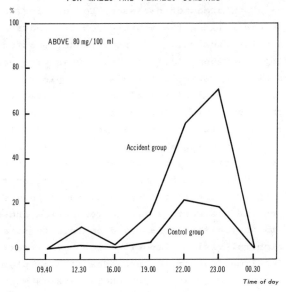

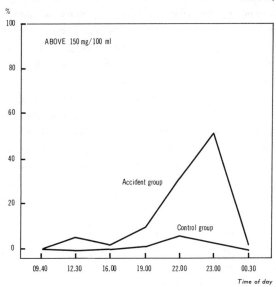

Perrine(19) has noted that "alcohol is consistently a neural depressant and therefore the apparent stimulating or facilitating effects are probably due to the depressant action of alcohol upon some inhibitory mechanism".

III.3.2 Psychological factors

The major psychological literature of interest to traffic safety are studies on vision, the prime source of information necessary for driving, on psychomotor skills, especially tracking, for controlling the vehicle, on information processing and cognition for integrating the two prior factors, and on attitude, emotion or set such as exhibited in changes in risk-taking behaviour. All of these areas have been extensively examined for the effects of alcohol. In general, reviews of simple visual acuity as, for example, in Wallgren and Barry(20) report that visual acuity is relatively insensitive to alcohol. An example of a thorough experimental study of this issue can be found in Verriest and LaPlasse(21). Moreover, as Burg(22) has noted, there appears to be little evidence for a close relationship between simple visual acuity and accident rate. There have been conflicting reports about the sensitivity of dark adaptation to alcohol, although a most recent study by Moskowitz, Sharma and Shapiro(23) still failed to find any significant evidence of such at 100 mg%. Glare recovery, following exposure to unusually bright sources of light, may require a significantly longer period under alcohol. Again, if so, it is not clear to what extent this would contribute to accident rates.

Examination of peripheral vision, important for both tracking and environmental search, has suggested impairment under the presence of a complex situation requiring attention to more than one factor. Studies of peripheral vision where no attention is required in foveal vision have failed to demonstrate any alcohol effects, e.g., Colson(24), King(25). However, when central vision is occupied with a task and subjects are simultaneously required to detect or recognize objects in peripheral vision, the presence of alcohol produces a sharp decrement in performance on peripheral vision, i.e., Von Wright and Mikkonen(26), Hamilton and Copeman(27) and Moskowitz and Sharma(28). The last study, by examining the effects of alcohol on peripheral vision as a function of the amount of information being processed in central foveal vision, demonstrated that the deficit is not a direct effect of alcohol on sensory input or transmission, but upon information processing capacity. Other examples of failures to recognize significant events in the environment when faced with tasks as complex as surveying the automobile driving scene can be gathered from studies using eye movement recording techniques. Buikhuisen et al.(29) studied eye movements of subjects viewing a film of traffic scenes, and Belt et al.(30) examined eye movement recordings in subjects while driving. Both reported a decrease in events perceived when under the influence of alcohol.

Another major aspect of driving is tracking. Again, the effects of alcohol are highly dependent on whether or not the tracking task is being executed by itself or in conjunction with other tasks in a divided attention situation. The BAC at which alcohol affects tracking tasks is much lower when the tracking task is being performed in conjunction with another task. For example, in a study by Pearson(31) subjects failed to exhibit a decrement on a compensatory tracking task at a BAC of 85 mg%, but did show an alcohol effect when the task was performed under hypoxia. Similarly, in a study by Chiles and Jennings(32) at peak BACs near 100 mg%, there was no decrement in tracking when the tracking task was performed by itself. However, when required to be performed in conjunction with a subsidiary task, there was a substantial and significant deficit in tracking. These results are in agreement with the review of Levine, et al.(33), which indicated that psychomotor tasks were the least sensitive to alcohol impairment in comparison with cognition or perceptual sensory tasks. While unusual demanding tracking tasks would show decrements with BACs as low as 40mg%, as for example, in Kielholz, et al.(34), these are atypically difficult tasks. On the other hand, in emergency driving situations where drivers were performing a difficult lane changing manœuvre and at the same time waiting for the appearance of an expected signal, Laurell(35) demonstrated substantial impairment at 48 mg% BAC.

The area which appears to be most sensitive to the effect of alcohol seems to be the central processing of information. In both the sensory visual tasks and in tracking tasks reviewed, impairment occurs at lower BAC levels when these tasks are combined with other tasks. This suggests that the alcohol impairment is in the ability to process the information necessary either for the correct analysis of the sensory information or the organisation of the motor output. Direct evidence for this interpretation has been given by two recent experiments. One, by Moskowitz and Murray(36), demonstrated that alcohol decreased the rate of information processing. This was further supported by an experiment by Moskowitz, Ziedman and Sharma(37) which examined visual search behaviour while viewing driving scenes in a simulator. At 75 mg% BAC, there was a 27 percent increase in the mean amount of time necessary for fixations or eye dwells, illustrating the increased time necessary for viewing an event under alcohol in order to extract the information from it. The increase in average dwell time was compensated for by a decrease in the number of fixations. With a decreased rate of information processing, fewer events can be observed in a given time.

It should be noted that when variables are examined which are sensitive to the effects of alcohol, such as information processing, division of attention, or visual search or tracking under dual task situations, impairment is found at BACs below 50 mg%. Since the nature of the deficits is in perception and central information processing, the fact that the individual is impaired at these low BAC levels may not be apparent to either himself or police authorities.

Although it is frequently reported that alcohol induces greater "risk taking", there is little evidence supporting this view. In one sense, the increased rate of accidents under the influence of alcohol does, indeed, make clear that imbibers are objectively under greater risk of having an accident. However, evidence is lacking that alcohol changes the willingness to assume risks, given that the individual is aware of the risks involved. Since there is strong evidence that alcohol impairs perception and information processing which would adversely adversely affect cognition and judgments, it becomes difficult to demonstrate that the frequently-observed increase in irresponsible behaviour under alcohol is due to "increased risk taking" rather than to decreased ability to evaluate the environment and the subject's own behaviour.

While earlier work by Cohen(38) suggested evidence for increased risk taking, recent studies with additional experimental controls have failed to find evidence for greater risk taking in a driving task(39) or in gambling(40).

III.3.3 Age differences

There are few empirical studies which can definitely clarify the nature of the interaction between age and the degree of impairment associated with a given BAC level. One of factors which interferes with a simple analysis of the issue is that younger persons have had less experience in driving as well as in drinking. Thus, Enslin(41) found younger subjects less impaired by alcohol (80 mg%) than older subjects on vision tests, but more affected on performance in a driving simulator. The author suggested that the greater resistance to an alcohol deficit in the simulator was based on the greater experience of the older drivers.

Moskowitz and Burns(42), using an information processing task which was newly learned by all subjects, found a greater alcohol deficit with increasing age. Craik(43) suggests a similarity between the nature of the deficits in information processing tasks produced by increasing age and by alcohol. The implication is that older drivers would be more likely to suffer impairment by alcohol in this area, so vital for driving.

It is possible that very young, inexperienced (in both driving and drinking) and elderly individuals are both more sensitive to the effects of alcohol than individuals in the prime of life, experienced at both driving and drinking, and not yet suffering the limitations of older persons. The experimental and epidemiological literature at this time is insufficient to provide an adequate answer.

III.3.4 <u>Drinking experience</u>

There is considerable evidence that experienced drinkers are less impaired by alcohol than inexperienced drinkers at any given BAC level (see Fig. 6). It demonstrates that the probability of having an accident <u>at any given blood alcohol level</u> is higher for the less frequent drinker. The results are in accord with an extensive literature(20) demonstrating the existence of tolerance to alcohol in experienced drinkers. Figure 6 also indicates that the more experienced drinkers are likely to achieve far higher BAC levels.

Figure 6
INCREASE IN RISK OF CRASHES WITH BAC FOR INDIVIDUALS
WHO REPORT DIFFERING DRINKING FREQUENCIES (12)

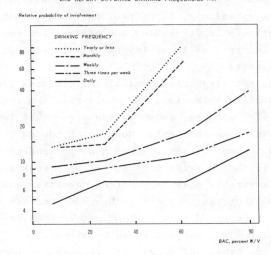

Examples from the recent experimental literature which report tolerance in experienced drinkers include the study by Goodwin, et al.(44) which found greater impairment on motor performance in light drinkers compared with heavy drinkers, after an alcohol dose of 1.2 g/Kg BW. Similarly, Moskowitz, Daily and Henderson(18) found greater impairment on body sway and hand steadiness in moderate drinkers compared with heavy drinkers at a series of BAC levels from 20 to 90 mg%. Further, a study by Burns and Moskowitz(45) examining light, moderate and heavy drinkers at BACs ranging from 30 to 130 mg%, found that the rate of increase of impairment with blood alcohol concentration was greatest for light drinkers and greater for moderate drinkers, in comparison with heavy drinkers. Twelve performance measures were examined, ranging from nystagmus to body sway.

These data suggest the importance of segregating accident probability data for different classes of drinkers, as data derived from heavy drinkers might greatly underestimate the dangers to moderate or infrequent drinkers from a given alcohol dose. It should be noted that, for all classes of drinkers, the probability of having an accident increases with any departure from zero BAC. There is no evidence in accident data that low BAC levels might enhance driving skills, a common misinterpretation of curves derived from mixing data from different drinking classifications.

III.3.5 Sex differences

There appears little epidemiological data from studies such as the Grand Rapids study, to suggest that there is any significant difference between the sexes in susceptibility to accidents under alcohol. It is important to note that such an analysis requires separating accident rates between the sexes from the differences between the sexes in annual driving mileage, drinking frequencies, age, and BAC levels at the time of accidents, all highly significant determinants of accident probabilities. Nor is there evidence from laboratory studies of important differences between the sexes in impairment under alcohol.

Burns and Moskowitz(46) examined five categories of performance tasks for differences in impairment at 100 mg% BAC and failed to find any statistically significant differences. In a study by Linnoila, Erwin, Logue, Gentry and Cleveland(47) which compared the sexes on tests of tracking, vigilance, simple reaction time and continuous performance, no consistent advantage was found for either sex with regard to alcohol impairment.

III.3.6 Self-evaluation of impairment

There is little evidence in the literature to suggest that self-evaluation of the degree of impairment induced by alcohol is a likely feasible deterrent to excessive drinking or to restriction of driving. While Frankenhaeuser, et al.(48) were able to demonstrate good correlation of subjective symptoms with BAC levels, others attempting to utilise the technique with heavy drinkers or alcoholics have been uniformly unsuccessful, e.g., Lovibond and Caddy(49), Silverstein, Nathan and Taylor(50).

The problem may be that the experienced drinker will exhibit less overt signs of impairment of body sway or cognitive clouding to cue himself to impairment. Unfortunately, the greatest degree of impairment under alcohol appears in the area of perception and information processing, areas which are less capable of self-observation. Moreover, as is frequently reported in the literature, subjects under alcohol frequently report more confidence in their skills performance, not less.

III.3.7 Areas requiring research

While the past decade has undoubtedly been the most productive period in the history of alcohol research, much remains to be understood. The fundamental nature of the influence of alcohol on the central nervous system remains unknown, as do many questions about physiological issues such as the acquisition of tolerance.

Of more immediate concern to driving and presumably more amenable to current research techniques are the following issues:

(1) What are the effects of the joint consumption of alcohol and the many drugs in current use?

(2) Many individuals have suffered hangover effects in the period when all the alcohol in the body has been metabolized. Are there objective impairments of skills in this period and are they correlated with the subjective hangover symptoms?

(3) Can we further define the nature and mechanisms of behavioural deficits produced by alcohol?

(4) What is the relationship between age and the degree and nature of alcohol impairment of skills?

(5) Can we reduce the BAC level associated with a given alcohol consumption through drugs?

III.4 Target Populations at Risk

One of the most important questions concerning alcohol and highway safety is whether high-risk drivers (or pedestrians) can be identified. The answer to this question depends upon the degree of specificity involved. If one is interested in identifying high-risk drinking drivers (HRDD) as a group, a sufficient number of studies have been conducted to permit relatively accurate descriptions of the relevant characteristics or variables (at least among American drivers). It is understandably much more difficult, however, to identify a specific individual as an HRDD. Nevertheless, some progress is being made at the individual level and promising results have been reported in a few recent American studies(14, 51-53).

Given the present state of knowledge, the basic pragmatic assumption is that a specific individual is probably at relatively high risk if his "relevant characteristics" are highly congruent with those of the high-risk group. This assumption leads to the use of psychometric methods in efforts to identify individual HRDDs before they become involved in serious problems on the highway. The rationale for this approach stems from the assumption that there are systematic differences between the HRDDs and non-HRDDs which can be measured by means of psychometric methods. More specifically, it is assumed that individuals who subsequently become labelled as HRDDs in terms of the ultimate criterion variables of highway crashes and convictions differ systematically on some combination of biographical, attitudinal, and personality variables which can be measured before the fact. Several studies in the United States have already demonstrated that some of this information can be obtained when the individual submits himself as an applicant for a driving licence or for its renewal(52, 54). For example, an ambitious three-year project has recently been launched by the Bureau of Motor Vehicles in Washington, D.C. in an effort to identify individual HRDDs as part of the examination and re-examination components of the driver licensing programme. Such a psychometric approach has great appeal because of its obvious administrative feasibility and potential cost/effectiveness, but its utility must in turn be evaluated on the basis of the validity of the underlying assumption noted above.

A number of psychometric and epidemiologic studies have been conducted over the years in attempts to uncover personal characteristics (such as "accident proneness") which are linked with crash involvement, but the present discussion is strictly limited to those studies in which alcohol was a primary variable. These studies fall roughly into three categories which differ in their respective methodological advantages and disadvantages:

(a) analysis of official record files (police and/or motor vehicle department);

(b) personal interview and/or testing of specifically identified target groups (e.g., convicted DWIs, hospitalized alcoholics, crash-involved drivers in "driver rehabilitation classes", and even the next-of-kin of fatally injured drivers);

(c) roadside research surveys using random or discretionary testing for alcohol (both case/control and non-case/control studies).

It should be stressed that because different subjects of the driving population are sampled using these three different sources of data, differing results are obtained. Only the last catagory of study using random testing can obtain results representative of all drinking drivers actually using the highways within a given region or nation. Therefore, the following review is limited to the most consistent findings from roadside research studies all of which were conducted in North America. More extensive reviews of such studies have recently been published elsewhere(55-59).

The personal variables most frequently studied are those which are relatively obvious and/or relatively straightforward and easy to obtain either from official records or from brief interviews. For the same reasons, these variables tend to have the highest potential utility for subsequent administrative and/or countermeasures purposes. The relevant variables tend to fall into three general classes, the first of which is essentially demographic and the second two of which are essentially behavioural: (a) biographical background variables (sex, age, etc.), (b) driving variables (driving history, record, and drinking-and-driving patterns), and (c) drinking variables (in particular, patterns of alcohol use in terms of quantity, frequency, and variability of consumption). Each class is considered below separately, but in terms of each of the other two classes.

III.4.1 Biographical variables

A number of studies (reviewed in (56) and (57) and/or cited below) have found significant relations between crashes, alcohol, and the following biographical variables: sex, age, marital status, and occupational level. Less consistent, but still potentially useful findings have been reported for such single and combined variables as race, ethnicity, religious affiliation, educational level, socio economic status, social stability/instability, social mobility, leisure activities, and contact with social agencies. The principal findings concerning each of these primary moderator variables are considered below.

Regarding sex, drinking-and-driving problems are clearly a predominantly male domain. In fact, by contrast to approximately equal representation in the adult population, males comprise a larger proportion of: licensed drivers (about two-thirds), drivers sampled during roadside surveys (about 80 percent), legally impaired (100 mg%) drivers sampled during roadside surveys (about 90 percent), fatally injured drivers (about 90 percent), as well as virtually all those convicted of driving while intoxicated (DWI) (about 98 percent)(9, 14, 60-62).

Regarding age, the general findings are that younger drivers with alcohol who get into trouble on the highways do so at lower average BACs than do their middle aged or older counterparts(14, 63). However, two extremely important additional factors must also be considered, namely, crash involvement and exposure. On the basis of his extensive review of the interrelations between age, alcohol, and crash involvement, Zylman(64) summarized the data from a number of studies showing that alcohol increases the probability of crash involvement among teenagers much more than among drivers age 20 to 24, who are in turn at higher risk than those in the range from 25 to 69, whereas the probability of crash involvement again rises among drivers aged 70 or older. In his definitive study of the interrelations of age, exposure, and alcohol involvement in nocturnal crashes, Carlson(65) has developed a method for analysing data from case/control studies to assess exposure and allow for a more accurate determination of the contribution of the other two factors. Regarding the reasons for the high crash involvement of drivers in the 16 to 25 age group, Carlson(65) concluded that these young drivers face two learning situations: first, learning to drive (with peak fatal crash involvement at age 18), and second, learning to drive after drinking (with peak alcohol-involved fatal crashes at age 21). These two learning situations result in crash involvement which is larger than can be attributed to exposure. Nevertheless, young drivers continue to have a disproportionately large number of crashes even after these two peaks in the learning period. Carlson concluded that the high crash involvement of drivers aged 16 to 25 corresponds to a high degree of night driving which he feels is the most significant single modifier variable after BAC itself. Thus the apparent over-representation of youth in the subpopulation of fatally injured drivers - both with and without alcohol - is partially attributable to their lifestyle which involves night driving for recreational purposes.

Regarding marital status, married drivers are under-involved in drinking and driving problems relative to unmarried drivers (single, divorced, separated, or widowed) when drivers under age 25 are excluded from the analysis. Divorced and separated male drivers are especially over-involved in drinking-and driving problems, as well as in alcohol usage in the nocturnal driving population(14, 56, 57, 61, 66).

Regarding occupational level, several studies(14, 61) have found that drivers from the lower levels are over-represented among those who have drinking and driving problems, especially DWI convictions. This pattern becomes even more pronounced when younger drivers (under age 25) are excluded from analysis.

III.4.2 Driving variables

A number of studies(52, 60, 65, 67) have found significant relations between alcohol, selected biographical variables, and the following driving variables: previous crashes, convictions, and suspensions. Regarding previous crashes, several investigators have found that drivers with alcohol-related problems (alcoholics, DWIs and fatally injured drivers with high BACs) have a higher incidence of crashes than random samples of the driving population(14, 60, 67). In the most comprehensive of these studies, Clark(60) reported that the DWI sample had the worst crash experience, with two-thirds of the sample having one or more crashes and with the average number of crashes being nearly three times higher than the average among a random sample of licensed drivers. She concluded that the group which misuses alcohol in the driving situation and is convicted of DWI is also a high-risk crash group prior to the incident which led to the conviction.

Regarding driving convictions, several studies have indicated that they are a more sensitive measure of deviant driving behaviour than crashes(14, 60, 67). In both the Michigan(60) and the Vermont(14) studies, the DWIs had significantly more previous driving convictions excluding the one for which they were sampled - than the two approximations of the driving populations obtained respectively by a sample of licensed Michigan drivers and by a sample of case/control drivers interviewed on Vermont highways. More specifically, the Michigan DWIs had four times as many convictions as the random samples of drivers. In fact, the Michigan DWIs averaged almost one conviction per year.

Driver fatalities in both studies(14, 60) also had more convictions for moving violations than the two random samples of drivers, but fewer than the DWI samples. Nevertheless, the driver fatalities with high BACs in Michigan were more similar to the DWIs in number of previous convictions, whereas those driver fatalities with no alcohol were more similar to the random sample of all licensed drivers.

It should be noted, however, that, in the Netherlands, studies concerning DWI recidivists have indicated that individual "predictability of their behaviour is low for practical purposes"(58).

Regarding licence suspensions, results similar to those for driving convictions discussed above were obtained in the Vermont study. For example, 60 percent of DWIs had already experienced one or more suspensions (during all years of driving) prior to the suspension in force at the time they were sampled, whereas only 14 percent of these DWIs had already experienced two or more previous suspensions. Hence, it can only be concluded that the overwhelming majority of individuals convicted for DWI were already well known to the courts and the motor vehicle officials.

In conclusion, these investigations of driving variables generally tend to support the popular assumption that past driving behaviour is the best _single_ predictor of future driving behaviour (see Fig. 7).

III.4.3 Drinking variables

Perhaps because of the relatively sensitive and stigmatized nature of the topic, very few studies are available in which data concerning reported drinking patterns were obtained from actual drivers, especially in conjunction with BAC data. The extent of the drinking pattern information obtained in previous studies ranges from quick and simple questions about drinking only on the day of the survey (e.g., whether or not; if yes, where and correct level(9, 66) to studies in which questions were asked about potentially very sensitive alcohol topics (e.g., frequency of "getting high" and of exceeding one's capacity, driving after drinking, having alcohol problems, hangovers, and blackouts)(2, 61). In other studies, very detailed questions were also asked about frequency and quantity of usual consumption of the major alcoholic beverage types, as well as typical occasions and places of drinking(14, 68, 69). Reviews and subsequent analyses of some of these studies have been presented by Cosper and Mozersky(70), Hurst(71) and Perrine(56, 57, 72).

The Vermont study(14) has been selected for the purposes of the present discussion because: (a) it contains the most extensive alcohol data for the widest range of the driving spectrum, and (b) it has the unique advantage of being able to validate aspects of reported drinking patterns by comparing them with actual BACs in samples of driver fatalities, case/control drivers and "clear-record" case/control drivers, as well as DWIs.

A drinking classification system based on reported usual frequency and quantity of alcohol consumption per sitting was developed in the Vermont study(14) to reflect the likelihood that a driver would attain an impairing amount of alcohol. The resultant _Quantity-Frequency Index_ (QFI) for preferred beverages is based upon that beverage which was reportedly consumed most frequently and in largest quantity, regardless of whether it was beer, liquor, or wine. (Regarding the fatally injured drivers, it should be noted that these data were obtained in interviews with next-of-kin.) The QFI data were compared and cross-tabulated with selected biographical variables and driving variables, as well as with obtained BACs. An overview of the reported drinking patterns is presented in Figure 8, in which the proportions of road-block case/control, clear record case/control, DWI, and deceased drivers are plotted as a function of a modified four-category (light, light-medium, medium, or heavy) QFI for preferred beverage. From this figure it is clear that as a group the DWIs are decidedly different in their self-reported drinking patterns from the other three samples, each taken as a group. Some of the more salient results of the QFI cross-tabulations with selected biographical variables and drinking and driving patterns are presented below on the basis of a composite summary across all four of these samples.

Regarding QFI and _sex_, the proportion of males to females increased as quantity and frequency of alcohol consumption increased. Regarding QFI and _age_, a surprisingly large proportion of the very young (i.e., teenaged) drivers could be categorized as heavy and frequent drinkers. The quantity of alcohol typically consumed decreased with increasing age. Regarding QFI and _marital status_, the proportion of married drivers decreased significantly as reported alcohol consumption increased.

Regarding QFI and _drinking and driving patterns_, two generalizations were offered by the investigators(14) as evidence that the BAC sampled at one point in time during the

Figure 7

PERCENT* OF «DRUNKEN»+ DRIVERS AND ADULT PEDESTRIANS
IN SELECTED SEGMENTS OF THE DRIVING POPULATION

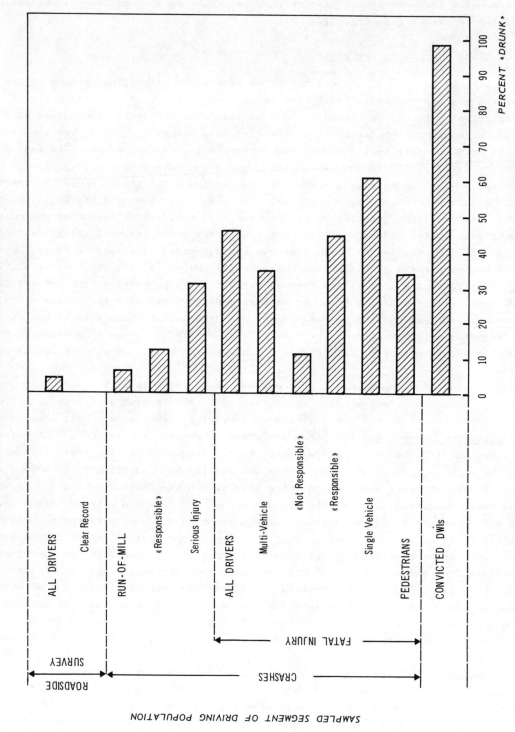

* Each proportion represents the average of relevant US studies reviewed in Chapter III-2, unless only one study was available.

+ Drunk = BAC of 100 mg % or greater.

Figure 8

PERCENT OF ROADBLOCK, CLEAR-RECORD, DWI, AND DECEASED DRIVERS WITH LIGHT, LIGHT-MEDIUM, MEDIUM, OR HEAVY QUANTITY-FREQUENCY INDEX FOR PREFERRED SEVERAGE

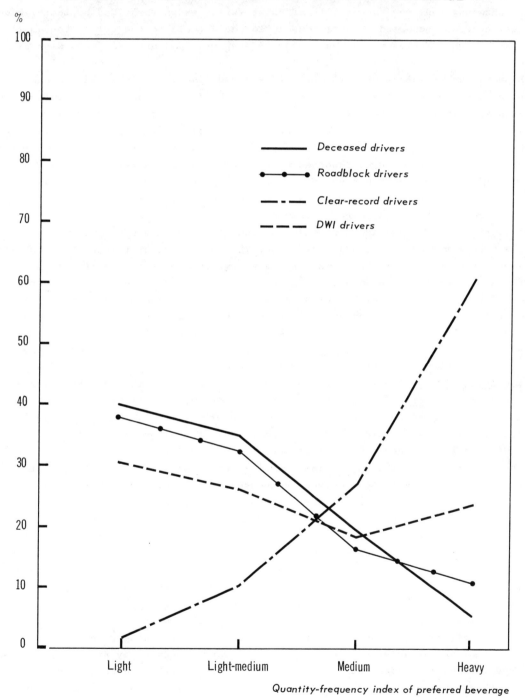

Source : Perrine et Coll. (1971).

study was a reliable indicator of usual patterns of driving after drinking: (a) the higher
the frequency of driving after drinking, the heavier and more frequent the reported usual
alcohol consumption, and vice versa; and (b) the lighter and less frequent the reported
usual alcohol consumption, the lower the frequency of driving after drinking, and vice
versa.

Perrine et al.(14) concluded from the analyses of the alcohol consumption data that
these variables are in fact useful in differentiating across the spectrum of drivers.
Further encouragement for the utility of these variables was provided by the high degree
of relation of the reported alcohol consumption data (QFI) to the _actual_ consumption data
(BACs) and to the driving variables (both self-reported and official record-check information).

Even further evidence of this utility resulted from a multiple discriminant analysis
of twelve selected variables (14). The four variables which were statistically significant in discriminating between the clear-record drivers and the DWI drivers were, in
order of importance: (a) the number of convictions for driving violations, (b) occupational level, (c) frequency of beer consumption, and (d) quantity of liquor consumption.
On the basis of a discriminant function using these four variables, 95 percent of the
clear-record drivers and 86 percent of the DWIs could have been correctly classified.
Thus, it was possible to determine classification "hits" and "misses" on the basis of a
weighted function which incorporated components from an individual's driving record, from
his socio-economic status, and from his reported patterns of alcohol use.

A subsequent study was conducted(52, 54, 73) in an attempt to use the results of the
above investigation(14) as the basis for the early psychometric identification of potential HRDDs. Accordingly, a questionnaire was developed and, in conjunction with the
Vermont ASAP and the official licensing examination, was given to four samples of appli-
cants for a new or renewal operator's licence, one sample of which being a group of drivers
convicted for DWI. The questionnaire, called the Vermont Driver Profile, obtained data
on the following variables: _biographical_ (sex, age, educational level of applicant and
both parents, employment status, occupational level, community type, marital status,
etc.); _driving history_ (in terms of experience, exposure, previous crashes, suspensions,
violations, etc.); _drinking history_ (in terms of frequency and quantity of alcohol
consumption, preferred beverage, crashes after drinking, etc.); and _attitudes_ (more
especially: attitudes toward accidents, violations, and alcohol; error-choice
items to indicate driving-related attitudes characterized as "risky" or "cautious").

The most significant results from the first stage of this study(52, 54) stem from
attempts to establish relations between responses on probable predictor variables and the
available validity criteria, i.e., the self-reported driving records of previous crashes,
citations, and suspensions from those individuals with prior driving experience. The
most important of these findings for all the male operators (excluding learners) are:
(a) significant variables regressed on number of _crashes in last 3 years_ (in order of
decreasing significance); crashes after drinking, age (negative), risky error-choice
(negative), number of citations in last 3 years, marital status and number of licence
suspensions; (b) significant variables regressed on _crashes after drinking_; combined
crashes, violations, and suspensions; age, risky error-choice, beer quantity, and wine
quantity (negative); (c) factor analysis indicated the following five factors accounted
for 65 percent of variance: 26 percent - beer (Quantity, Quantity-Frequency, and as
Preferred Beverage), 16 percent - wine and liquor (Q and Q-F), education and alcohol
attitude (high values on each variable associated with high values on each other variable),
9 percent - driving record (crashes, convictions, suspensions, crashes after drinking),
8 percent - mother's education, and marital status, 7 percent - attitudes toward accidents
and violations.

The DWIs differed from all other drivers on almost every variable analysed (by means of multiple discriminant analysis, as well as the above methods). As a group, the DWIs were: generally older; less well-educated, with less well-educated parents; more likely to be widowed, divorced, or separated; and more likely to be unemployed. Regarding driving variables, DWIs reported having had more crashes after drinking, more licence suspensions, and more crashes and citations in previous 3 years. Regarding drinking patterns, DWIs reported heavier consumption of beer, liquor, and preferred beverage (typically beer), but highest proportion of individuals who do not drink wine.

On the basis of these results, it was concluded that this psychometric approach to identifying HRDDs in conjunction with driver licensing programmes is both technically feasible and appears sufficiently valid to warrant continued refinement for wider implementation(52, 54). As noted above, a full-scale project using a computer-based psychometric questionnaire is currently being conducted in conjunction with the driver licensing programme in Washington, D.C.

Another psychometric questionnaire was developed and used by many ASAPs for court procedures to aid in identifying problem-drinking drivers from among the drivers arrested (but not yet sentenced) for DWI(51). Thus, this so-called Mortimer-Filkins test has been used in a number of ASAPs as part of pre-sentence investigations of DWI in attempted classifications of drinkers for sentencing and referral purposes.

In an attempt to determine which variables provide the best discrimination between problem drinkers and social drinkers, the Mortimer-Filkins interview and questionnaire procedures have been used at three ASAPs in conjunction with biographical, driving and drinking variables which already had demonstrated utility in previous studies. These data were analysed by multiple discriminant analyses in an effort to determine the relative importance of these variables in the search for the minimum information necessary to differentiate validly between problem and social drinkers. The following variables (in rank order of decreasing value of the discriminant loading) were reported(53) to be especially significant - and therefore relatively important - in the statistical differentiation between these two types of drinkers in the South Dakota study: Mortimer-Filkins score, drinking pattern, prior DWI convictions, BAC at the time of arrest, and prior public intoxication convictions. The following variables were also statistically significant, but had appreciably smaller discriminant loadings (and thus were relatively less important in the differentiation): age, marital status, work pattern, prior convictions for other crimes, prior reckless driving convictions, and prior licence violation convictions. Thus, in this official government report, it was concluded that "the most valid, reliable, and efficient pre-sentence investigation factors are the Mortimer-Filkins test score (interview and questionnaire), BAC at time of arrest, and driver and arrest records", although it was also acknowledged (regarding the South Dakota study) that the client's drinking pattern is a "major discriminatory data element"(53, p. 17).

By way of conclusion, what can be said regarding the initial question: can we in fact identify the high-risk drinking driver? On the basis of the evidence reviewed above, it would seem possible to specify some of the most relevant characteristics of the HRDD (at least in America), as one who: (1) drives at least occasionally at high BACs, (2) frequently consumes beer (and in generous quantity), (3) consumes a high quantity of liquor at one sitting, (4) seldom if ever drinks wine, (5) has had at least one prior crash after drinking, (6) has one or more prior DWI conviction, and (7) has one or more prior non-DWI conviction. Furthermore, we can specify some of the characteristics of the target population in which such HRDDs would be expected to be overrepresented: male, under 40 years of age (especially those in their 30's), lower socio-economic status, lower educational level, divorced or separated, and heavy drinking especially at public bars. The most important <u>characteristics of the risk situation</u> can be specified in terms of: nocturnal driving especially Friday and Saturday nights and travelling from a bar, tavern, or other public drinking establishment. Although not specifically reviewed in the above studies, the most frequently occurring <u>characteristics of alcohol-involved crashes</u> (especially at high BACs) are: nocturnal, involving damage to the front end of the vehicle, hitting a stationary object, running off the road, or hitting another vehicle at an intersection.

Finally, since convicted DWI repeaters comprise one important and readily identifiable group, they should perhaps be selected for immediate attention and rehabilitation efforts. As a second priority, drivers convicted of their first DWI should be closely examined in an attempt to differentiate between those who will be candidates for future DWI violations and those who will not. Studies are required to determine what programme characteristics are most appropriate for the specific groups of drivers concerned. According to several sources(53, 74) different countermeasures and treatments are appropriate for each of these major types of first-offender DWIs.

References

1. McCarroll, J.P., and Haddon, W., Jr., A Controlled Study of Fatal Automobile Accidents in New York City. J. Chronic Bis. 15:811-826, 1962.

2. Borkenstein, R.F., Crowther, R.F., Shumate, R.P., Ziel, W.G., and Zylman, R., The Role of the Drinking Driver in Traffic Accidents. Indiana University, Dept. of Police Administration, Bloomington, Indiana, 1964.

3. Perrine, M.W., Drinking and Driving: A Comparison of Deceased Drivers and Roadblock Control Motorists. Proceedings of the 5th International Conference on Alcohol and Traffic Safety. H.F. Schulz Verlag, Freiburg, Germany, 1969.

4. United States Dept. of Transportation. Alcohol Safety Action Projects: Evaluation of 1972 operations. Vol. I (Summary). NHTSA Technical Report, February, 1974. (See also Ref. 53.)

5. Stroh, C.M., Roadside Surveys of Drinking-driving Behaviour. Proceedings of Conference on Medical, Human and Related Factors Causing Traffic Accidents, Including Alcohol and Other Drugs. Ottawa, Ontario, Canada: Traffic Injury Research Foundation of Canada, May, 1972.

6. Stroh, C.M., Roadside Surveys of Drinking-driving Behaviour: A Review of the Literature and a Recommended Methodology. Unpublished manuscript, Road Safety Branch, Ministry of Transport, Ontario, September, 1972.

7. Storie, V.J., The Role of Alcohol and Human Factors in Road Accidents. 5th International Conference of the Int. Assoc. for Accidents and Traffic Medicine. London, September, 1975.

8. Carlson, W.L., Chapman, M.M., Clark, C.D., Filkins, L.D., and Wolfe, A.C., Washtenaw County BAC Roadside Survey. Report # HERI-71-126. Highway Safety Research Institute. University of Michigan, 1971.

9. Clark, C.D., Compton, M.J., Douglass, R.L., and Filkins, L.D., A Tree Year Comparison of Alcohol Related Driving Behaviour in Washranaw County, Michigan. HIT LAB Reports 4(2):1-14, Highway Safety Research Institute, University of Michigan, 1973.

10. Codling, P.J. and Sampson, P., Blood Alcohol in Road Fatalities,Before and After the Road Safety Act 1967. Supplementary Report 45UC. Dept. of the Environment, Transport and Road Research Laboratory, Crowthorne 1974.

11. Hurst, P.M., Estimating the Effectiveness of Blood Alcohol Limits. Behav. Res. Highway Safety 1:87-99. 1970. (See also Ref. 71.)

12. Hurst, P.M., Epidemiological Aspects of Alcohol in Driver Crashes and Citations. In Perrine, M.W., ad., Alcohol, Drugs, and Driving. NHSTA Technical Report, DOT HS 255-2-489, United States Dept. of Transportation, 1973.

13. Allsop, R.E., Alcohol and Road Accidents. Ministry of Transport, Road Research Laboratory Report N°. 6. Harmondsworth, 1966.

14. Perrine, M.W., Waller, J.A. and Harris, L.S., Alcohol and Highway Safety: Behavioural and Medical Aspects. NHTSA Technical Report, DOT HS-800-599. United States Dept. of Transportation, 1971.

15. Clayton, A.B., Booth, A.C. and McCarthy, P.E., A Controlled Study of the Role of Alcohol in Fatal Adult Pedestrian Accidents. 7th International Conference on Alcohol, Drugs and Traffic Safety, Melbourne, January, 1977.

16. Sedman, A., Wilkinson, P., Sakmar, E., Weidler, D., and Wagner, J., Food Effects on Absorption and Metabolism of Alcohol. Journal of Studies on Alcohol, 37, 1197-1214, 1976.

17. Hurst, P.H., and Bagley, S.K., Acute Adaptation to the Effects of Alcohol. Quarterly Journal of Studies on Alcohol, 33, 358-378, 1972.

18. Moskowitz, H., Daily, J., and Henderson, R., Acute Tolerance to Behavioral Impairment by Alcohol in Moderate and Heavy Drinkers. Technical Report HS-009-2-322 for the National Highway Traffic Safety Administration, Dept. of Transportation, Washington, D.C., 1974.

19. Perrine, M.W., Alcohol Influence on Driving-Related Behavior: A Critical Review of Laboratory Studies of Neurophysiological, Neuromuscular, and Sensory Activity. Journal of Safety Research, 5, 165-184, 1973

20. Wallgren, H., and Barry, H., III, Actions of Alcohol. Vol. I and II. Elsevier, Amsterdam, 1970.

21. Verriest, G., and LaPlasse, D., New Data Concerning the Influence of Ethyl Alcohol on Human Visual Thresholds. Experimental Eye Research, 4, 95-101, 1965.

22. Burg, A., Vision and Driving: A Report on Research. Human Factors, 13, 79-87, 1971.

23. Moskowitz, H., Sharma, D., and Shapiro, M., A Comparison of the Effects of Marihuana and Alcohol on Visual Functions. In: Lewis, M.F. (ed.). Current Research in Marihuana. Academic Press, New York, 1972.

24. Colson, A.W., The Effect of Alcohol on Vision. Journal of the American Medical Association, 115, 1525-1527, 1940

25. King, A.R., Tunnel Vision. Quarterly Journal of Studies on Alcohol, 3, 362-367, 1943.

26. Von Wright, J.M., and Mikkonen, V., The Influence of Alcohol on the Detection of Light Signals in Different Parts of the Visual Field. Scand. J. Psychol., 11, 167-175, 1970.

27. Hamilton, P., and Copeman, A., The Effect of Alcohol and Noise on Components of a Tracking and Monitoring Task. British Journal of Psychology, 61, 149-156, 1970.

28. Moskowitz, H., and Sharma, S., Effects of Alcohol on Peripheral Vision as a Function of Attention. Human Factors, 16, 174-180, 1974.

29. Buikhuisen, W., and Jongman, R.W., Traffic Perception under the Influence of Alcohol. Quarterly Journal of Studies on Alcohol, 33, 800-806, 1972.

30. Belt, B.L., and Krenek, R.F., Driver Eye Movement as a Function of Low Alcohol Concentrations. Driving Research Laboratory, The Ohio State University. Columbus, Ohio: 1969.

31. Pearson, R.G., Alcohol-hypoxia Effects upon Operator Tracking, Monitoring, and Reaction Time. Aerospace Medicine, 39, 303-307, 1968.

32. Chiles, W.D., and Jennings, A.E., Effects of Alcohol on Complex Performance. Report N°. AM69-14, Federal Aviation Administration, Office of Aviation Medicine, Civil Aeromedical Institute, Oklahoma City, 1969.

33. Levine, J.M., Greenbaum, G.D., and Notkin, E.R., The Effect of Alcohol on Human Performance: A Classification and Integration of Research Findings. American Institute for Research. Washington, D.C., 1973.

34. Kielholz, P., Goldberg, L., Hobi, V., and Reggiani, G., Teilsimulation zur Prüfung der Beeinträchtingung der Fahrtüchtigkeit unter Alkohol. Dutsch. Med. Wschr., 101, 1725-1731, 1971.

35. Laurell, H., Effects of Small Doses of Alcohol on Driver Performance in Emergency Traffic Situations. Report N°. 68A, National Swedish Road and Traffic Research Institute, 1975.

36. Moskowitz, H., and Murray, J., Alcohol and Backward Masking of Visual Information. Journal of Studies on Alcohol, 37, 40-45, 1976

37. Moskowitz, H., Ziedman, K., and Sharma, S., Visual Search Behavior While Viewing Driving Scenes under the Influence of Alcohol and Marihuana. Human Factors, 18, 417-432, 1976.

38. Cohen, J., Chance, Skill and Luck. London, Penguin Books, 1960

39. Snapper, K., and Edwards, W., Effects of Alcohol on Psychomotor Skill and Decision-making in a Driving Task. Paper presented at the Society of Automotive Engineers Congress, Detroit, MI, 1973.

40. Sjoberg, L., Alcohol and Gambling. Psychopharmacologia, 14, 284-298, 1969.

41. Enslin, M.D., Problem Drivers: The Effects and After Effects of Alcohol on Driver Proficiency. Special Report PERS 222, Council for Scientific and Industrial Research, Johannesburg, South Africa, 1975.

42. Moskowitz, H., and Burns, M., The Effect of Alcohol upon the Psychological Refractory Period. Quarterly Journal of Studies on Alcohol, 32, 782-790, 1971.

43. Craik, F.I.M., Similarities between the Effects of Aging and Alcoholic Intoxication on Memory Performance, Construed within a "Levels of Processing" Framework. In: Birnbaum, I.M., and Parker, E.S. (eds.), Alcohol and Memory, Hillsdale, N.J., Lawrence Eribaum Associates Press, (in press).

44. Goodwin, D.W., Powell, B.J., and Stern J.A., Behavioral Tolerance to Alcohol in Moderate Drinkers. American Journal of Psychiatry, 127, 87-89, 1971.

45. Burns, M., and Moskowitz, H., Psychophysical Tests for DWI Arrest. Report to the National Highway Traffic Safety Administration, Southern California Research Institute, Los Angeles, CA, 1977.

46. Burns, M., and Moskowitz, H., Gender-related Differences in Impairment of Performance by Alcohol. Paper presented at the National Council on Alcoholism Conference, San Diego, CA, May, 1977.

47. Linnoila, M., Erwin, C., Logue, P., Gentry, W. and Cleveland, W., Gender-related Effects of Alcohol on Performance. (unpublished study)

48. Frankenhaeuser, M., Dunne, E., Bjurström, H., and Lundburg, U., Counteracting Depressant Effects of Alcohol by Psychological Stress. Psychopharmacologia, 38, 271-278, 1974.

49. Lovibond, S.H., and Caddy, G.R., Discriminative Aversive Control in the Moderation of Alcoholics' Drinking Behavior. Behavior Therapy, 1, 437-444, 1970.

50. Silverstein, S.J., Natan, P.E., and Taylor, H.A., Blood Alcohol Level Estimation and Controlled Drinking by Chronic Alcoholics. Behavior Therapy, 5, 1-15, 1974.

51. Mortimer, R.G., Filkins, L.D., Kerlan, M.V. and Lower, J.S., Psychometric Identification of Problem Drinker. Quarterly Journal of Studies on Alcohol, 34; 1332-1335, 1973.

52. Perrine, M.W., The Vermont Driver Profile: A Psychometric Countermeasure for Early Detection of Potential High Risk Drivers. In Israelstram, S., and Lambert, S. (Eds.) Alcohol, Drugs, and Traffic Safety. Addiction Research Foundation of Ontario, Toronto, Canada, 1975.

53. United States Dept. of Transportation, National Highway Traffic Safety Administration. Alcohol Safety Action Projects: Evaluation of Operations - 1974. Vol. II, Chapter 5, Technical Report, DOT-HS-801-728, 1975. (See also Ref. 4.)

54. Perrine, M.W., The Vermont Driver Profile: A Psychometric Countermeasure for Early Identification of Potential High Risk Drivers. National Highway Traffic Safety Administration, Technical Report, DOT Contract FH-11-7543, 1973.

55. Carr, B., Borkenstein, R.F., Perrine, M.W., Van Berkom, L.C., Voas, R.B., International Conference on Research Methodology for Roadside surveys. National Highway Traffic Safety Administration, Technical Report, DOT HS-801-220, 1974.

56. Perrine, M.W., Alcohol and Highway Safety. In Alcohol and Health: Special Report to the United States Congress (2nd ed.), Secretary of Health, Education, and Welfare (Ed.). DHEW Publication; U.S. Government Printing Office, Washington, D.C., 1974.

57. Perrine, M.W., Alcohol Involvement in Highway Crashes: A Review of the Epidemiologic Evidence. In Clinics in Plastic Surgery, R.D. Schultz (Ed.). M.B. Saunders, Philadelphia, 1975.

58. SWOV. Drinking and Driving. Institute for Road Safety Research, SWOV, Technical Report, Voorburg, Netherlands, 1976.

59. Voas, R.B., Roadside Surveys, Demographics and BACs of Drivers, In Israelstram, S., and Lambert, S. (Eds). Alcohol Drugs and Traffic Safety. Addiction Research Foundation of Ontario, Toronto, 1975.

60. Clark, Cheryl D., A Comparison of the Driving Records and Other Characteristics of Three Alcohol Involved Populations and a Random Sample of Drivers. Highway Safety Research Institute, University of Michigan, HIT LAB Reports 2 (10), 1-5, 1972.

61. Wolfe, A.C., Characteristics of Alcohol-impaired Drivers. Society of Automotive Engineers, Report 750878, 1975.

62. Wolfe, A.C., Characteristics of Late-night Weekend Drivers: Results of the United States National Roadside Breath-Testing Survey and Several Local Surveys. In Israelstram, S., and Lambert, S. (Eds). Alcohol, Drugs, and Traffic Safety. Addiction Research Foundation of Ontario, Toronto, 1975.

63. Voas, R.B., Alcohol, Drugs and Young Drivers. United States Dept. of Transportation, National Highway Traffic Safety Administration, Technical Report, 1974.

64. Zylman, R. Youth, Alcohol, and Collision-Involvement, Journal of Safety Research 5, 58-72, 1973.

65. Carlson W.L., Age, Exposure, and Alcohol Involvement in Night Crashes, Journal of Safety Research 5, 247-259, 1973.

66. Carlson, W.L., Alcohol Usage of the Nighttime Driver, Journal of Safety Research 4, 12-25, 1972.

67. Filkins, L.D., Clark, C.D., Rosenblatt, C.A., Carlson, W.L., Kerlan, M.W., and Mason, H., Alcohol Abuse and Traffic Safety: A Study of Fatalities, DWI Offenders, Alcoholics, and Court-related Treatment Approaches. United States Dept. of Transprtation, National Highway Safety Bureau, Technical Report FH-11-6555 and FH-11-7129, 1970.

68. Damkot, D.K., Perrine, M.W., Whitmore, D.G., Toussie, S.R., and Geller, H.A., On-the-Road Driving Behaviour and Breath Alcohol Concentration, Vol. 1., National Highway Traffic Safety Administration, Technical Report, DOT HS-364-3-757, 1975.

69. Perrine, M.W., Methodological Considerations in Conducting and Evaluating Roadside Research Surveys. National Highway Traffic Safety Administration. Technical Report, DOT HS-800-471, 1971.

70. Cosper, R., and Mozersky, K., Special Correlates of Drinking and Driving, Quarterly Journal of Studies on Alcohol, Supplement N°. 4, 58-117, 1968.

71. Hurst, P.M., Estimating the Effectiveness of Blood Alcohol Limits. In Alcohol, Drugs, and Driving, M.W. Perrine (Ed.). National Highway Traffic Safety Administration, Technical Report, DOT HS-801-096, 1974. (See also Ref. 11.)

72. Perrine, M.W., The Spectrum of Drinking Drivers. In Alcohol and Highway Safety, Patricia F. Waller (Ed.). North Carolina Symposium on Highway Safety. University of North Carolina Press, Chapel Hill, North Carolina, 1972.

73. Perrine, M.W., The Driver Profile: Using Driver Licensing as a Countermeasure for Highway Crashes Involving Alcohol. Proceedings of the Department of Transportation Forum on Traffic Safety Alcohol Countermeasures. Washington, D.C., 1971.

74. Spoerer, E., Rehabilitation von Alkoholauffälligen Kraftfahrern in Nordamerika. Bundesanstalt für Strassenwesen, Technical Report, 7517/1, Cologne, 1976.

IV

DRUGS

IV.1 Introduction

Since very little research has as yet been conducted on the effects of drug use on road safety, the aim of this chapter will be to examine the kinds of drugs that probably are important to road safety, in terms both of the extent of consumption and of their effect in impairing driving performance.

Very few attempts have been made to relate the use of drugs to the occurrence of accidents. The most comprehensive reviews of the subject(1, 2, 3)(*) indicate that unequivocal figures concerning the incidence of drug use by drivers involved in accidents are not available. Few drugs have undergone rigorous laboratory testing with the measurement of their levels in body fluids. Also few investigators have used similar criteria for selecting their experimental populations. Therefore, comparisons of the data between laboratories are difficult.

An important point to note is that, to date, there have been few determined efforts to associate the use of psychotropic drugs by drivers with specific driving errors or with responsibility for accidents. This would be an essential step in establishing the potential hazard of driving and drug use.

The following Tables 3 to 5 review studies which have attempted to relate both drug use in the driving population and drug use among those drivers who have been involved in fatal or non-fatal accidents.

Classifications of drugs can be established in numerous ways, and rationales are given for alternative systems. No present classification of drugs is fully satisfactory. Even a chemical classification of drugs is imperfect. It is difficult to define the point at which a structural derivative becomes pharmacologically so dissimilar from the parent compound that it can no longer be regarded as a derivative. The dose of a drug can determine its effect and classification, e.g., in an adult, amylobarbital in a dose of 30 mg is a sedative but 100 mg of the same drug is a hypnotic. Regardless of pharmacological activity, legislators and international conventions have created drug classifications suitable for their purposes.

Due to these difficulties in classifying drugs a simplified WHO classification is used in this document.

(*) See list of references at the end of this Chapter.

TABLE 3

INCIDENCE OF DRUG USE: GENERAL POPULATIONS

Author & Reference	Type of Study	Incidence of Drug Use	Drug Type(s)

Parry (4)
 	
1968
	General population: over 18 years
	(i) N = 3,990
	(ii) N = 2,649
	(a) Use of psychotropic drugs
	       in the past 12 months
	(b) Use of psychotropic drugs
	       at any time
	(c) % of total prescriptions
	       represented by psychotro-
	       pic drugs
		
		25 %
		
		48 %
		
		14 %
			Sedatives
			Tranquilizers
			Stimulants
			(includes pres-
			cribed and over-
			the counter
			drugs)

Traffic Laws Commentary(5)
 	
1965
	(a) Smith, Kline, French - U.S.
	       "driving population"
	
	       Use of prescribed drugs at
	       any one point in time
	(b) U.S.D.H.E.W. - 1963
	       U.S. use of over-the-
	       counter drugs at any one
	       point in time
		10 % - 20 %
		
		1 $\frac{1}{2}$ x "prescri-
		bed drugs"
			"prescribed
			drugs"
			
			over-the-
			counter

Chelton and Whisnant(6) 1966	Acute alcoholic patients N = 100	38 % (by analyses) 9 % (by question- ing)	Barbiturates Tranquilizers (major and minor)

Milner(7)
 	
1969
	N = 4,584
	753 (16.4 % on prescription
	       drugs)
	of those on drugs
	    85 % of males use alcohol
	    60 % held driving licences
	    71 % females used alcohol
	    42 % held driving licences
		335 (7.3 %)
		
		18 (0.4 %)
		280 (6.1 %)
		181 (3.9 %)
		Conclusion:
		   57 % males
		   35 % females
		at risk of drink-
		ing and driving
		while taking
		drugs
			Tranquilizers
			(major and
			minor)
			
			Stimulants
			Sedatives
			Antidepressants

Rees(8) 1966	Survey of 1,190 motorists (927 males, 263 females) % use > 3 months within past 5 years % taking drugs currently	 males 3.4 % females 5 % 2.3 %	Sedatives Tranquilizers Antidepressants

TABLE 3 (Continued)

Author & Reference	Type of Study	Incidence of Drug Use	Drug Type(s)
Alha(9) 1971	Examination of urine N = 100 subjects arrested for drunken driving 1969-70	26 (23.6 %) 26 (23.6 %) 10 (9 %) 7 (6.3 %) 6 (5.4 %) 21 (19.1 %)	Barbiturates Benzodiazepines Meprobamate Solvents Phenothiazine derivatives Miscellaneous drugs
Waller, Lamborn, and Steffenhagen (10) 1974	N = 1,271 surveys of drug usage and driving habits of university students	49 % For frequent users of canabis 25 % of driving while "high" occurred under the combined effects of marijuana and alcohol.	Users of cannabis during the past year.
Glauz and Blackburn(11) 1975	Roadside survey driving popul-ation with provision of blood and urine samples 78 % of 1,500 participated; 840 blood samples and 1,029 urine samples. Breath samples and lip swabs also requested 41 drugs plus marijuana screened	Breath test: 37 % had been drinking 4 % had BAC level $\geq$ 100 mg%. 48 (4.6 %) or urines positive 9.2 % positive 53.3 % positive	Ethanol Meprobamate, secobarbital phenobarbital, methamphetamine, codeine, chlor-pheniramine, diphenthyldantoin, Phenylpropanola-mine, amitriptyl, methaqualone, methylphenidate, diazepam Marijuana Nicotine
Crespy and Neyroud(162) 1972	Survey of psychotropic drugs; prescriptions of physicians	30 %	Hypnotics, Sedatives, Tranquilizers

TABLE 4

INCIDENCE OF DRUG USE: NON-FATAL ACCIDENTS

Author & Reference	Type of Study	Incidence of Drugs	Drug Type(s)
Finkle et al. (12) 1968	N = 10,436 Drug use by drivers Questioning confirmed by blood/urine samples Biochemical technique not adequate for some drugs	2,559 (25 %) positive for drugs In 1,406 (13 % of total) drugs were legally "dangerous drugs" When BAC was <150 mg% but clinically there was "intoxication" 159 (22 %) were positive for drugs	In order of frequency: tranquilizers analgesics stimulants hormones sedatives and hypnotics anti-infectives vitamins antidiabetics antihistaminics anticoagulants narcotic analgesics
Gupta and Kofoed (13) 1966	Number of people charged with "driving under influence" where there was 0 % blood alcohol concentration.	barb. tranq. 1958 1 0 1962 9 0 1964 18 7	Barbiturates Tranquilizers
Reinartz (14) 1962	Questioning of 500 drivers involved in traffic accidents (auto, cycle, etc.) % auto drivers (N = 296) using drugs in past 24 hours % total having taken variety of drugs in past 24 hours	15.2 % 12.6 %	Sedatives Hypnotics Stimulants Miscellaneous
Wagner (15) 1962	Medical examination and questioning of 2,060 drivers under influence of alcohol % admitting to drug use in past 24 hours	11 %	Sedatives Hypnotics Analgesics Miscellaneous
Wangel (16) 1962	Questioning of 6,067 drivers in general traffic accidents % of drug use in past 24 hours	15 %	Tranquilizers Hypnotics Analgesics Antibiotics, etc.
Gilbert (17) 1973	Hospitalized patients after accidental injury. Blood specimens from N = 460 tested for drugs and alcohol.	35 (7.6 %) 16 (3.5 %) 14 (3 %) 12 (2.5 %) 7 (1.5 %) 25 % patients with BAC levels ≥50 mg% are likely to be using sedatives such as barbiturates or diazepam	Salicylates Barbiturates Diazepam Chlordiazepoxide Phenothiazines

TABLE 4 (Continued)

Author & Reference	Type of Study	Incidence of Drugs	Drug Type(s)
Haffner and Lunde(18) 1974	Hospitalized accident victims N = 74	7 (9.5 %) 31 (41.9 %) 8 (10.8 %)	Diazepam Ethanol Both diazepam and ethanol
Neyroud(163)	Questionning of 962 hospitalized drivers injured in traffic accidents; % having taken psy-chotropics drugs in past 24 hours	8 %	Tranquilizers Hypnotics Antidepressants Stimulants

TABLE 5

INCIDENCE OF DRUG USE: FATAL ACCIDENTS – AUTO AND AVIATION

Author & Reference	Type of Study	Incidence of Drugs	Drug Type(s)
Braunstein et al.(19) 1968	183 fatally injured auto drivers	1.5 %	Barbiturates
Briglia(20) 1955	95 traffic deaths (auto and cycle)	3 %	Barbiturates
Davis and Fisk(21) 1966	179 fatal single vehicle accidents (drivers killed "immediately")	8 cases (4.5 %) 4 of the posi-tive cases had BAC $>$ 80 mg% carbon monoxide detected in 3 of the positive cases	Barbiturates Glutethimide Caffeine Aminophyllin
State of California Highway Patrol(22) 1967	772 fatal single vehicle accidents (death within 15 minutes of acci-dent)	84 (11 %) of males positive for drugs 18 (2.3 %) fe-males positive for drugs 61 % of those positive for drugs had BAC $\geq$ 80 mg%.	Barbiturates Tranquilizers Stimulants Diphenylhydantoin Caffeine

TABLE 5 (Continued)

Author & Reference	Type of Study	Incidence of Drugs	Drug Type(s)
Sunshine et al.(23) 1968	Fatal vehicular accidents (death within 12 hours of accident) N = 157	2.6 % positive for drugs 1.3 % > 10 % carboxy. Hg. 17.3 % between 5 and 10 % carboxy Hg. 17.7 % BACs > 10 mg%	Barbiturates Amphetamines
Hossack(24) 1972	400 fatal accident victims between June 70 and May 71 Autopsy evidence 100 selected for presence of drugs in blood.	4 (1 %) 2 (0.5 %) 1 (0.25 %) 1 (0.25) 7 of 8 (87.5 %) had a BAC level such that this alone probably contributed to the accident.	Amphetamines Barbiturates Bromureide Chloroquine
Turk, McBay and Hudson(25) 1974	Blood and urine examination of fatally injured drivers and pedestrians for alcohol and drugs N = 67 drivers and N = 33 pedestrians	33 (49.2 %) drivers positive for 20 (60.6 %) pedestrians positive for 4 (6 %) positive for drugs in drivers 7 (35 %) positive for drugs (in pedestrians)	Ethanol Ethanol Phenobarbital, propoxyphene, salicylate and chlorpromazine Phenobarbital, meprobamate, amobarbital, secobarbital & salicylates.
Woodhouse(26) 1974	Analysis of blood, urine, and bile of fatally injured drivers: screening for 46 commonly abused drugs by TLC, GLC, and Mass Spec. Blood N = 682 Bile N = 526 Urine N = 517	Blood Bile Urine 2.9 % 4.6 % 5.2 % 1.32% 0.57% 0.58% 0.15% 1.14% 35% 0.29% 2.09% 1.35% 0 % 0.57% 0.58% 8.4 % 17.3 % 54.9 % 12.8 % 19.8 % 22.1 % 0.44% 0 % 0.38% Tests for cannabis performed on hand and nasal swabs. Positive results. 11.8 % for hand swabs 38.4 % for the nasal swabs 58 % had ingested 47 % had BAC level ≥ 100 mg%	Sedatives and Hypnotics Stimulants Antihistamines & decongestants Tranquilizers Narcotic analg. Nicotine Aspirin Miscellaneous drugs Alcohol Ethanol

IV.2 Classification

(1)   Sedatives/Hypnotics   Barbiturates, benzodiazepines, carbamates, gluthethimide, ethyl and some higher alcohols;   methaqualoné.

(2)   Tranquilizers   some overlap with 1.1 benzodiazepines, phenothiazines, meprobamate.

(3)	Antidepressants	Certain potent enzyme inhibitors known as monoamine-oxidase inhibitors or MAOI; polycyclic compounds such as amitriptyline, imipramine, dexepin, and maprotiline.
(4)	Anaesthetics	Ultra-short acting barbiturate, trichloroethylene, nitrous oxide, cyclopropane, ether, chloroform, fluothane, penthrane and enthrane.
(5)	Narcotics (excluding cannabis and cocaine)	Includes opium alkaloids such as morphine, its derivatives, e.g., heroin and synthetic substitutes for the opium derivatives such as pethidine and methadone.
(6)	Hallucinogens	Most are potent drugs for the relief of pain. Lysergide, certain ring substituted amphetamines known by a variety of initials, e.g., S.T.P., Bufotenine and mescaline. Certain derivatives of ethyl and methyl tryptamine such as psilocybin.
(7)	Cannabis	Marijuana, hashish, bhang, kif, ganja.
(8)	Stimulants (including cocaine)	Amphetamines, methylphenidate, phenmetrazine, chlorphentermine, mephentermine, mazindol.
(9)	Other drugs	Various anti-histamines, cardiovascular drugs, cathartics and diuretics, hormones, antidiabetic drugs, and antihypertensives.
(10)	Volatile liquids	Liquid and gaseous substances used in industry, certain pesticides; nitrous oxide, airplane glue, nailpolish remover; in particular carbon monoxide gas.

IV.3 Consumption and Past Trends

To estimate the significance of drug use to traffic safety, international, national, and regional statistics and special studies concerning sale and consumption patterns of drugs have to be considered. However, the main emphasis has to be given to consumption of drugs by motorists and occurrence of drugs in victims of traffic accidents.

As mentioned in the WHO report, an increase in the cost and amount of drug consumption has been a matter of serious concern in all countries studied, although the national data are not directly comparable.

The need for periodical collection of information is obvious, but this is time consuming and expensive. It is thus advisable to select data of greatest value and least complexity.

General international statistics

No reliable information on drug consumption which allows international comparisons is available. The only information from different countries is a list of per capita annual expenditures for drugs (WDMM-1975). This comparison is not meaningful for the following reasons: the price of given drugs varies greatly from country to country; the proportion of drugs prescribed that are actually consumed may vary from country to country; the proportion of the population that consumes these drugs is not known; and the proportion of the population that consumes these drugs and has access to an automobile is not known. A number of drugs readily available in one country are strictly controlled in others. The average dosage and duration of drug use and the mileage driven under the influence of a drug varies from country to country.

It does not seem reasonable to seek international data for comparison at the present time. There is some information concerning drug involvement in traffic accidents within any nation, and thus national statistical collections are of the highest priority for the present time.

National statistics

These should have a standard data base in order to reveal fluctuations and trends over the years. Subdivision into certain therapeutic groups is performed in some countries already.

Engels and Siderius(27) reviewed several studies of the consumption of drugs in six European countries (Austria, France, Hungary, Netherlands, Sweden, and Great Britain). In Denmark the health authorities have registered the use of certain stimulants, sedatives and tranquilizers every 5th year since 1960(28). Sources of information were manufacturers, importers, wholesale dealers and pharmacies, supplemented by a one-day's prescription study. The study revealed a trend to decreasing use of barbiturates but increased use of tranquilizers and antidepressives.

Regional analyses

This may be carried out within countries, allowing for more detailed analysis, e.g., by a study of ways of distribution of drugs (over-the-counter, by prescription, through hospitals, etc.).

Detailed study were performed in France through the Market Research Institute CREDOC, by Rosch et al.(29) and by ONSER(161, 162). It included groupings for the main pharmaceutical products and additionally analyzed medical reasons for consumption.

Another, less detailed study was performed by Lazar(30) from Hungary.

Surveys based upon prescriptions

Collected from National Health Services, pharmacies or physicians and subdivided by sex and age, socio-economic status, etc., or by diseases, such studies could be performed with a special view to traffic safety. In some countries a commercial drug monitoring service (e.g., IMS) operates a continuing survey of drug sales, the medical indications for these sales are obtained by means of information derived from selected doctors and pharmacists. Because the material has considerable commercial value to manufacturers, it is protected by legal confidentiality.

Swaren and Smedby from Sweden(31, 32) by extrapolation from a regional study estimated the monthly drug consumption of one million people expressed in numbers of normal doses. This resulted in the following figures: Analgesics: 7.32 million; sedatives: 2.13 million; barbiturates and other hypnotics: 1.82 million; antispasmodics: 1.27 million; antihypertensives: 0.67 million and antidepressants and CNS stimulants: 0.37 million.

Special studies among consumers

Examined by means of questionnaires or through interviews or both, this will reveal actual consumption, not sales of drugs. The method has limitations because of incomplete returns, and incorrect answers due to forgetfulness, misunderstandings, or disinterests.

An example of a smaller study carried out in a country medical practice, that of Rees(8) in Wales should be mentioned. Such studies could easily be carried out on a larger scale and in such a manner as to make them comparable within countries and across national borders.

<u>Roadside studies</u>

These are discussed in Chapter II of this report and the results of drug studies are presented in Table 3.

<u>Hospital studies on victims of traffic accidents</u>

These enable thorough reviews and more or less complete chemical examinations, but the materials will be selected.

Several important results from such studies are published and have revealed that from 3.1 percent to 16 percent of the victims have been "drug positive". Drugs have been considered causative for the accidents in 4 - 5 percent. The variance of the results of these studies may be explained by different analytical methods (see Ref. 33 and 163).

<u>Medico-legal-toxicological examination in fatal traffic accidents</u>

These studies can yield complete information, provided that necessary expertise and equipment are available. The material at one's disposal for such studies is selected, because fatal cases do not represent <u>all</u> traffic accident victims. Legal authorities request toxicological examination only from a positive point of view, rather than based on a random selection of cases. Some results of these studies are indicated in Table 6.

TABLE 6

<u>RESULTS OF SCREENING FOR DRUGS IN VICTIMS OF FATAL TRAFFIC ACCIDENTS</u>

Author : Year Country	N =	Drug positive	Screening for
Naess-Schmidt 1971 Denmark	240	3.3 %	Barbiturates (4 pos.) Meprobamate (4 pos.) 82 for organic bases (0) 142 for salicylates (0)
Whitlock 1971 Australia	119 74	0 0	Barbiturates Amphetamines
Braunstein et al. 1968 United States	168	1.5 %	"Total spectrum of drugs" Barbiturates (2 pos.) Diphenylhydant (1 pos.)
Kaempe and Dalgaard 1972 Denmark	200	14 %	Liver, blood and urine screened for drugs, which were considered the likely cause of accident in 4 cases

From Astrup and Retpen (33).

IV.4 <u>Social Attitudes Toward Drug Usage</u>

Drug using behaviour and social attitudes towards drugs in society are related, and because of the deleterious effects of many kinds of drugs on driving skills, it is expedient to consider the components of motivation for drug use.

In effect, most people living in industrialised societies have employed since child-hood some forms of drug. These may modify mood by relieving discomfort or pain, counter-act feelings or tiredness, or alternatively lessen feelings of anxiety. Examples include caffeine in coffee and tea, nicotine in tobacco and ethanol, in addition to numerous preparations of analgesics sometimes combined with mild psychoactive substance.

While it can be conjectured that in some instances drugs used non-medically are really forms of self-medication for persons with basic feelings of unhappiness, or who are experiencing discomfort from daily stress, it is equally clear that customs, culture and the perceived habits of family members, friends, and immediate social groupings lar-gely determine the prevalence and the specific patterns of drug use in a society.

During the past fifteen years there has been a broadening of drug use to chemicals which were formerly considered exotic, adventurous or capable of producing new kinds of bodily or psychic sensations. Others sought feelings of power - while still others sought tranquility. There have occurred several periods of widespread drug use, especially by young persons who have variously employed stimulants such as cocaine and methampheta-mine, sedative-euphoriants such as cannabis, hallucinogenic compounds of several forms, and narcotics such as heroin or dilandid.

In addition, psychopharmacology has made available a host of new psychoactive medi-caments to combat pathological anxiety, mental depression, and other forms of mental illness that formerly would have occasioned short or long terms in psychiatric hospitals and institutions. Physicians worldwide have greeted these agents with gratitude, but unfortunately with some degree of over-enthusiasm, and exaggerated expectations of ther-apeutic effectiveness. The effect is the presence of a large number of individuals who are still capable of holding a driving permit, but who are consuming large amounts of psychoactive drugs, often different types simultaneously, over long periods of time. While these persons are usually improved over their non-medicated state, they are commonly still unstable, and may from time to time employ alcohol in addition to their prescribed medication or vary their doses without medical advice to do so. Over-the-counter drugs add another dimension to the problem.

However, whether drug-using behaviour stems from medical or non-medical sources, negative effects on driving skills may be logically expected.

With the plethora of drugs now available for use, it seems clear that it is incumbent to assess carefully the varying liability of each class of drug, and some spe-cific drugs, as their use will adversely affect driving behaviour and abilities.

IV.5 Sedative-Hypnotics

Definition

The term "sedative-hypnotic" as used in this chapter refers to any drug that is used in order to induce or maintain sleep, or in low doses for daytime sedation. It should be pointed out that sedative-hypnotics overlap with minor tranquilizers. All barbiturates have the "-al" ending in American usage, and the "-one" ending in British usage.

Epidemiology

Extent of use. Estimates of the extent of sedative-hypnotic use are mainly based on questionnaire studies. Therefore, the figures given are probably underestimates of the true ones. The most commonly used sedative-hypnotics vary from country to country. The barbiturates are the most commonly used ones in United States, whereas in Scandinavia

the benzodiazepines are used more often than the barbiturates(34, 35). About 40 percent
more barbiturates equal to 1.6 thousand million 100 mg dosage units, are used illicitly(36).
According to a 1974 New York State survey(37) the incidence of illicit barbiturate use
among the population aged 14 and over was 2.6 percent. The definition for incidence of
use was the taking of these drugs at least six times during the previous month. The incidence of legal barbiturate use rose markedly with increasing age. For the sample in
this United States survey, barbiturates were most often used as part of a therapeutic
regimen by persons who belonged to the middle or lower socioeconomic classes. Twenty-two
percent of the users took the drugs in a manner other than as prescribed.

Three American surveys have found that 4.4 percent of the population aged between
18 and 74 years(36) and 17 to 19 percent of college students(38, 39) use barbiturates.

The incidence of non-barbiturate sedative-hypnotic use in the New York State survey
was 1.4 percent of the population. Elderly women were the group using these drugs most
commonly(37). The use of the benzodiazepine derivatives marketed as hypnotics is rapidly
increasing in the United States.

Involvement in traffic accidents. The estimates about the role of sedative-hypnotics
in traffic accidents vary considerably. Questionnaire studies have demonstrated either
a 1.5 - 2 times increased rate of traffic accident involvement(40) or no increase in the
number of traffic accidents among sedative-hypnotic users over non-users(40). As above,
some studies point out a considerable over-involvement of barbiturate users among drivers
in fatal accidents(41), whereas other studies find a very low involvement rate of barbiturate users(42, 43).

It should be stressed that there are no hospital studies available concerning the
involvement of sedative-hypnotic users in traffic accidents. This is a considerable void,
because the extent of use of barbiturate and nonbarbiturate hypnotics is largest among
middle-aged and elderly people.

There are at present no data concerning the involvement of benzodiazepine hypnotics
in traffic accidents.

Laboratory studies

The intermediate and long-acting barbiturates used as sedative-hypnotics have been
shown to impair the following skills in healthy volunteers: simple auditory(44) and
visual-motor coordination(45,44), digit symbol substitution, and symbol copying(46).

Barbiturates also attenuate oculomotor function. Nystagmus has been induced by low
doses of barbiturates, and these drugs can interfere with eye convergence. Eye movements
become jerky after low doses of barbiturates(47). During angular acceleration, 100 mg of
secobarbital induced more errors in a tracking task and enhanced vestibular nystagmus(48).

Simulated driving and flying, and closed course vehicle handling tests have shown
that skills are impaired following low doses of barbiturates in healthy volunteers(49, 50,
51, 52). For a comprehensive review of the subject of barbiturates and driving, see
Sharma(53).

Few studies have been carried out to compare the effects of inadequate sleep with
the effects of barbiturates on the morning following their use as hypnotics. Studies on
the effects of sleep deprivation have demonstrated that there is no significant impairment
of psychomotor skills related to driving after sleep deprivation of one night or more(54).

100 mg of amylobarbital did not impair choice reaction coordination, or information-
processing performance on the following morning in healthy, trained volunteers(54). The
drug, although present in the blood of all subjects, did not accumulate during the two-week
administration period.

In the same study the nonbarbiturate hypnotics gluthimide and diphenhydramine-methaqualone had effects similar to those of amylobarbital. There is dose-dependent impairment, particularly of the motor components of various tests related to driving, even 12 hours after administration.

In some psychomotor tests the decrement in performance was significant for secobarbital, but not for flurazepam. With long administration of secobarbital, both the effectiveness of the drug as a hypnotic and the decrement in driving performance decreased considerably(45).

The benzodiazepine-hypnotics nitrazepam and flurazepam after long term use impaired psychomotor skills to a greater extent than other hypnotics studied(54, 55, 56). The active metabolites of these drugs were demonstrated to accumulate in the bodies of the volunteers. The hazards of these drugs may be more pronounced in older subjects(57). These drugs, unlike barbiturates, may also slow eye movements(58). This may become critical in dense traffic.

Concluding remarks

The epidemiological evidence of the role of sedative-hypnotics in traffic accidents remains controversial. This is because of the inadequate methodologies that have been used so far; at present no hospital studies and no roadside surveys are available.

Laboratory studies on healthy volunteers have demonstrated that barbiturates can and do impair skills related to driving. In a few studies the accumulation in the body of active metabolites of the benzodiazepine hypnotics has been accompanied by an impairment of skills related to driving. This impairment on the morning after the drug use has been more severe than that caused by deprivation of one night's sleep. Most sedative-hypnotics increase the hazards of alcohol even if the drinks are ingested as long as ten hours after the drugs have been taken.

IV.6 Tranquilizers

Definition

The term "tranquilizer" as used in this chapter means two different classes of drugs: the neuroleptics, antipsychotics, or major tranquilizers (e.g., chlorpromazine); and the minor tranquilizers, ataractics or anxiolytic agents (e.g., diazepam). Some of the minor tranquilizers are also used as hypnotics, sedatives or anticonvulsants. There is an overlapping of indications for use of these diffrient classes of drugs.

Epidemiology

There are no epidemiological data available on the subject of major tranquilizers and traffic safety.

Extent of use of minor tranquilizers. At present over 50 million prescriptions are written annually in the United States for diazepam alone(59). In the New York State survey of 1971 the incidence of the use of minor tranquilizers (anxiolytic agents) was 3.8 percent, that of major tranquilizers 0.5 percent, and that of antidepressants 0.3 percent(60). The annual consumption of diazepam per person is about 30 tablets in Sweden, and only slightly less than 20 tablets per person in Finland and Norway. The consumption of diazepam represents more than 50 percent of the total consumption of tranquilizers in the Scandinavian countries mentioned above(34). Several studies reveal that 20 to 70 percent of patients use their medication irregularly rather than as prescribed(61, 7). This is by no means a special feature of psychiatric patients.

Involvement in traffic accidents. There are only a few studies elucidating the relative accident risk in road traffic of drivers using tranquilizers. Furthermore, from most of the studies it is impossible to calculate the accident risk caused by a particular drug, because the tranquilizer users in general have more emotional and social problems that the rest of the population(40). These problems by themselves may well increase traffic accident risk.

In a Finnish questionnaire study it became evident that patients using psychotropic drugs had a significantly greater risk of road accidents. The ingestion of alcohol with the medication at least once a week further increased this risk(62).

In a Norwegian hospital study conducted in the city of Oslo, a significant amount of diazepam was found in the serum of 11 percent of persons injured in road accidents(63). The drug was found in combination with alcohol in a further 7 percent of victims. Significantly less diazepam (2 percent) was found in the reference group.

In a recent American study of drivers involved in fatal accidents, tranquilizers were detected in 2.59 percent of the drivers(64), i.e. no over-representation of tranquilizer users was found.

The minor tranquilizers have a moderate potential for abuse. Because tolerance develops to the desired effects of the drug, the abuser is liable to increase the dose. Some of the side effects of the drugs are not diminished to the same extent as the desired ones, and an over-user or abuser of tranquilizers can be a dangerous driver. There are, however, no studies available describing the extent of risk of traffic accidents among tranquilizer abusers.

Laboratory studies

Mental disorders as such impair driving ability(65). How these states by themselves and drugs added to these states affect negatively or positively skills related to driving is not presently known, even at the laboratory level.

The common neuroleptics or major tranquilizers used for the treatment of psychotic patients are relatively nonspecific in their actions on the central nervous system.

The psychomotor skill which is most affected following administration of a single dose of a neuroleptic is information-processing capacity. This is the case with the short-term administration of all the neuroleptics studied in different laboratories: chlorpromazine, thioridazine, haloperidol, promethazine, fluphenazine, and flupenthixole(66, 67, 68, 69, 70). The impairment of information-processing capacity is severe with all these drugs, and the differences between the individual agents given in roughly equipotent doses are not significant. At the beginning of treatment, side effects arising from both central and peripheral sites of action are observed; these include changes in blood pressure and heart rate, impaired vision, and alertness. Many of the initial deleterious side effects of neuroleptics are overcome by the body as a result of adaptation or tolerance after 10 - 14 days of regular drug use. The information-processing capacity is also restored after this adaptation. No data are available on the long-term effects of large doses of neuroleptics commonly used for the treatment of psychotic patients on the psychomotor skills related to driving. Studies in this area should be promoted in view of the increasing importance of depot neuroleptics in ambulant therapy of severely disturbed patients.

However, for persons on chronic therapy, neuroleptic drugs should continue to be used regularly even if driving during the course of treatment is necessary; withdrawal symptomatology may be more dangerous than the effects of the drug in tolerant persons.

Bernheim and Michiels(71) gave 20 subjects 5 mg diazepam three times daily for four days. On the fourth day, they found increased reaction times using a choice-reaction apparatus (eleven different stimuli, visual/acoustic) and slower psychomotor skills with a two-hand test apparatus. Also they found that diazepam enhanced the effect of a BAC of 35 mg%.

A single 2 mg dose of lorazepam decreased performance in a psychomotor exercise (tracking). Functions of the peripheral visual apparatus (accomodation, visual field, oculomotor balance) were not impaired(72).

Schoene(73) studied visualsensory performance (spacial vision, fusion ability, capacity for convergence and accomodation) in subjects given chlordiazepoxide or phenobarbitone, and alcohol (160 - 70 mg%) together. Phenobarbitone was found to enhance the effect of alcohol in lowering performance only as regards fusion ability. In the other visual tests, there was no evidence of potentiation by the drug.

Legg, Malpas and Scott(74) doubt the relevance of these studies and refer to their own studies, which show that cognitive and psychomotor performance is diminished in normal subjects after a single dose of a tranquilizer, but not in anxious patients receiving the drug for a period of time. It is thus quite possible that the effect of tranquilizers on performance relevant to driving behaviour can be different in healthy subjects from that in patients.

Zirkel, McAtee, King and van Dyke(70) found in 22 subjects that administration of 400 mg meprobamate four times a day for one week impairs performance in a digit symbol test and greatly enhances the lower of performance due to alcohol (50 mg%) in cognitive functions.

The main danger with these drugs is thus clearly in the effect produced by combination with alcohol. This applies also to the other psychotropic drugs, particularly those with sedative properties.

Concluding remarks

The validity of the laboratory studies is somewhat limited. In most of the studies the subjects have been healthy volunteers and, because of this, drug-disease interaction has been excluded. The laboratory setting may lead to overestimates of deleterious drug effects(75). On the other hand, the young subjects that have been studied may well be more capable of compensating for the deleterious effects of drugs on their driving skills than older persons who commonly receive them(76).

After the ingestion of a tranquilizer it is difficult to find a correlation between the blood levels of the drug and possible impairment of skills(77). This is due to the rapid appearance of active metabolites in the body and to certain peculiarities in the distribution of the drug within the body(78). Therefore legislation directed against tranquilizer use and driving is much more difficult to devise than against drinking and driving.

The only hospital study conducted so far has demonstrated an over-representation of diazepam users among the drivers involved in road accidents. Diazepam plus alcohol seems to be specifically hazardous.

IV.7 Antidepressants

Definition

Drugs used for the treatment of depressive type affective disorders are referred to as antidepressants in this report. MAO inhibitors, tricyclic and polycyclic antidepressants are representative of this class of drugs.

Epidemiology

There are no epidemiological data available concerning antidepressants and traffic safety; as regards the extent of use, in Switzerland 900,000 prescriptions for antidepressants were written in 1973(79). In virtually all developed countries depression has become a major medical concern and antidepressive chemotherapy is a very common practice.

Laboratory studies

In spite of the increasing therapeutic use of antidepressants, there are few studies concerning driving ability after the use of these drugs(80, 81). Their results indicate that antidepressants in the low doses used for the treatment of neurotic depression do not usually impair driving skills. Some of the more sedative antidepressants (e.g. doxepin, and amitryptiline) can cause substantial impairment of information-processing capacity in susceptible individuals(82).

Concluding remarks

Particularly at the beginning of the treatment with antidepressants, sedative side effects may impair driving ability. As tolerance develops, these effects tend to disappear after a few weeks of therapy. However, during the first 3 - 4 weeks of treatment, it is commonplace to note changes in sleep patterns, drowsiness and sedation which all impair altertness and stimulus receptiveness. During this period, abstention from driving is recommended.

IV.8 Anaesthetics

Definition

The problem of impairment of driving ability by anaesthetics is only relevant in the case of outpatients anaesthesia, which is indicated for minor surgical or painful therapeutic or diagnostic procedures including dental surgery.

Hence local anaesthetics, neuroleptic analgesics and some narcotic analgesics are dealt with in this context.

As premedication and for sedation, benzodiazepine tranquilizers such as diazepam are often used either alone or in combination with analgesics. As noted in the chapter "minor tranquilizers", the impairment produced depends on the dose administered and the time elapsed since the administration.

Epidemiology

There are only very few epidemiological data(83). In Finland diazepam, propanidid and thopentone are the most commonly used anaesthetics. In North America, the benzodiazepines are widely employed for sedation, to be followed by either local anaesthetics or short-acting general anaesthetics such as thiopentone and nitrous oxide.

Laboratory studies

Local anaesthetics can result in increased reaction times and in impaired psychomotor performance(84). Lidocaine impairs driving ability for 1 - $1\frac{1}{2}$ hours, and long-acting local anaesthetics such as bupivacaine and etidocaine administered without adrenaline produce impairment for at least 2 hours(74). At 2 hours after injection, 0.2 mg fentanyl

(but not 0.1 mg) had an adverse effect on choice-reaction-time(85). Hence, the recommendation not to drive a car for at least 2 hours after local anaesthesia for dental surgery
(83, 86) seems adequate.

Neuroleptic analgesics are not recommended for use in outpatients because recovery
is delayed up to 24 hours(83). Intravenous agents such as thiopentone and methohexitone
are considered to impair driving ability for up to 24 hours(87, 83), while propanidid(88)
does so for only 3 - 4 hours and alphadione(83) for 8 hours after anaesthesia.

Subjects who have been exposed to nitrous oxide and halothane show decreased performance in terms of attention and memory(89).

After general anaesthesia, patients should refrain from driving for at least 10 hours
and in some instances for 48 hours(83) depending on the length of the procedure and agents
employed.

IV.9 Narcotics Excluding Cannabis and Cocaine

Definition

For the purposes of this section the term "narcotic" excludes cannabis and cocaine
although both these drugs are specified as narcotics under the United Nations Single
Convention on Narcotic Drugs, 1961.

With these exclusions the narcotic drugs here considered consist of opium and its
derivatives as well as some synthetic substitutes for opium derivatives such as pethidine
and morphine. Most are potent drugs for the relief of pain. They are all capable of
producing psychic and physical dependence.

The phenanthrene derivatives of opium and their synthetic substitutes may produce
drowsiness, inability to concentrate, and depending on the subject, affect mood and personality, induce apathy or euphoria. These effects are potentially detrimental to driving
ability, although there are no experimental studies of these effects on driving skills.
Only in the case of codeine and methadone have these effects been evaluated at all(90, 91,
92).

Epidemiology

Driving records of methadone maintained patients in New York State were compared
with peers of the same socioeconomic group who had never been heroin addicts or methadone
patients(93). It was found that methadone maintained patients had essentially the same
number and types of accidents as the control group. Their accident records were also
examined for the period while they were heroin users, and no evidence was found for increased accident rate during that period. Criticism of this study involves the nature
of the control group who, although not opiate addicts may have been users of other drugs.

Laboratory studies

Reaction times of 18 male and 9 female methadone patients were compared with control
groups(92), and it was found that the median reaction time of methadone subjects was
either equal to or shorter than those of control groups. Studies currently being conducted by Moskowitz, Sharma and Baloh are comparing methadone maintained patients with former
heroin addicts who are currently on abstinence programmes and are thus not taking any
drugs. In a compensatory tracking task, in a battery of visual tasks and a short-term-
memory test no differences were found between methadone maintained subjects currently
receiving between 60 and 80 mg daily who have been in the programme at least one year,

and comparable control groups who are not under any drugs.

Before tolerance develops a user is adversely affected by the opiates. As drug effects wear off addicts experience severe withdrawal symptoms which may disrupt all forms of behaviour, including those associated with driving.

IV.10 Hallucinogens

Definition

The term "hallucinogen" refers to any drug that induces hallucinations, e.g. D-Lysergic acid diethylamide (LSD), Mescaline and Psilocybin. Also certain ring substituted amphetamines known by a variety of initials (STP, DOM) are included in this class.

Epidemiology

There are no data concerning the involvement of hallucinogen users in traffic accidents.

Because hallucinogens are not used therapeutically in outpatient treatment, their importance lies in illicit use.

Laboratory studies

There are few studies available for the hallucinogens. While a large number of papers on hallucinogens were examined, the overwhelming majority of them were concerned with reports of subjective states. Subjects under the influence of LSD reported the occurrence of very strong emotional reactions, without any apparent stimulation from the outside. They also reported depersonalisation phenomena feeling unable to control their emotions and thoughts, feeling detached from the real world, experiencing perceptions of the real world as having an unreal quality and experiencing an altered body image. Finally, they experienced mainly visual hallucinations. Such reports, while suggesting possible difficulties while driving, certainly make it hard to predict how the drug would influence actual performance. Woody(94) reported 3 cases of patients who had reported episodes of visual disturbance while driving. Subjects were active hallucinogenic drug abusers, although none had actually taken any of the substances within the preceding 10 hours. Rather, they appeared to have had flashbacks, which can be described as either retrograde hallucinations or prolonged emotional after-images. The importance was the fact that the subjects reported that they reacted to these visual disturbances as though they were real, either by stopping the car immediately or by driving off the road. Experimental studies of the effects of hallucinogens using objective measurements were not performed on effects which could be easily related to driving performance.

A prime conclusion, after examining a considerable number of relatively recent papers regarding hallucinogenic drugs, is the surprising lack of research that has utilised an end point of objective skills and performance.

IV.11 Cannabis

Definition

Drugs of the cannabis type include all natural cannabis derivatives and their synthetic substitutes.

Epidemiology

It was estimated(95) that by 1972, roughly 15 percent of the United States population aged eleven and over had used marihuana at least once; perhaps half of these are currently using marihuana to some extent. According to recent epidemiological studies(96, 97, 98), the majority of marihuana users have driven while under the influence of the drug. To date, difficulties in measuring the levels have prevented drug-driving epidemiological studies similar to those performed for alcohol(e.g., 99).

Comparison of accident rates for marihuana users with those for non-users has been employed as an alternate method of obtaining estimates of the role of marihuana in accident causation. Such studies have yielded divergent results. Waller(100, 101) and McGlothlin(36) reported that the accident rates for users were typical of all drivers within the same age range, while Crancer et al.(102) found above-normal accident rates for users.

There are other difficulties in drawing conclusions from these studies, apart from the disagreement regarding results. In many respects drug users may not be typical with regard to control groups quite apart from the use of the related variable drug which is under study. Thus, even if marihuana users are shown to have a higher accident rates than nonusers of any drug it would be difficult to ascribe this solely to the use of marihuana.

Laboratory studies

According to the reports of some studies, marihuana appears to have some effect on motor control such as decrements in hand and body steadiness(103), impairment in phoria and duction tests of oculomotor control(104) and of tapping speed(105). The loss of motor control of vehicles seems unlikely, however, since the reported decrements were quite small.

A more relevant task for driving than motor control is the tracking of complex functions. An extensive study of human operator tracking characteristics was made by Reid et al.(106) employing single-axis compensatory tracking. A small increase was found in random output under 88 mcg delta-9 THC/kg bodyweight, while a lower dose of 21 mcg/kg had no effect. 200 mcg/kg THC bodyweight significantly decreased the performance of subjects in a tracking task, with the degree of impairment being approximately the same as that in subjects with blood alcohol levels midway between 0.075 percent and 0.15 percent(107). Furthermore, performance decrements in pursuit tracking tasks beginning at 5 mcg/kg THC have been demonstrated in a number of investigations(108, 105, 103, 109, 110, 111). The greater sensitivity of pursuit tracking to marihuana may be related to the greater perceptual demands of such tasks in contrast to compensatory tracking. It should be noted that since sensorimotor tasks involve both perceptual and motor demands, deficits can be due to impairment of either or both aspects.

Studies of simple sensory functions with anticipated stimuli that have low demands for information analysis generally demonstrate no performance decrement in subjects under marihuana. Marihuana has no effect upon visual brightness threshold(112), depth perception(113), dark adaptation or visual acuity(104), whereas thresholds of awareness and pain levels for electrical stimulation can be lowered(114).

When the subject is given stimuli that demand constant attention there is considerable evidence of a performance decrement under marihuana(115). Also, detection of intermittent random signals in either or both central and peripheral vision is impaired(116, 117) as is recognition of previously presented material(118, 119, 120).

Another perceptual function affected by marihuana is sustained attention or vigilance. Sharma and Moskowitz(121) examined performance in an observing task. Initial performance was impaired and continued to decline over the one-hour experimental session. Under a dose of 200 mcg/kg THC, there was more than a 100 percent increase in errors by the end of the session. A further study(107) demonstrated by means of eye-movement recording that the errors occur at some fairly central point in the information-processing system.

In a simulator study(122), the subjects were required to simultaneously perform a tracking task while monitoring light signals. The responses measured were the latency in responding with the brake to stop in response to light signals, and response with the accelerator to start up lights, the number of gear changes, and the speed. Three orally ingested doses of marihuana (8, 12 and 16 mg delta-9 THC) were compared with a dose of 70 grammes of alcohol. Marihuana primarily caused a failure or delay in responding to signals from the environment rather than affecting car control or tracking aspects. These results are in accordance with those of Kielholz et al.(105) who found, in a complex tracking task, that quality and speed of information-processing were impaired rather than simple motor functions.

In another simulator study, Moskowitz et al.(123) used a car mounted on a chassis dynamometer facing a screen on which a film of a 31 mile drive was projected. To further complicate the situation, appropriate responses had to be given to four lights that appeared intermittently in the peripheral visual field. It was found that in the presence of peripheral stimuli tracking ability was impaired.

Marihuana in doses of 0,50, 100 and 200 mcg/kg delta-9 THC was administered in the form of a cigarette. There was no decrement under marihuana in any of the parameters relating to manipulation of the steering wheel, accelerator or brake. The response to the peripheral light signal detection task, however, showed an increasing delay, which, was linearly related to the drug dose. Moreover, the number of incorrect responses, indicating misinterpretation of the signal, increased significantly under marihuana, reaching a maximum of 70 percent more errors with the highest dose.

From actual car-driving studies, further findings are available regarding the effects of marihuana on driving performance. A pilot project(124) by the North Carolina Highway Safety Research Center failed to find any performance decrement under "a relatively high" dose of THC. In another study(96) observers, both in the car and on the course, were unable to perceive any impairment of performance.

Klonoff(125) performed the most extensive study involving subjects in cars both on a closed driving course and in actual city traffic, using doses of 4.9 and 8.4 milli-grammes delta-9 THC. In a series of quite stringent closed-course driving tasks, perfor-mance decrements were found primarily at the higher dose. Driving performance on the city streets was scored by observers. Eleven dimensions were used for scoring performance. Of these, marihuana appeared to have a significant effect on judgement, care and concen-tration. The finding of great variation in performance among the subjects taking the drug confirmed the results of Kieloholz et al.(108, 105) who demonstrated the personality-specific action of cannabis.

Decision making is another dimension of significance for driver performance. Sub-jective reports suggest that, in many situations, marihuana has a tranquilizing rather than a stimulating effect and that little evidence exists to support the notion that marihuana increases aggressiveness(96).

Two simulator studies have examined the effect of marihuana upon risk taking.

Subjects attempted to overtake less. When the opportunity for overtaking occurred, however, the time taken by subjects to reach a decision increased greatly under marihuana.

The author concluded from his findings that marihuana produces a state of decreased willingness to take risks(126).

Ellingstad et al.(127) examined the risk-taking under marihuana and reported similar results. Thus, the data from studies of risk-taking do not suggest that there is an increase under marihuana.

Concluding remarks

Results from car driving tests and car simulators and experimental reports from more abstract laboratory tasks are consistent. Perceptual functions of importance for driving are clearly impaired to a marked extent by marihuana. This would be expected to interfere with the ability of drivers to monitor the environment for important signals and potential dangers. Tracking aspects of driving would also be affected to some extent by the impairment of perceptual functions necessary for their control. Since motor performance per se appears less affected by marihuana, the motor aspect of tracking is less likely to be affected. No evidence was found to support the notion that emotional or attitudinal changes under marihuana would be likely to lead to increased risk taking in the driving situation.

The evidence presented for a decrement in driving performance skills, supported by reports from experienced users of self-awareness of impairment, would be expected to lead to some increase in accident probability. The dosages used in the experimental studies reported have been typical of low to moderate dosages of social users. There are frequent users of far heavier dosages who could be expected to exhibit greater degrees of impairment.

IV.12 Stimulants

Definition

Central stimulants or analeptics are used to reduce tiredness and the need to sleep, and to increase activation and drive. In ambulant adult patients they are used therapeutically as anorectics. Stimulants (mainly amphetamines) are used illicitly. The main symptoms of cocaine are restlessness, reduced need to sleep and the subjective feeling of increased ability to concentrate. Higher doses produce psychomotor disturbances and tremor. There are neither epidemiological nor laboratory studies of its effects on driving ability.

Laboratory studies

The effect of stimulants on driving ability has been investigated in only a very few studies: performance in psychomotor tests (tracking task:48) is improved by amphetamine, as are concentration and attention(128, 129), but the ability to inhibit vestibular nystagmus by visual fixation is impaired(48). Baumler(130) showed that even a small dose of methylphenidate increased the "hope of success" and decreased the "fear of failure" in a projective test of achievement motivation. Another serious effect of amphetamine as regards road safety is the interference with counter-adaptation to optically induced distortion as produced by windscreens and corrective lenses(131).

Concluding remarks

Although these effects do not impair the psychomotor components of driving ability, central stimulants must still be considered as dangerous if used while driving a car. The subjective feeling of increased efficiency and the risk-taking behaviour may result in a high accident risk in critical situations. The use of stimulants to overcome tiredness during long drives and for night driving may be dangerous. Because they eliminate the natural signs of tiredness unexpected attacks of sleep can occur as the stimulant effects wears off.

IV.13 Other Drugs

These include some drugs that in certain countries may not require a prescription. In the context of this report, attention is paid to those drugs that are used therapeutically for their effects on the C.N.S. It must not be forgotten, however, that drugs used for purposes other than their action on the C.N.S. may play a role in traffic accidents because of side effects or adverse reactions.

Further it should be noted that it may be the symptoms of the illness being treated rather than the effects of the drugs that may have dangerous consequences on driving. Some drugs and their effects on driving ability are cited:

Antihistamines have a C.N.S. depressant effect that is sometimes very prolonged and so common that one might classify them as sedatives. Mainly used for the relief of allergic conditions such as hay fever and urticaria, they are also used for travel sickness. They may enhance the effects of other depressant drugs, particularly alcohol. However, these sedatives effects are not experienced by all individuals and may diminish after a short period of treatment. Newer agents such as clemastine and chlormezanone have less potential for psychomotor decrements.

A number of cardiovascular drugs may impair driving ability in its widest sense as a result of their main effects: bradycardia (which may cause faintness), disturbances of heart rate, hypotension, disturbances of gastrointestinal function, etc. Beta-adrenoceptor blockers have inconsistent effects on psychomotor functions and reaction-time(132).

Some commonly used drugs often cause changes in blood pressure especially in older persons. These include a variety of sedatives, tranquilizers of the pneuothizaine type, antidepressants, coasolidators, used in the therapy of hypertension and diuretics (133).

Hormones, e.g. the corticosteroids, may cause severe mental disturbances. The severity of the disturbances that may be suffered by diabetics being treated with insulin or newer oral antidiabetic drugs and not eating properly should be emphasized.

There are a number of drugs which have marked side effects on vision.

Atropine and homatropine given by any route - even instilled into the eye for optical examination - paralyse the intrinsic muscles of the eye so that the eye cannot adapt for clear vision. Atropine is particularly long-acting.

Hyoscine has a similar effect on the eye. It can cause hallucinations in overdose. It is sometimes used for travel sickness.

Nalidixic acid (which is used for the treatment of urinary tract infections), antimalarial and antiparasitic drugs if taken over a long period, amiodarone (which is used to prevent angina), antiepileptic and the antitubercular drug ethambutol all impair both colour vision and visual acuity. Hydroxyquinolines, in wide use in some countries as a prophylactic against amoebic infestation and travellers diarrhoea, may cause serious visual problems if used over extended periods of time.

Hence driving ability must be assessed in each individual patient by the prescribing physician who is aware of all facets of the patient.

IV.14 Volatile Liquids

Solvents, such as ethyl acetate and esters, trichlorethylene, benzene, and benzole impair driving ability even in low concentrations. Not only does the industrial use of these solvents lead to impaired performance, but they are commonly abused as well. So called "glue-sniffing" may lead to severe intoxications, lesions of the liver, broncho-pneumonia, and organic brain syndromes.

As regards carbon monoxide, Naess-Schmidt(133) reviewed the literature and reported one epidemiological study from Denmark. He concluded that low concentrations of carbon monoxide such as produced by smoking do not increase the risk of an accident. Although some detrimental effects on vigilance and attention are recognized, the only severe carbon monoxide intoxication resulting from e.g. leakages of engine exhausts can seriously inter-fere with driving ability.

IV.15 Drug Interaction

Few studies have been made on the interaction of different drugs on driving perfor-mance, although potentiation or antagonism between the effects of many drugs are well known. There is clinical evidence, for instance, that certain antidepressants (e.g. trimipramine and amitriptyline) enhance the sedative effects of barbiturates. Treatment with a combin-ation of an antidepressant and a major tranquilizer may lead to mutual potentiation by an inhibition of metabolism(134, 135).

A number of difficulties are encountered in attempting to measure these interventions: the pharmacokinetic and pharmacodynamic interactions are largely unknown, although attempts have been made to develop models to understand how different drugs affect the absorption, distribution and metabolism of each other. Interactions may be dose-dependent; and epi-demiological studies have to reveal the combinations and doses of drugs commonly used together.

Interactions with alcohol

The drug most commonly consumed in combination with other drugs is alcohol. In this report only those results concerning the behavioural effects of the combined use will be mentioned; the pharmacokinetic studies in the narrower sense are reviewed elsewhere(136).

Epidemiology

There is some evidence that about 10 to 16 percent of drunken drivers have been using drugs other than alcohol during driving(137, 139, 140) while 11 to 25 percent of arrested drinking drivers have been using drugs as well(139, 140). More than half of patients using tranquilizers drink alcohol(7).

Sedatives and hypnotics

Virtually all sedative-hypnotics increase the hazards of alcohol(140, 55). There is strong evidence for potentiation between the deleterious effects of barbiturates and alco-hol(141, 138). In some individuals serious changes in mood have been reported(138).

Tranquilizers

The most important danger of tranquilizers as regards road safety lies in their potentiation of the effects of alcohol(142).

This detrimental interaction has been demonstrated in a number of studies for different major tranquilizers(143, 76, 68, 144, 145, 70) and minor tranquilizers(71, 139, 51, 76, 144, 146).

Chlordiazepoxide shows only a mild synergistic effect with alcohol(45, 76). There are no results that show an antagonistic effect between alcohol and any tranquilizer, including the benzodiazepines. It seems reasonable to warn seriously every patient for whom tranquilizers are prescribed about the alcohol-potentiating effects of the drug(142).

Antidepressants

Just as for the tranquilizers, one of the detrimental effects of antidepressants on driving ability lies in their synergistic effects with alcohol. This interaction is important for amitriptyline and doxepin(147, 76, 82).

Anaesthetics

Even low blood alcohol levels markedly augment the detrimental effect of trichloroethylene on performance related to driving(148). Although there are no studies on the interaction between local anaesthetics and alcohol, patients should be warned not to use alcohol shortly after minor outpatient anaesthesia.

Narcotics

Interaction effects of narcotics and alcohol have not been investigated except in the case of codeine(90, 91), which has been shown to increase the effects of alcohol.

Cannabis

In a field study using an instrumented car, it was shown that alcohol in combination with cannabis adversely affects performance in many ways(146). Other investigations conclude that a combination of these drugs results in much worse performance than is observed after either agent alone(149, 110).

Stimulants

Between stimulants (e.g. amphetamine) and alcohol an antagonistic action can be expected. Regarding skills related to driving there is no clear evidence of such an antagonism(150, 151, 152), nor of a synergistic effect(150).

Oral contraceptives may decrease the rate of metabolism of alcohol, so that the expected duration of impairment may be prolonged beyond usual periods of time (153).

Insulin or an oral hypoglycemic agent may create a dangerous degree of mental confusion, and lack of coordination during the period of sobering-up after ethanol (ethyl alcohol) consumption, as a state of hypoglycemia may occur.

Most antihistamines enhance the effects of alcohol(154, 76, 146, 155). Hence, even small doses of alcohol can result in an inability to drive a car when combined with antihistamines (taken, for example, for travel sickness).

Patients taking disulfiram should not drive a car after drinking alcohol. There are a number of substances which, when combined with alcohol, cause the same symptoms

as disulfiram: nitrofuzarone, griseofulvin, some oral antidiabetic drugs(157), phenyl-
butazone and analgesics containing aminophenazone or phenacetin(156). These drugs, which
are frequently prescribed, are not detrimental to driving ability when used alone and in
therapeutic doses, though there is a considerable danger as regards road safety when
combined with alcohol. A number of antiprotozoal agents, such as metronidazole(158, 159,
160) and the antineoplastic agent procarbazine also possess disulfiram-type properties,
thus leading to an adverse reaction when ethanol is consumed concomitantly.

After chronic consumption of alcohol, drug metabolism may be accelerated. This is
the case for some antiepileptic agents, anticoagulants, and oral antidiabetic drugs. To
prevent hyperglycemia or an epileptic attack for example, the dose of these drugs has to
be adjusted according to the amount of alcohol consumed.

References

1. Goldberg, L. and Harvard, J.D.L., Alcohol and Drugs. The Effects of Alcohol and
Drugs on Driver Behaviour and their Importance as a Cause of Road Accidents. OECD
Road Safety Research, Paris, 1968.
2. Kibrick, E. and Smart, R.G., Psychotropic Drug Use and Driving Risk. A Review and
Analysis. J. Safety Res., 1970, 2, 73-85.
3. Perrine, M.W. (Ed.), Alcohol, Drugs and Driving. Final report. Psychological
Research Foundation of Vermont, Inc., 1974.
4. Parry, H.J., Use of Psychotropic Drugs by U.S. Adult. Public Health Rep. 33 (10),
799-810, October, 1968.
5. Traffic Laws Commentary. Drugs and Driving, N°. 65-1, pp 1-17, April 30, 1965.
6. Chelton, L.G. and Whisnant, C.L., The Combination of Alcohol and Drug Intoxication.
South Med. J. 59(4), 393, 1966.
7. Milner, G., Drinking and Driving in 753 General Practice and Psychiatric Patients on
Psychotropic Drugs. Brit. J. Psychiat. 115 (518): 99-100, January, 1969.
8. Rees, W.D., Psychotropic Drugs and the Motorist. Practitioner 196, pp 704-706, 1966
9. Alha, A., 1971. Recent Trends in Drunken Driving in Finland.
10. Waller, J.A., Lamborn, K.R. and Steffenhagen, R.A., Marihuana and Driving among Teenagers. Repeated Use Patterns, Effects and Experiences Related to Driving. Accident
Analysis and Prevention 6 (2): 141-61, 1974.
11. Glauz, W.D., and Blackburn, R.R., Drug Use among Drivers. Midwest Research Institute,
1975.
12. Finkle, B.S., Biasotti, A.M. and Bradford, L.W., The Occurrence of some Drugs and
Toxic Agents Encountered in Drinking Driver Investigations. J. Forensic Sci. 13(2),
236-245, 1968.
13. Gupta, R.C. and Kofoed, J., Toxicological Statistics for Barbiturates, Other Sedatives
and Tranquilizers in Ontario. A 10 Year Survey. Canad. Med. Ass. J. 94 (16), 863-
865, 1966.
14. Reinartz, E.F.K., Ueber die Einwirkung von Medikamenten bei 500 Kraftfahrzeugunfällen
in Frankfurt A.M. (The influence of drugs on 500 car accidents in Frankfurt A.M.).
(German). Gesamtherstellung: Ditters. Bürodienst, p. 27, 1962.
15. Wagner, H.J., Die Bedeutung der Untersuchung von Blut-bzw. Harnproben auf Arzneimittel
nach Verkehrsunfällen auf Grund der Ueberprüfung von 2060 Personen (Significance
of urine and blood tests for drugs after traffic accidents (2060 persons tested.)
(German) Arneimittelforschung 11: 992-995, 1962.
16. Wangel, J., Alcohol, Road Traffic and Drugs in Denmark, 1960. Proc. 3rd International
Conference on Alcohol and Road Traffic, pp 162-165, 1962.

17. Gilbert, J.A.L., 1973. Collection of Baseline Data on Effect of Alcohol Consumption on Traffic Accidents. Discussion. Conference on Medical, Human, and Related Factors Causing Traffic Accidents, Including Alcohol and Other Drugs. Montreal, Canada Proceedings 49-54. May 30-31, 1972.

18. Haffner, J.F.W., Bø, O. and Lunde, P.K.M., Alcohol and Drugs Consumption as Causal Factors in Road Traffic Accidents in Norway. Journal of Traffic Medicine 2(4); 52-6, 1974.

19. Braunstein, P.W., Weinberg, S.B. and Cortivo, L.D., The Drunk and Drugged Driver versus the Law. J. Trauma 8(1) 83-90, 1968.

20. Briglia, R.J., Toxicological Screening Programme of Coroner's Cases in Sacramento County, Sacramento, California. Sacramento County Coroner's Office, p. 14, 1966.

21. Davis, J.H. and Fisk, A.J., The Dade Country, Florida, Study on Carbon Monoxide, Alcohol and Drugs in Fatal Single Vehicle Automobile Accidents. Florida: National Association of Coroners' Seminar, July, 1966.

22. State of California Highway Patrol. The Role of Alcohol, Drugs and Organic Factors in Fatal Single Vehicle Accidents (Final Report), p. 130, June, 1967.

23. Sunshine, I., Hodnett, N., Hall, C.R. and Rieders, F., Drugs and Carbon Monoxide in Fatal Accidents. Postgrad. Med. (43(3)), 152-155, 1968.

24. Hossack, D.W., Investigation of 400 People Killed in Road Accidents with Special Reference to Blood Alcohol Levels. Medical Journal of Australia 2:255-58, 1972.

25. Turk, R.F., McBay, A.J. and Hudson, P., Drug Involvement in Automobile Driver and Pedestrian Fatalities. Journal of Forensic Sciences 19(1) 90-7. 1974.

26. Woodhouse, E.J., Incidence of Drugs in Fatally Injured Drivers. Final Report. Midwest Research Institute, 1974.

27. Engel, A. and Siderius, P., The Consumption of Drugs. Report of a Study 1966-1967, WHO EURO, 3101, 1969.

28. Andersen, A.H. and Johansen, P.J., Medicine Consumption in Denmark on the asis of Analysis of Prescriptions on 28.IX.1971. Ugeskr. Laeg., 136, 2204, 1974.

29. Rosch, G., Rempp, J.J. and Magdelaine, M., Une enquête par sondage sur la consommation médicale, Consommation, N°. 1, 1966.

30. Lazar, J., Népegészegugy (Public Health). 47 264, 1966.

31. Swaren, U., Health Insurance and Drug Consumption (1965). State Official Committee's Report (SOU), 28, Stockholm, 1966.

32. Smedby, B., Prescription Study. Consumption of Drugs During one Year for a Sample of Persons Studied through Prescription Data, 1963

33. Astrup, S. and Retpen, J.A.B., Drugs and Traffic Safety. A Survey of Epidemiological Studies. To be published (in Danish). Retsmed. Institute. DK-8000 AARHUS.

34. Idanpaan-Heikkita, J. and Salonen, R., Uni-ja rauhoittavien Laakkeider kaytto Suomess. Ruotsissa ja norjassa. Suom Laak Lehti 27, 3304-3307, 1972

35. Lorman, A.J., Drugs, Driving and the Law. A Report to the Governor and General Assembly of Virginia, Charlottesville, Va., 1973.

36. McGlothlin, W.H., Amphetamines, Barbiturates, and Hallucinogens; An Analysis of Use, Distribution, and Control. Drug enforcement administration, United States Dept. of Justice, SCID - TR - 9, 1973.

37. Chambers, C.D. and Inciardi, J.A., An Assessment of Drug Use in the General Population. Special Report N°. 2. State Narcotic Addiction Control Commission, New York, 1973.

38. Holroyd, K. and Kahn, M., Personality Factors in Student Drug Use. Journal of Consulting and Clinical Psychology, 42, 236-243, 1974.

39. Goode, E., Trends in College Drug Use: Report from one Campus. In the Proceedings of the First National Conference on Student Drug Surveys, Baywood Publishing Co., 1972.

40. Nichols, J.L., Drug Use and Highway Safety: A Review of the Literature. COT-HS-O-800-580, United States Dept. of Transportation National Highway Traffic Safety Administration, Washington, D.C., 1971.

41. Report on Alcohol, Drugs and Organic Factors in Fatal Single Vehicle Traffic Accidents. State of California Highway Patrol, Final Report, 1967.

42. Kaye, S., Blood Alcohol and Fatal Traffic Accidents in Puerto Rico. Report to DOT, FHWA Region L. Delmar, N.Y., 1970.

43. Kouble, R.K., Analogue 1000. FBI Law Enforcement, 1969, 38, 12-22.

44. Goodnow, R.E., Beckner, H.K., Brazier, M.B., Mosteller, F. and Tagiure, R., Physiological Performance Following a Hypnotic Dose of a Barbiturate. Journal of Pharm. Exp. Ther., 102, 55-61, 1951

45. Goldstein, A., Searle, B.W., and Shimbe, R.T., Effects of Secobarbital and of d-Amphetamine on Psychomotor Performance of Normal Subjects. J. of Pharm. Exp. Ther., 130, 55-58, 1960.

46. Kornetsby, C., Vates, T.S. and Kessler, E.K., A Comparison of Hypnotic and Residual Psychological Effects of Single Doses of Chlorpromazine and Secobarbital in Man. J. Pharm. Exp. Ther. 127, 51-54, 1959.

47. Rashbass, C., Barbiturate Nystagmus and the Mechanisms of Visual Fixation. Nature, 183, 875-898, 1959.

48. Schroeder, D.M., Collins, W.E. and Elam, G.W., Effects of Secobarbital and d-amphetamine on Tracking Performance During Angular Acceleration. Ergonomics, 17, 613-621, 1974.

49. Betts, T.A., Clayton, A.B. and McKay, G.M., Effects of four Commonly Used Tranquilizers on Low Speed Driving Performance Tests. Brit. Med. J., 4, 580-584. 1972.

50. McKenzie, R.E. and Elliot, L.L., Effects of Secobarbital and Diamphetamine on Performance During a Simulated Air Mission. Aerospace Medicine 36, 774-779, 1965.

51. Kielholz, P., Goldberg, L. Im Obersteg, J., Pöldinger, W., Ramseyer, A. and Schmid, P., Fahversuche zur Frage der Beeinträchtigung der Verkehrstüchtigkeit durch Alkohol, Tranquilizer und Hypnotika. Dtsch. Med. Wschr., 94, 301-306, 1969.

52. Loomis, T.A. and West, T.C., Comparative Sedative Effects of Barbiturates and Some Tranquilizing Drugs on Normal Subjects. J. Pharm. Exp. Ther., 122, 525-531, 1958.

53. Sharma, S., Barbiturates and Driving. J. Accident Analysis, in press, 1975.

54. Saario, I. and Linnoila, M., Effects of Subacute Treatment with Hypnotics alone or in Combination with Alcohol, on Psychomotor Skills Related to Driving. Acta Pharmacol. and Toxicol., 38, 382-392. 1976.

55. Saario, I., Linnoila, M. and Mäki, M., Interaction of Drugs with Alcohol on Human Psychomotor Skills Related to Driving: Effect of Sleep Deprivation on two Weeks Treatment with Hypnotics. J. Clin. Pharmacol., 15, 52-59. 1975.

56. Bond, A.J. and Lader, N.H., Residual Effects of Hypnotics. Psychopharmacologia, 25, 117-132, 1972.

57. Linnoila, M., Drug Interaction on Psychomotor Skills Related to Driving Hypnotics and Alcohol, Am. Med. Exp. et Biol. Fenn. 51, 118-124, 1973.

58. Gentles, W. and Thomas, E.L., Effect of Benzodiasepines on Saccadic Eye Movement in Man.

59. Greenblatt, D.J. and Shader, R.I., Drug Therapy: Benzodiazepines. N. Engl. J. Med., 291, 1011-1015, 1974.

60. Chambers, C.D. and Inciardi, J.A., An Assessment of Drug Use in the General Population. New York State Narcotic Addiction Control Commission, New York, 1971.

61. Ayd, F.J., Jr., Single Daily Dose of Antidepressants. J.A.M.A., 230, 263-264, 1974.

62. Mäki, M. and Linnoila, M., The Effect of Drugs on Driving of Psychiatric Out-patients. Liikennneturvan tutkimuksia, 25. Liikenneturva, Helsinki, 1975.

63. Bø, O., Haffner, J.F.W., Langard, O., Trumpy, J.H., Bredesen, J.E. and Lunde, P.K.M., Ethanol and Diazepam as Causative Agents in Road Traffic Accidents. Proceedings 6th International Conference on Alcohol, Drugs and Driving, Toronto, 1974.

64. Woodhouse, E.J., The Incidence of Drugs in Fatally Injured Drivers. DOT-HS-801016. United States Dept. of Transportation, Washington, D.C., 1974.

65. Eelkema, R.C., Brosseau, J., Koshnick, B.S. and McGee, C., A Statistical Study on the Relationship between Mental Illness and Traffic Accidents - A Pilot Study. Am. J. Public Health, 60, 459-461, 1970.

66. Boucsein, W., Experimentelle Untersuchungen zum Problem interindividueller Reaktions-differenzen auf Psychopharmaka. Unveröff. Doktorarbeit. Giessen, 1971. Universitat Basel, 1972.

67. Linnoila, M., Effects of Diazepam, Chlordiazepoxide, Thioridazine, Haloperidole, Flupenthixole, and Alcohol on Psychomotor Skills Related to Driving. Ann. Med. Exp. Biol. Fenn., 51 125-132, 1973.

68. Milner, G. and Landauer, A.A., Alcohol, Thioridazine, and Chlorpromazine Effects on Skills Related to Driving Behaviour. Brit. J. Psychiatry, 118, 351-352, 1971.

69. Safer, D.J. and Allen, R.P., The Effect of Fluphenazine in Psychologically Normal Volunteers: Some Temporal Performance and Biochemical Relationships. Biological Psychiatry, 3, 237-249, 1971.

70. Zirkle, G.A., King, P.D., McAtee, O.B. and Van Dyke, R., Effects of Chlorpromazine and Alcohol on Coordination and Judgement. J.A.M.A., 11, 1496-1499, 1959.

71. Bernheim, J. and Michiels, W., Effets psycho-physiques du diazépam (VALIUM) et d'une faible dose d'alcool chez l'Homme. Schweiz. Med. Wschr., 103, 863-870, 1973.

72. Bell, R.W., Dickie, D.S., Stewart-Jones, J. and Turner, P., Lorazepam on Visuo-motor Co-ordination and Visual Function in Man. J. Pharm. Pharmac., 25-87-88, 1973.

73. Schoene, J., Ueber die Beeinflussung verschiedener optischer Funktionen durch Alkohol und Arzneimittel. Inaug.-Dissertation, Frankfurt/M., 1970.

74. Legg, N.J., Malpas, A. and Scott, D.F., Effects of Tranquilizers and Hypnotics on Driving. Br. Med. J., 417, 1973.

75. Richter, R. and Hobi, V., Die persönlichkeitsspezifische Wirkung eines Tranquilizers. Arzneimittelforschung, 26, 1136-1138, 1976.

76. Linnoila, M., Effect of Drugs and Alcohol on Psychomotor Skills Related to Driving. Ann. Clin. Res., 6, 7-18(c), 1974.

77. Linnoila, M., Saario, I. and Mäki, M., The Effect of two Weeks Treatment with Diazepam and Lithium, alone or in Combination with Alcohol, on Psychomotor Skills Related to Driving. Eur. J. Clin. Pharmacol 7, 337-342, 1974.

78. Klein, E., van der, Kinetics and Distribution of Diazepam and Chlordiazepoxide in Mice. Arch. Int. Pharmacodyn., 178, 193-215, 1969.

79. Kielholz, D., and Hobi, V., Medikamente und Fahrverhatten. Therapeutische Umschau, 34, 803-812, 1977.

80. Landauer, A.A. and Milner, G., Desipramine and Imipramine, alone and together with Alcohol in Relation to Driving Safety. Pharmakopsychiat., Neuropsychopharmakologie, 4, 265-275, 1971.

81. Patman, J., Landauer, A.A. and Milner, G., The Combined Effect of Alcohol and Amitryp-tyline on Skills Similar to Motor-car Driving. Med. J. Australia, 2, 946-949, 1969.

82. Seppälä, R., Linnoila, M., Elonen, E., Mattila, M.J. and Mäki, M., The Effect of Tricyclic Antidepressants and Alcohol on Psychomotor Skills Related to Driving. Clin. Pharm. Ther., 17, 515-522, 1975.

83. Kortilla, K., Recovery and Skills Related to Driving after Minor Out-patient anes-thesia. Unpubl. Academic Dissertation, Helsinki, 1975.

84. Tetsch, P., Reaktionszeitmessungen bei Zahnärztlich-chirurgischen Eingriffen in Analgosedierung. Dtsch. Zahnärzt.Z., 28, 618, 1973.

85. Ghoneim, M.M., Mewaldt, S.P. and Thatcher, J.W., The Effect of Diazepam and Fentanyl on Mental, Psychomotor and Electroencephalographic Functions and their Rate of Recovery. Psychopharmacologia (Berl.), 44, 61-66, 1975.

86. Tetsch, P., Machtens, E. and Voss, M., Reaktionszeitmessungen bei operativen Eingriffen in örlicher Schmerzausschaltung. Schweiz. Mschr. Zahnheilk., 82, 229, 1972.

87. Haas, E., Freusher, H. and Stickstroct, M., Vergleichende elektronystamographische und psychophysische Untersuchungen nach intravenosen Kurznarkosen mit Thiopental, Methohexital und Phenoxyessigsäure-amid. Anaesthesist, 12, 346, 1963.

88. Rittmeyer, P., Weitere Untersuchungen zur Frage der Strassenverkehrstüchtigkeit nach Propanidid-Narkosen. Anestesiology and Resuscitation, 4, 298, 1965.

89. Bruce, D.J., Bach, M.J. and Arbit, J., Trace Anesthetic Effects on Perceptual, Cognitive, and Motor Skills. Anesthesiology, 40, 453, 458, 1974.

90. Linnoila, M. and Häkkinen, S., Effects of Diazepam and Codeine, alone and in Combination with Alcohol, on Simulated Driving Clinical Pharmacology and Therapeutics, 15, 368-373, 1974.

91. Linnoila, M. and Mattila, M.J., Interaction of Alcohol and Drugs on Psycho-motor Skills as Demonstrated by a Driving Simulator. British J. of Pharmacology, 47, 671-672, 1973.

92. Gordon, N., Reaction Time of Methadone-treated Ex-heroin Addicts. Psychopharmacologia, 16, 337-344, 1970.

93. Blomberg, R.D. and Preusser, D.F., Drug Abuse and Driving Performance. Report N°. DOT-HS-800-754, NHSTA, U.S. DOT, Washington, D.C., 1972.

94. Woody, G., Visual Disturbances Experienced by Hallucinogenic Drug Abusers while Driving. American J. of Psychiatry, 127, 683-686, 1970.

95. Secretary of Health, Education and Welfare, Marijuana and Health. 3rd Annual Report to the United States Congress, DHEW Pub. N°. ADM-74-50. Washington, D.C., 1974.

96. Le Dain Commission. Cannabis: A Report of the Commission of Inquiry into the Non-medical Use of Drugs. Information Canada, 1972.

97. Smart, R.G., Marijuana and Driving Risk among College Students. Journal of Safety Research, 6, 155-158, 1974.

98. Waller, J.A., Lamborn, K.R. and Steffenhagen, R.A., Marihuana and Driving among Teenagers: Reported Use Patterns, Effect and Experiences Related to Driving. Accident Analysis and Prevention, 6., 141-161, 1974.

99. Borkenstein, R.F., Crowther, R.G., Shumate, R.P., Ziel, W.B. and Zylman, R., The Role of the Drinking Driver in Traffic Accidents. Indiana University, Bloomington, 1964.

100. Waller, J.A., Chronic Medical Conditions and Traffic Safety: Review of the California Experience. New England Journal of Medicine, 273, 1413-1420, 1965.

101. Waller, J.A. and Goo, J.T., Highway Crash and Citation Patterns and Chronic Medical Conditions. Journal of Safety Research, 1, 13-27, 1969.

102. Crancer, A., and Quiring, D.L., Driving Records of Persons Arrested for Illegal Drug Use. Report 011. State of Washington, Dept. of Motor Vehicles, Administrative Services, May, 1968.

103. Liplinger, G.F., Manno, F.E., Rodda, B.E. and Forney, R.B., Dose Response Analysis of the Effects of Tetrahydrocannabinol in Man. Clinical Pharmacological Therapeutics, 12, 650-657, 1971.

104. Moskowitz, H., Sharma, S. and Schapero, M., A Comparison of the Effects of Marihuana and Alcohol on Visual Functions. In M.F. Lewis (Ed.), Current Research in Marihuana, New York, Academic Press, 1972.

105. Kielholz, P., Hobi, V., Ladewig, D., Miest, P. and Richter, R., An Experimental Investigation about the Effect of Cannabis on Car Driving Behaviour. Pharmakiopsychiat., 6, 91-103, 1973.

106. Reid, L.D., Ibrahim, M.K.F., Miller, R.D., and Hansteen, H.W., The Influence of Alcohol and Marihuana on a Manual Tracking Task. Society of Automotive Engineers Congress, Technical Paper N°. 730092, Detroit, Michigan, 1973.

107. Moskowitz, H., Ziedman, K. and Sharma, S., Marihuana Effects on Visual Scanning Patterns, in the Driving Situation. Unpublished.

108. Kieholz, P., Goldberg, L., Hobi, V., Ladewig, D., Reggiani, G. and Richter, R., Cannabis and Driving Ability. German Medical Monthly, 3, 38-43, 1973.

109. Manno, J.E., Kplinger, C.F., Bennett, I.F., Haine, S. and Forney, R.B., Comparative Effects of Smoking Marihuana and Placebo on Human Motor and Mental Performance. Clinical Pharmacological Therapeutics, 11, 808-815, 1970.

110. Manno, J.E., Kiplinger, G.F., Scholz, N. and Forney, R.B., The Influence of Alcohol and Marihuana on Motor and Mental Performance. Clinical Pharmacological Therapeutics, 12, 202-211, 1971.

111. Roth, W.T., Tinklenberg, J.R., Whitaker, C.A., Darley, C.F., Kopeli, B.S. and Hollister, L.E., The Effect of Marihuana on Tracking Task Performance. Psychopharmacologia, 33, 259-265, 1973.

112. Caldwell, D.F., Myers, S.A., Domino, E.F. and Mirriam, P.E., Auditory and Visual Threshold Effects of Marihuana in Man. Perceptual Motor Skills, 29, 755-759, 1969.

113. Clark, L.D. and Nakashima, E.N., Experimental Studies of Marihuana. American Journal of Psychiatry, 125, 379-384, 1968.

114. Hill, S.Y., Goodwin, D.A., Schwin, R. and Powell, B., Marijuana: CNS Depressant or Excitant. American Journal of Psychiatry, 131, 313-315, 1974.

115. Casswell, S. and Marks, D., Cannabis Induced Impairment of Performance of a Divided Attention Task. Nature, 241, 60-61, 1973.

116. Sharma, S. and Moskowitz, H., Effect of Marihuana on the Visual Autokinetic Phenomenon. Perceptual Motor Skills, 35, 891-894, 1972.

117. Moskowitz, H., Sharma, S. and McGlothlin, W., The Effects of Marihuana upon Peripheral Vision as a Function of the Information Processing Demands upon Central Vision. Perceptual Motor Skills, 35, 875-882, 1972.

118. Abel, E.L., Marijuana and Memory. Nature, 227, 1151-1152, 1970.

119. Abel, E.L., Effects of Marijuana on the Solution of Anagrams, Memory and Appetite. Nature, 231, 260-261(a), 1971.

120. Abel, E.L., Retrieval of Information after Use of Marihuana. Nature, 231, 58(b), 1971.

121. Sharma, S. and Moskowitz, H., Marihuana Dose Study of Vigilance Performance. Proceedings 81st Annual Conference AM. Psychological Ass., 1035-1036, 1973.

122. Rafaelsen, O.L., Bech, P., Christensen, J., Christrup, H., Nyboe, J. and Rafaelsen, L., Cannabis and Alcohol: Effects on Simulated Car Driving. Science, 1/9, 920-923, 1973.

123. Moskowitz, H., McGlothlin, W. and Hulbert, S., The Effect of Marihuana Dosage on Driver Performance. Institute of Transportation and Traffic Engineering Report UCLA-END-7341. UCLA, Los Angeles, 1973.

124. Anonymous. Pilot Study of Marihuana Effects is Conducted. The Accident Reporter, February, 1972.

125. Klonoff, H., Marijuana and Driving in Real-life Situations. Science, 186, 317-324, 1974.

126. Dott, A.B., Effect of Marihuana on Risk Acceptance in a Simulated Passing Task. Public Health Services Report. ICRL-RR-TI-71-3DHEW, Pub. N° HSM 72-10010. Washington, D.C., 1972.

127. Ellingstad, V.D., McFarling, L.H. and Struckman, D.L., Alcohol, Marijuana and Risk Taking. Report DOT-HS-191-2-301, Vermillion, University of North Dakota, Human Factors Laboratory, North Dakota, 1973.

128. Blum, B., Stern, M.H. and Melville, J.K.I., A Comparative Evaluation of the Action of Depressant and Stimulant Drugs on Human Performance. Psychopharmacologia, 6, 173-177, 1964.

129. Strasser, H. and Müller-Limmorth, W., Physiologische Veränderungen und Regelleis-tungsverhalten älterer Probanden während kontinuierlicher Tracking-Tätigkeiten nach Zufuhr einer zentral aktivierenden Substanz. Arzneimittel-Forschung. 23, 406-415, 1973.

130. Bäulmer, G., Beeinflussung der Leistungmotivation durch Psychopharmaka: 1. Die 4 bildthematischen Hauptvariablen. Z. exp. und angw. Psychol., 22, 1-14, 1975.

131. Fischer, R. and Hill, R.M., Psychotropic Drug-Induced Transformations of Visual Space. Int. Pharmacopsychiat., 6, 28-37, 1971.

132. Ogle, C.W., Turner, P. and Markomihelakis, H., The Effects of High Doses of Oxpren-olol and of Propranolol on Pursuit Motor Performance, Reaction Time and Critical Flicker Frequency. Psychopharmacologia, 46, 295-299, 1976.

133. Naess-Schmidt, T.E., Alcohol, Carbon Monoxide and Drugs in Road Fatalities. Blutalkohol, 8, 318-336, 1971.

134. Gram, L.F., Effects of Neuroleptics on the Metabolism of Tricyclic-antidepressants. Proceedings of the 10th Collegium Internationale Neuro-psychopharmacologium (C.N.I.P.), Quebec, 1976.

135. Perel, J.M. and Hurwic, M.J., Interactional Influences on the Kinetics of Anti-depressants. Proceedings of the 10th Collegium Internationale neuro-psychopharma-cologium (C.N.I.P.), Quebec, 1976.

136. Wallgren, H. and Barry, H.,III Actions of Alcohol, I & II, Elsevier, Amsterdam, 1970.

137. Kessler, A., Der gemeinsame Einfluss von Arzneimitteln und Alkoholgrenzkonzentra-tionen auf die Verkehrssicherheit anhand der Ueberprunfung von 2500 Fallen. Unveröffentlichte Doktorarbeit, 1963.

138. Kielholz, P., Goldberg, L., Jm Obersteg, J., Pöldinger, W., Ramseyer, A. and Schmid, P., Strassenverkehr, Tranquilizer und Alkohol. Dtsch. Med. Wschr., 92, 1525-1531, 1967.

139. Chelton, L.G. and Whisnant, C.L., The Combination of Alcohol and Drug Intoxication. South Med. J., 59-393, 1966.

140. Finkle, B.S., Drugs in Drinking Drivers. J. Safety Res., 4, 179, 1969.

141. Doenicke, A., Beeinträchtigung der Verkehrssicherheit durch Barbiturat-Medikation und durch die Kombination Barbiturat/Alhohol. Arzneimittel-Forschung, 12, 1050-1054, 1962.

142. Kielholz, P. and Hobi, V., Beeinflussung der Fahrtüchtigkeit durch Psychopharmaka. Therapeutische Umschau, 31, 606-613, 1974.

143. Doenicke, A., and Sigmund, W., Prüfung-der Verkehrssicherheit nach Verabreichung von Fluphenazindihydrochlorid und Alkohol. Arzneimittel-Forschung, 14, 907-912, 1964.

144. Saario, I., The Effect of two Weeks Treatment Bromazepam or Thioridazine, alone or in Combination with Alcohol on Psychomotor Skills Related to Driving. In preparation.

145. Seppälä, T., The Effect of two Weeks Treatment with Cholopromazine and Sulphiride, alone or in Combination with Alcohol, on Human Psychomotor Skills Related to Driving. In preparation.

146. Smiley, A.M., Combined Effects of Alcohol and Common Psychoactive Drugs. Field Studies with an Instrumented Automobile. National Research Council, National Aeronautical Establishment, 1974.

147. Landauer, A.A., Lauri, W. and Milner, G., The Effect of Benzoctamine and Alcohol on Motor Skills Used in Car Driving. Forensic Science, 2.275-283, 1973.

148. Vernon, R.J., and Ferguson, R.G., Effects of Trichlorethylene on Visual Motor Performance. Archives of Environmental Health, 18, 894-900, 1969.

149. Ling, G.M., Interaction Between Alcohol and Drugs and their Relationship to Driving. Discussion. Conference on Medical, Human and Related Factors Causing Traffic Accidents, Including Alcohol and other Drugs, 131-135, 1973.

150. Hughes, F.W. and Forney, R.B., Dextro-amphetamine, Ethanol and Dextro-amphetamine-ethanol Combinations on Performance of Human Subjects Stressed with Delayed Auditory Feedback (DAF). Psychopharmacologia, 6, 234-238, 1964.

151. Kaplan, H.L., Forney, R.B., Richards, A.B. and Hughes, F.W., Dextro-amphetamine Alcohol and Dextro-amphetamine-alcohol Combination and Mental Performance. Alcohol and Traffic Safety. Proceedings of the 4th International Conference on Alcohol and Traffic Safety, 211-214, December 6-10, 1965.

152. Rutenfranz, J. and Janzen, G., Ueber die Kompensation von Alkoholwirkungen durch Coffein und Pervitin bei einer Psychomotorischen Leistung, Internationale Zeitschr. F. Angewandte Physiologie Einschl. Arbeitsphysiologies, 18, 62-81, 1959.

153. Morgan-Jones, B., Jones, M.K. and Paredes, A. University of Oklahoma Health Science Centre, Paper presented at the meeting of the 15th annual reunion Da Sociadad Mexicana de nutricion y endocrinologia, Alcupolco, Mexico, November, 1975.

154. Hughes, F.W. and Forney, R.B. Comparative Effect of Three Antihistamines and Ethanol on Mental and Motor Performance. Clinical Pharmacology and Therapeutics, 5, 414-421, 1964.

155. Tang, P.C. and Rosenstein, R. Influence of Alcohol and Dramamine, alone and in Combination, on Psychomotor Performance US Army Aeromedical Research Unit, 1967.

156. Burkhardt, G. and Reimann, W. Menschen unter Alkowirkung im Strassenverkehr und am Arbeitsplatz. Steinkopf, Dresden, 1973.

157. Truitt, E.B. et al. Disulfiram like Actions Produced by Hypoglycemic Sulfonyeureau Compounds. Q. Journal Stud. Alcohol, 23, 197-207, 1962.

158. Strassman, H.E. et al. Metronidazole Effect on Social Drinkers. Q. Journal Stud. Alcohol, 31, 394, 1970.

159. FDA Reports of Suspected Adverse Reactions to Drugs Nº 700301 - 064-01001 Metronidazole, 1970.

160. ITIL, T.I. et al. Central Effects of Metronidazole. Psychiatric Research Report Nº 24 American Psychiatric Research Association, March, 1968.

161. Crespy, J., Influence de la consommation de médicaments sur la conduite automobile. Etudes bibliographiques. ONSER, Arcueil, 1974.

162. Crespy, J., Neyroud, M., Etude sur la consommation de psychotropes en France à partir d'une enquête auprès des médecins généralistes. Rapport interne, ONSER, Arcueil, 1973.

163. Neyroud, M., Consommation de médicaments par les usagers de la route: comportements et risques. Note de synthèse, ONSER, Arcueil, 1976.

COUNTERMEASURES

V.1   Legislative Countermeasures

V.1.1 Alcohol

Legislation against drinking and driving is aimed at reducing the number of drinking drivers on the road by defining a certain behaviour as illegal and by stipulating the methods of detection and punishment of this behaviour. The definition of illegal behaviour is thus a major part of a legislation. There are basically two methods of defining impairment. The first is a verbal description of impairment based on simple behavioural observations and other evidence (e.g. erratic driving behaviour) to prove an offence. The second is a definition based on a legal BAC limit. Evidence based on verbal description may also be supported by information on BAC. The difficulties in providing sufficient evidence for conviction can be eliminated, however, with a legal BAC limit. A number of countries are changing or have changed from a general verbal description of drunken driving to a statutory BAC limit (See Table 7). As indicated, some countries employ more than one level in an effort to reflect the seriousness of the offence - with more severe consequences for higher BAC levels.

The choice of a particular legal limit is viewed as a compromise between the need for a low limit from the traffic safety point of view, and the political and practical problems of enforcing the limit. A limit of 80 mg% was originally considered as being the ideal compromise. It was selected primarily as a result of studies(1)(*) which found that accident risks increased significantly among drivers whose BAC was 80 mg% and higher. Tolerance to alcohol however, is a critical factor. For mor   ienced drinkers, the level may be higher but beyond 100 mg% evidence suggests what all drinking drivers are impaired to an extent that their accident risk is definitely increased. Conversely, inexperienced drinkers (which by implication includes   n   rs) are at greater risks than average at levels as low as 50 mg%. The legal limit   50 mg% presently employed by some countries, is justified on the basis of recent evidence (see Chapter III). Even when a BAC limit is adapted, however, there are still important legislative differences between countries.

The penalties for committing an offence under the impaired driving legislation is one example. All countries impose fines and/or jail sentences on those convicted of impaired driving. In some countries, however, there is no penalty for refusing to submit to a chemical test while in others a refusal can either carry the same penalty as a conviction for impairment or, only result in a suspension of the driver licence. When evaluating the effectiveness of penalties, consideration must be given to the extent to which they are effective as a general deterrent in discouraging drinking-driving among all drivers and as a special deterrent in changing the behaviour of a convicted driver(3).

(*) See list of references at the end of this chapter.

TABLE 7

STATUTORY LIMITS AND PENALTIES IN OECD COUNTRIES

Country	Statutory BAC Limit (mg%)	Fines	Jail Sentences	Licence Suspension
Austria	80	5,000-30,000 Sh(1)		6 months
Belgium	80	100-1,000 F	15 days-6 months	8 days-5 years
Canada	80	$50-$2,000	14 days-2 years	2 months-3 years
Denmark	80/120	1 month's net income		$1\frac{1}{2} - 2\frac{1}{2}$ years
Finland	50/150	Mean income 34 days	2 - 4 months	Maximum 2 years
France	80/120	Minimum 1,000FF Maximum 40,000 FF	Minimum 1 month Maximum 4 years	Minimum 15 days Maximum 6 years
Germany	80/130	Maximum 3,000 DM		3 months - 5 years
Japan	50	Maximum 50,000 Y	Maximum 2 years	Maximum 3 years
Netherlands	50	Maximum 10,000 Fl.	Maximum 3 months	5 - 10 years
Norway	50		21 days	2 years
Sweden	50/150	Minimum 1/100th of annual income	Maximum 6 months	1 year for 50/ 2 years for 150
Switzerland	80		Maximum 6 months	Minimum 2 months
United Kingdom	80	Maximum £100	Maximum 4 months(2)	Minimum 1 year
United States	100(3)	Minimum 0 to $100 Maximum $500 to $1,000	Generally 1 year	Generally 1 year

(1) The minimum and maximum fine, sentence and suspension period are presented in each case. In most cases the minimum figure represents penalties levied against a first offence. With repeated offences, the penalties increase.

(2) Some laws stipulate fines and/or jail sentences.

(3) Two states have a limit of 80 and two others have two limits, 100 and 150.

The general deterrent effects of penalties alone are difficult to identify, primarily because drinking behaviour will also be influenced by level of enforcement and public education campaigns. Research suggests however that it may be effective in changing the drinking-driving patterns of moderate or social drinkers but not of the problem drinker(4). The special deterrent effect of penalties is also in doubt. Studies by Buikhuisen(5) and Steenhuis(6) have indicated that the effect of penalties in changing behaviour is small or non-existent.

Another difference in legislations is the method employed by enforcement agencies in detecting an impaired driver. Whichever statutory BAC limit is in force, the police are faced with the task of detecting drivers who are just above the statutory limit. To do this, proper screening methods are required. In this respect, there are remarkable differences between countries in the manner with which police may request a test for BAC determination and the method employed to determine the BAC (e.g. screening tests or quantitative tests; breath or blood sample).

In the British Road Safety Act of 1967, the police were empowered to demand a qualitative breath test (i.e. roadside test) if they suspected that the driver had been drinking. The qualitative test could then be followed by a quantitative test which could result in a charge being laid if the BAC was 80 mg% or greater. The effect of this legislation was demonstrated by an immediate reduction in the proportion of casualties during drinking hours. It was unfortunately followed, however, by a slow decline in the following years(7).

Other countries such as Canada(8), France(9) and Australia(10) have introduced legislation that appears to have had no effect. The ineffectiveness of the Canadian law has been attributed to the inability of the police to detect impaired drivers which the United Kingdom law considered. Germany, on the other hand, recorded a reduction in relative number of injury accidents following the introduction in 1973 of an 80 mg% law. The fuel crisis a few months after the introduction of the law (driving on Saturday nights and Sundays was prohibited) however, presented problems in evaluating the effectiveness.

These examples firstly show the need for proper research to determine the effect of a legal change. Secondly, while not accurately documented, they demonstrate that effectiveness of a particular BAC limit is dependent on a combination of factors such as level of enforcement, penalties, and method of detecting a drinking driver. In addition, drinking legislation which controls the sale and consumption of alcohol can also influence drinking driving. This has been demonstrated by the effect on road accident patterns of lowering the legal drinking age and changing hotel-bar closing times (see Chapter V.4). For these reasons, an international comparison can only lead to tentative conclusions on the effect of the various factors.

With respect to existing legislations, however, the major problem appears to be the apparent inability to detect an offender. For someone driving under the influence of alcohol or drugs, the risk of apprehension is very small. Borkenstein(11) estimates that only one out of 2000 violators is detected and charged. In a study by Beitel et al.(12) only one in fifty drivers with a BAC above 200 was detected. Even when an impaired driver is detected, they may not be charged. Borkenstein(13) cites that, for the two drivers a policeman typically arrests each year for impaired driving, he refrains from charging 75 to 100 more whom he suspects.

The problem is also related to the policeman's inability to determine whether the driver is impaired by definition of the law. A Swedish experiment(14) has shown that the police have a great deal of difficulty in determining whether a driver is above the legal limit when he is only slightly so. Eleven out of fifteen policemen considered the individual to be below the legal limit. To help alleviate this problem, some countries have passed legislation to allow the use of roadside screening devices (RSDs).

With or without RSDs, however, legal questions arise as to what constitutes "reasonable cause" for police officers to stop a driver and demand a test for the presence of alcohol. In some countries, reasonable cause is defined as suspected impairment. Accordingly, the probability of a driver being apprehended is small as long as he does not have an accident or does not display erratic or abnormal driving behaviour. In an effort to resolve this problem, some countries (e.g. Canada) have redefined "reasonable cause" from suspected impairment to suspected drinking. Among the European countries only Finland, Sweden, Denmark and Switzerland allow routine breath testing without reasonable cause for suspicion of drunk driving. The testing is not necessarily random; drivers are usually screened at times and places where the probability of drivers being impaired is the greatest. For practical purposes, only Sweden makes use of this possibility.

A radical way of increasing the chances of detection is provided by routine testing at road blocks. Few countries allow such a practice, however, and even fewer countries make use of it.

In general, the effect of enforcement will benefit from a simple and fast method of determining BAC and greater powers to the police in detecting the drinking driver. A current hypothesis is that legislation is most effective as a general deterrent in encouraging drivers not to drive after drinking. To this end, the drinking-driver must be led to believe that his chances of being detected and charged with impaired driving are high.

One method of influencing risk perception would be to increase enforcement levels. If enforcement is used indiscriminantly, however, an increase in the number of drunken driving cases may subsequently lead to an overloading of the judicial system. Enforcement must be examined closely, therefore, to determine the optimum level at which drivers perceive a change in the risks of detection.

With respect to the specific deterrent effort of legislation, consideration should be given to reducing the time interval between which a driver is detected and subsequently appears in court. It has been suggested that, as this interval increases, the individual becomes less sensitive to the seriousness of the offence. In addition, the upper limit of a penalty for impaired driving must be compatible with those for other traffic violations. For example, if an impaired driving charge carried a heavier penalty than for a "hit and run" offence, the incidence of the latter offence may increase.

At present, there are four different legislation which are or have been critically assessed. These are the Dutch, Scandinavian, British and United States legislations.

A 50 mg% limit was introduced in the Netherlands in 1974 and a series of roadside surveys during week-en nights has shown a decrease in drinking and driving one year after the introduction. At the same time, the number of fatal accidents during nighttime fell considerably in 1975. This is probably due to the new legislation since the trend of fatal accidents during the daytime was quite different(2).

In the case of the Scandinavian legislation, efforts have been made to determine whether Sweden and Norway have been able to control the drinking-driving problem by means of laws which stipulate the use of prison sentences as the routine penalty. Ross(15) created a controversy when he concluded that there was no adequate proof for the proposition that the Scandinavian laws per se deterred people from drinking and driving. Klette(16), however, questioned this conclusion on the basis that two main conditions for using the interrupted time-series analysis employed by Ross were missing.

Klette also refers to a 1976 study by Votey who examined the deterrent effects of law enforcement and control of alcohol consumption in relation to drunken driving in Norway and Sweden by using economic models and simultaneous analysis. The conclusions quoted from Klette(16) are that Votey's results indicate that Norwegian and Swedes respond to law enforcement and this this factor rather than control of alcohol consumption and sales has the greater influence on accidents.

The results from roadside surveys suggest, however, that the Scandinavian laws may be affecting drinking-driving behaviour. Data from Finland(17), Norway(18) and Sweden(19) indicate that the percentage of drinking-drivers is low in relation to the percentages found in the Netherlands and North America. For example, in Norway, only 1 percent of the drivers tested were found to have BACs above 100 mg% as compared to 6 percent in the Netherlands. It is evident, therefore, that a careful examination of the studies on Scandinavian laws is necessary before any conclusions can be drawn.

Great Britain has demonstrated that legislation can be effective. Of greater concern, however, is the finding that this effect has declined with time. Over the first seven years following the introduction of the British legislation, it was estimated that the total savings in casualties decreased from 42,500 in the first year to 6,000 in the seventh.

Ross(20) believes that drivers after a while realized that the risk of apprehension was much lower than they were led to believe by the information campaigns when the law was introduced. Other explanations are also possible. Sabey and Codling(7) point out that there is an essential difference between older and younger drivers. The older drivers continued to respect the legislation to a considerable extent, while the incidence of high drinking levels amongst younger drivers has increased more sharply. It is perhaps relevent that in recent years many of the younger drivers (certainly those under 20 years) started driving after legislation had come into force, so will not have benefitted from the publicity accompanying the introduction of legislation.

This indicates that there is a continuing need to reinforce legislative programmes. A United Kingdom Government Committee of Inquiry(21) set up in 1974 to review the law on drinking and driving reported as its main recommendations:

(i) To remove the present artificial limitations on the power of the police to stop and test drivers.

(ii) To determine blood alcohol by means of breath analysis devices at police stations - with blood analysis as an optional final test, should the motorist request one.

(iii) To require offenders in the high-risk categories to apply to the court for restoration of their licences, and to show that they did not present an undue risk as drivers because of their drinking habits.

(iv) To mount a permanent programme of publicity and education.

The overriding factor, however, is evaluation. As the United Kingdom Committee recommended, there is a need to extend research on drinking related to driving, and to monitor the evolving situation in order to gauge the results of education and enforcement over the years. Variables such as statutory BAC limits, level and methods of enforcement and punitive actions must be scientifically examined within the context of each country's problem with respect to drinking and driving.

In the United States, the response to the impaired driving problem has been to create an alcohol safety action programme(22) which emphasizes the use of traditional enforcement and judicial practices. The uniqueness of the programme is its endeavour to organize community safety organizations into an effective system to control the drunk driver. To this end, a control system was designed which would deter the social drinker, and at the same time, provide a means to identify and put into treatment the problem drinker who, because he had lost control of his drinking, could not be deterred from drunk driving through traditional legislative action.

An ASAP project provided a community with a director to coordinate the activity of its agencies in the four areas concerned with impaired driving: enforcement, the judicial system, the alcoholism treatment community, and organizations responsible for public information programmes in traffic safety. The project provided funds to a co-operating organization so that each could carry out its mission within the system. The police were given support to increase arrests in order to deter the social drinker and to bring more problem drinkers into the system. Funds were provided to the courts to handle the increase in the impaired driving charges and to provide them with the means of diagnosing problem drinkers. Treatment agencies were provided with support to handle the increased flow of clients from the court system and funds were provided for public information programmes designed to obtain public support for the ASAP system. The changes in enforcement were also publicized in an effort to increase its effectiveness in deterring the social drinker.

Each project was evaluated by comparing the three years prior to its initiation with the three years of project operation which followed. Twenty-four or 70 percent of the 35 projects showed a reduction in the night-time crashes below the trends projected from the base period. Of these 24 ASAPs, 11 or 45 percent showed a statistically significant reduction during the same years in which the ASAPs were in operation. A comparison was also made with a specially selected group of 10 sites, chosen on the basis of their similarity to the ASAP sites on some 24 different characteristics which were believed to predict night-time crashes. For this comparison group, half of the sites had more accidents and half had less than the projected levels from the baseline period. Only one comparison site, however, had a statistically significant reduction in accidents.

With respect to legislative countermeasures, the ASAP projects have demonstrated that enforcement levels can be increased up to 300 percent without changing existing legislation. This increased enforcement combined with public education campaigns did produce a small effect as reflected by a reduction in crashes. The ASAP projects have also demonstrated that the fines collected from impaired drivers can be used to support an increased enforcement programme and to streamline the court's system for dealing with impaired drivers.

Even though it has not clearly emerged from the research, it may be assumed, by way of conclusion, that legislation will have an influence on drinking and driving if the driver's perception of his chances of being detected, charged and convicted of impaired driving are high.

V.1.2 Drugs

Most countries (Switzerland is an exception) include within their road traffic legislation a prohibition against driving while impaired by a drug. Such legislation is predicated on the fact that many types of drugs produce either primary or secondary effects which among others may alter vision, change blood pressure and thus induce dizziness, lower blood sugar and thus impair coordination, or induce drowsiness as a side effect.

There are no known correlations, however, between blood levels of drugs and recognized degrees of driving impairment. For example, some drugs such as the tricyclic anti-depressants produce drowsiness as a side effect for only a few weeks. Psychotropic drugs such as opiates, benzodiazepines and other sedative hypnotics and other minor tranquil-izers induce their own metabolism and thus produce a tolerance. Many drugs are generally detected in higher concentration in urine than in plasma or saliva. However, the relationship between drug concentrations in the body fluids and performance is not clear at present.

In view of the difficulties in quantifying drug concentrations, it seems unlikely that the offence of driving while impaired under a drug must continue to be documented on the basis of an agreed battery of functional tests that correlate with levels of impairment of those physiological skills deemed to be important to the driving task.

V.2 Information, Education and Rehabilitation Programmes

V.2.1 Public information programmes concerning alcohol and driving

Background and description

In the context of this report, public information and education programmes refer to efforts to affect road user behaviour by means of various mass media campaigns. Such programmes differ from more "formal" educational programmes, which are described in subsequent sections, in that mass media approaches involve no face-to-face interaction between the sources and the recipients of the communication.

Mass communication programmes for the promotion of greater traffic safety take many forms and can serve a variety of immediate functions. They may, for example, be designed to: (A) transmit information to the public; (B) modify the attitudes of the public toward safe driving practices; or (C) facilitate or eradicate various forms of driving behaviours. In all cases the ultimate goal of such programmes should be to reduce traffic crashes and/or the consequences thereof.

The design and effectiveness of road safety campaigns were studied in the framework of the OECD Road Research Programme. A first report(23) contains analyses of safety campaigns conducted prior to 1971 and reviews research and experience in this field. As a follow-up activity, a conference on the design of safety campaigns was organised by the Italian Ministry of Public Works, and held in Rome in October 1971(55). Finally, in 1975, a manual(56) was published by the OECD; it sets out to give a systematic presentation of the various stages in the preparation of such campaigns, their design and implementation and how their effectiveness can be measured, all of which aspects require consideration if the campaign is to be effective. In addition, the 1974 U.S./DOT report on "The Use of Mass Media for Highway Safety"(24) should be mentioned; this report which represented an update of some of the concepts included in the 1971 OECD study.

Evaluation problems

From the literature contained in the above and other sources, it appears that while public information programmes may have considerable potential as an effective highway safety measure, the amount of scientific information available concerning the effectiveness of such campaigns is limited. One of the most apparent problems involves the criteria often used to evaluate such programmes. As was already indicated, the ultimate goal and criterion of effectiveness of any such safety campaign must be a reduction in the number and/or severity of crashes. Highway crashes, especially the more serious ones, are relatively rare events and are subject to marked statistical fluctuations over-time and from site-to-site. This, in combination with variance in reporting likelihood and procedures, makes such an event a difficult dependent variable to use for many research projects. Hence intermediate criteria of campaign effectiveness have often been used. Some of these include:
- increase in traffic knowledge;
- enhancement of safety compatible attitudes;
- recall of the content of medial messages;
- recall of the media used;
- change in reported driving behaviour;
- behaviour change recorded through roadside alcohol surveys.

Only the latter two measures, in addition to crashes, can be considered as meaningful criteria by which to measure the effectiveness of media campaigns. The 1971 OECD report points out that perhaps one of the most blatant errors made in the evaluation of these programmes is to mistake the amount of public and official interest generated by the campaign for its true effectiveness. Effectiveness, the report points out, must inevitably be assessed in terms of what actually happens on the road as a result of the campaign itself, in that, any behaviour which one attempts to modify by means of the campaign must be related to the probability of crash involvement.

A serious problem involved with evaluating their effectiveness is that such campaigns are rarely carried out without some accompanying change in laws, level of enforcement or modification of the traffic environment. Almost no such combination programme has been carried out in a fashion such that the individual effects of these different components can be assessed. Because of this situation, very little has been learned from the results of such programmes which can be used for the planning of future media campaigns.

Another major failure of attempts to evaluate mass media campaigns in the past has been the inability to obtain external control groups of persons not exposed to such media efforts in order to compare subsequent crash rates or crash related behaviours. Most frequently before and after measures have been used in the evaluation of such programmes. Unfortunately, such procedures cannot account for potentially more influential factors affecting crashes and behaviour. Some of these factors include changes in weather conditions, population density, enforcement and reporting procedures, and numerous other conditions.

Results of media campaigns conducted to combat alcohol-related crashes
a. Combined campaigns

As indicated, few media campaigns have been implemented in isolation. Some of the most significant media programmes have been accompanied by changes in legislation and/or enforcement as well. One of the earliest of such programmes which appeared to be successful in reducing drinking and driving and its consequences was carried out at an air base in the United States(25). In this programme, a media campaign was carried out which stressed that driving after drinking was not masculine or brave. Rather, according to the campaign material, such behaviour was indicative of a weak or disturbed personality. An increase in the enforcement of base regulations against drinking and driving accompanied the media efforts. In addition, offences and referrals for diagnosis and treatment were publicized via call meetings, bulletin boards and the base newspaper. Using a before and after approach, the results of the campaign evaluation indicated significant reductions in total accident rate, total injury rate, and driver injury rate. These reductions appeared to be in sharp contrast to the experience of a nearby base and to local, state, and national trends.

Another example of a major public information effort was carried out in the United Kingdom in conjunction with the Road Safety Act of 1967. In this programme, a large scale media campaign was implemented to publicize the introduction of the 80 mg% BAC level for presumed intoxication. The campaign also emphasized new measures to be taken by the police (e.g. the use of roadside breath testers) to apprehend violators. Subsequent evaluations indicated a significant change in motorist awareness and behaviour(26) and a reduction in deaths and injuries(27) as a result of the entire effort. Unfortunately, there was no way of separating the effects of the media campaign from the effects of the law change or of any change in enforcement level. In addition, it appeared that the effects of the programme began to dissipate after 18 months. Recent investigations(28, 7) suggested that the situation may now be similar to what it was previous to the enactment of the 1967 law.

An example of a recent public information campaign which was accompanied by other countermeasures but which was designed such that inferences concerning individual countermeasure effect could be made, comes from the Vermont Alcohol Safety Action Project (ASAP) in the United States(24).

The Vermont programme employed much of the mass communications design methodology recommended in the 1971 OECD report. It also used roadside survey techniques to identify pertinent characteristics of high risk groups and to evaluate the results of the campaign in terms of changes in drivers' BAC levels.

The state was divided into 3 separate areas, one of which would receive public information and a variety of other countermeasures; one of which would receive public education alone; and one of which would receive none of these programme efforts. Subsequent evaluation suggested changes in both countermeasure areas with respect to increased knowledge levels and fewer drivers with blood alcohol concentrations greater than 50 mg percent. While these changes were indicated for both experimental groups and not for the control group, the numbers involved in the roadside survey data were small and not subjected to adequate statistical tests. Still this project demonstrates the type of programme design which permits individual evaluations of concomitant countermeasures.

b. Isolated campaigns

It is somewhat more difficult to find examples of isolated media campaigns in the drinking and driving area which have been evaluated. One such programme was carried out in Edmonton, Canada, during the month of December, 1972 and was reported by Farmer[29]. In this campaign evaluation a control city (Calgary) was used and initial results suggested a trend towards reduced blood alcohol levels among Edmonton drivers apparently as a result of the campaign.

Another campaign was conducted in 1973 in 9 towns in Ontario, Canada[30], using 9 other towns as control areas. The campaign appeared to result in increased public awareness and modified public opinion but the effectiveness of the programme on known crash related behaviours was not adequately assessed.

Obviously some media campaigns have failed to produce any effect at all. Resource documents in this area suggest that such results can be attributed to improper use of accident causation theory; behaviour modification theory; or mass communication theory [23, 24]. Most campaigns, however, appear to have been either not evaluated or improperly evaluated due to inadequate research designs or methodological errors in data collection, processing, or interpretation. As a consequence, these campaigns have added little to the body of knowledge necessary to develop future campaigns.

Mass communication theory and previous campaign experience

Mass media programmes should be designed in accordance with sound mass communication principles. The original OECD report[23] discusses communication theory in view of past campaign results in a variety of areas including:

   (i)   target behaviour (what we want to change);
  (ii)   target audience (who we want to change);
 (iii)   types of appeals (how we motivate change);
  (iv)   message content (what is said and how);
   (v)   activation techniques (how to make the audience participate);
  (vi)   media selection (where we present the message); and
 (vii)   campaign timing (when and how long we present the message).

All of the above are important considerations which should be studied in detail by persons designing a mass media campaign. However, recent attempts have been made to extract the most salient information from past experience with safety campaigns. In attempting to compare those evaluated safety campaigns which have had a measurable effect upon road user behaviour with campaigns that have failed to demonstrate such effects, a number of characteristic differences are suggested. Such an analysis by Wilde (1972) has suggested the importance of the following campaign characteristics.

   a)   Instructiveness. The message has to inform the recipient concretely and unambiguously what precise behaviour is being advocated. Encouragements such as 'safety first', 'no accident please', 'safety is no accident', etc., cannot be expected to have a positive effect because they do not communicate what one should do, however, much one might be interested in safety.

b) <u>Immediacy</u>. The message should reach the road user at the very time and in the very place where it may be translated into behaviour. Reducing the temporal and spatial gap between message and pertinent situations would seem to place real-time radio, posters, signs, and billboards at an advantage over television and the printed press.

c) <u>Personal relevance</u>. The message should be perceived by the recipient as personally relevant to him rather than to some generalized "other" (the alcoholics, the young males, 'the other guy', etc.) and should clearly indicate in what respect the advocated behaviour is in his own interest.

d) <u>Facilitation of modelling and social imitation</u>. Driving and other road use does not take place in isolation but in social interaction situations in which the behaviour of the individual is strongly influenced by his perception of the behaviour of others. In order for desirable behaviour to enhance this process of imitation, it should be conspicuous.

This conspicuousness implies public and overt commitment to the desired behaviour on the part of the individual(57). This condition will reduce the likelihood of rapid extinction of the behaviour involved.

With regard to the form of the message, L'Hoste(31) has suggested that the use of fear arousal should only be used after careful consideration. He points out that:

- the effects of messages using fear vary from person to person and that they may sometimes produce defensive avoidance reactions, especially in people with anxious predispositions; and

- fear arousal messages seem to have a good deal of immediate impact but may not be retained as well as messages in other forms.

L'Hoste suggests that to have the greatest probability of modifying attitudes and behaviour the messages should:

(i) give precise and useful information;
(ii) reach the target audience at the most favorable time for implementing the recommended behaviour;
(iii) involve the target personally;
(iv) have strong credibility;
(v) use humor and fear in moderation; and
(vi) encourage a collective awareness of the problem.

<u>Conclusions</u>

In spite of a considerable apparent potential for being an effective highway safety measure, it appears that little scientific information is available concerning the effectiveness of various types of public information programmes in modifying drinking and driving behaviour. It is important to note for both this section and the section dealing with formal education and rehabilitation programmes that most public information campaigns have been aimed at social drinkers. It appears to be the consensus of persons working in this area that problem drinkers are too difficult to reach through such efforts and that only formal treatment can deal with such persons. In the 1971 OECD report(23), for example, it is stated that:

"Little effect may be expected in general from safety campaigns directed at particular problem groups such as alcoholics... these individuals have already demonstrated such a considerable resistance against the pressures exerted by their immediate environment, medical intervention, as well as from society in general that mild and general educational approaches such as used in safety campaigns cannot have any substantial effect. Consequently, campaigns on drinking and driving should be directed at "normal" (i.e., social) drinkers...".

Evidence which will be presented in the section concerning formal education programmes appears to support this view to some degree.

Finally, as noted in the 1974 review by the United States Department of Transportation(24), practitioners of the mass media should be reminded that it is only from scientific campaign evaluation that we will eventually learn how to use the mass media for desirable modification of road user behaviour. There is no valid substitute for this information generating procedure just as there is no learning without feedback. This is why all resistances against evaluation measurement, financial and otherwise, must be overcome if a truly serious effort at safety promotions is to be made.

V.2.2 Public and formal education programmes concerning drugs (other than alcohol) and driving

With regard to drugs other than alcohol, there are few driver oriented educational programmes in existence. Further, there are virtually no adequate evaluations of such programmes available. The greatest amount of activity in this area appears to be in the secondary school driver education system in the United States where data on drugs other than alcohol is presently being integrated into various curricula. In no other country surveyed is drug information a component of official driver education programmes in the schools(*). There are indications, however, that in Denmark, Sweden and the Federal Republic of Germany, this subject is dealt with in commercial driving schools. It is interesting to note that in most nations, even though no great emphasis is placed on it, drug information comprises a portion of the driving licence examination. No information is available concerning public education programmes aimed at drugs and driving or on rehabilitation programmes for drivers convicted of driving under the influence of drugs other than alcohol.

V.2.3 Formal alcohol education programmes for drivers

The integration of information concerning alcohol into secondary school driver education curricula in the United States has recently received much emphasis. A variety of curricula components specific to alcohol have been developed and are now being included in the secondary school driver education system. None of such programmes has been evaluated to date. A survey of European programmes has suggested that in no country is alcohol information an obligatory component of the public school driver education system. In the Federal Republic of Germany, however, driver education programmes are beginning to incorporate alcohol information. Obviously, the effects of such programmes have not yet been even initially assessed.

(*) Information obtained from Belgium, Denmark, the Federal Republic of Germany, the Netherlands, Norway, Sweden and the United Kingdom.

V.2.4 <u>Formal education and rehabilitation programmes for drinking drivers</u>

<u>Background</u>

Education and rehabilitation programmes for (usually convicted) drinking drivers were first noted in the literature as a result of an educational programme begun in Phoenix, Arizona(32).

Since that time, court-based referral programmes have proliferated in the United States and Canada. In the United States, for example, a large scale programme called the "DWI Counter-attack" programme has developed from the DWI Phoenix concept and now includes more than 500 schools across the nation. In addition, the United States Department of Transportation's ASAP programme has resulted in the development of a large number of schools and other types of rehabilitation referral programmes in nearly every state. In fact, most of the information available concerning the effectiveness of education and rehabilitation programmes comes from the 35 alcohol safety action projects in the United States.

Education and rehabilitation programmes have been implemented on a more extensive scale than that on which they have been evaluated. In the United States, where more than a quarter of a million persons have been assigned to attend such programmes as part of the Alcohol Safety Action Projects (ASAPs) many of these programmes were completed without being rigorously evaluated. This has been even more so the case with non-ASAP DWI education programmes in the United States and the situation is similar in other nations implementing programmes for drinking drivers.

Even when valid experimental designs have been developed for evaluating such programmes, local opposition to procedures such as random assignment and no-treatment control groups has resulted in compromised and equivocal results. Another major problem which has plagued such evaluation studies has been the lack of adequate numbers of persons in both the "treatment" and "no-treatment" groups so that small effects could be documented if, in fact, they existed.

Just as was the case in the public information area, the ultimate goal of education and rehabilitation programmes for drinking drivers must be a reduction in the number and/or consequences of highway crashes. Also, as was the case with media campaigns, crashes have been difficult to use as evaluative criteria because of their rarity and the incompleteness with which such events are recorded. As a result, there have been a variety of criteria employed to evaluate the effectiveness of this area of effort. Such criteria have included:

- increased knowledge about alcohol;
- improved attitudes towards drinking and driving;
- reductions in alcohol-related driving violations; and
- reductions in subsequent crash involvement.

More recently, several attempts are being made to evaluate the effectiveness of these programmes in terms of reductions in drinking problems not related to driving (e.g., job status, health, etc.).

<u>Evaluations of non-ASAP education and rehabilitation efforts</u>

With regard to evaluation of <u>education</u> programmes for drinking drivers, one of the first recorded controlled studies of such a programme was conducted in Phoenix, Arizona(33).

This study suggested that the DWI Phoenix programme was effective in reducing subsequent violations among those persons exposed to it (as compared with a control group) but no indication of a crash reduction effect could be demonstrated. Further subsequent

evaluations have been conducted on this programme throughout the years as a part of Phoenix' participation in the ASAP programme. These subsequent evaluations appear to have
confirmed the earlier study's findings.

Unfortunately, there have been few adequate evaluations of more recent forms of this
programme which constitute the "DWI counter-attack" programme. One recently reported
evaluation conducted in the State of New York(34) used several paper and pencil instruments to evaluate the effectiveness of the New York "DWI counterattack" programme. This
study reported improvements on a drinking and driving-knowledge inventory, an opinion
(attitude) survey and various behavioural description scales. Many of these improvements were noted for non-problem, potential problem and definite problem drinkers alike.
However, non-problem drinkers appeared to show significantly greater improvement on these
scales. No measures of arrest or crash reduction were reported.

In Canada, the Alberta Impaired Drivers' Programme (AIDP) evaluation study looked at
the effectiveness of an alcohol education programme in that country(35). Although the
study had found no significant reduction in alcohol-related arrest recidivism associated
with the programme, drivers who completed the course were reported as having significantly
reduced traffic and criminal code convictions other than alcohol impaired driving.

With regard to other forms of referral programmes for drinking drivers, a study
conducted in Denver, Colorado(36) found that persons referred to rehabilitation programmes
had no fewer subsequent alcohol related driving arrests than persons who received the
more traditional penal sanctions. A longer term study conducted in the State of California,
however, found evidence that more comprehensive rehabilitation programmes (e.g. Alcoholics
Anonymous and multiple modality programmes) appeared to result in significantly fewer
alcohol related arrests and crashes for persons referred to them(37).

Taken together, the above studies provide some minimal information which suggests
that education and rehabilitation programmes for drinking drivers probably improve knowledge levels and attitudes towards drinking and driving, and there is very limited evidence
that violation and/or crash involvement may be reduced. There are suggestions that social
drinkers may be changed more by educational programmes than are problem drinkers and that
comprehensive programmes may be more effective than more brief efforts.

Evaluations of ASAP education efforts

As already noted, by far the bulk of studies available concerning the effectiveness
of education and rehabilitation programmes comes from the 35 Alcohol Safety Action Projects in the United States. With regard to purely educational programmes, for example,
more than 30 studies have been reported between 1972 and 1974 concerning the effectiveness
of such programmes in increasing the knowledge levels of drinking drivers exposed to
them(38). Virtually all of these studies have indicated that statistically significant
improvements in knowledge levels have resulted from being exposed to the educational
programmes. While some studies were methodologically less sound than others, it appears
safe to conclude that alcohol education programmes do result in desirable knowledge level
changes.

A similar, yet somewhat more equivocal, situation exists with regard to the effects
of such programmes on attitudes towards drinking and driving. Over the same three-year
period, at least 21 attitudinal studies were conducted in various ASAP localities(38).
Seventeen (81 percent) of these before-and-after studies reported desirable changes in
attitudes towards drinking and driving following exposure to the programmes. One primary
reason why these studies are less interpretable than the knowledge-oriented studies is
that most of the persons being tested probably assumed that they were still under the
control of the court and were understandably prone to say what they perceived the programme

officials wanted to hear. Another major problem involves the inherent difficulty involved
in defining and measuring attitudes. These results are, however, consistent with the
earlier findings by Malfetti and Simon(34). Somewhat more closely related to the ultimate programme objective or reduced crash involvement are reductions in subsequent alcohol-
related violations. From 1972 through 1974 there were fifty-four analytic studies conducted on the effects of ASAP education schools in terms of reduced violations for the education exposed groups(38). As Figure 9 indicates these analytics were viewed relative to
their methodology as well as their results. The studies were then categorized as being
either methodologically weak (w) or methodologically sound (s). Two-thirds(36) of these
studies were judged as being methodologically weak. Of these weak studies, 44 percent(16)
reported that the groups exposed to the educational programmes had fewer subsequent alcohol-related driving arrests than did the non-exposed control groups. Of the 18 methodologically sound studies, only 22 percent(4) reported positive results for the educational
programme. This finding, that the number of positive results is indirectly proportional
to the amount of experimental control exercised, has been previously reported with regard
to evaluations in the general alcohol rehabilitation area(39).

Attempts to combine the data from several of the ASAPs in order to assess the relative
effectiveness of various types of education schools for large numbers of both problem and
non-problem drinkers have been reported by Nichols and Reis(40) and by Ellingstad and
Springer(38). These studies have suggested that non-problem drinkers referred to education programmes have lower subsequent arrest rates for alcohol-related offences than
similar persons not assigned to such schools. It appeared to make little difference
whether these "social" drinkers were assigned to brief lecture type schools or to longer,
more interactive schools. Problem drinkers fared less well in that there was little
evidence that those sent to education programmes had any fewer subsequent rearrests than
those not sent to these programmes. Within the problem drinker group, however, the type
of school these persons were exposed to appeared to make a great deal of difference. More
specifically, as Figure 10 shows, problem drinkers assigned to lecture (type 3) programmes
had significantly more rearrests than those assigned to more therapy-like, interactive
(type 1) schools.

Finally, with regard to alcohol educational schools, studies which have attempted to
assess the effectiveness of these programmes in terms of reducing crashes have been methodologically similar to those which have examined subsequent arrests. In the ASAP experience, 12 crash studies were received from 1972 to 1974. One-quarter(34) of these studies
were judged as being suitably controlled. None of the controlled studies to date has
reported statistically significant reductions in subsequent crashes for the educational
groups. Small sample sizes have obviously been an inherent problem in these studies.

Evaluations of more generalized ASAP rehabilitation efforts
There are a variety of programme types to which convicted drinking drivers may be
sentenced by the courts. They range from out-patient programmes (e.g. school, group
therapy, individual therapy, and chemotherapy) to long-term in-patient programmes. While
most of the referrals at any location are to education programmes, the effectiveness of
other alternatives have also been examined. A number of ASAP studies have been conducted
wherein clients were grouped relative to whether they had been assigned to any form of
rehabilitation (e.g., school, group therapy, chemotherapy, etc.), versus whether they had
not been so assigned. Thus, a large component of the effort examined by such studies also
included education programmes. Of the 35 studies submitted by ASAP projects concerning
the effectiveness of overall rehabilitation in reducing subsequent rearrests, less than
one-third(41) were considered methodologically sound. Four (40 percent) of these relatively sound studies suggested that the overall decision of sending a person to some form of

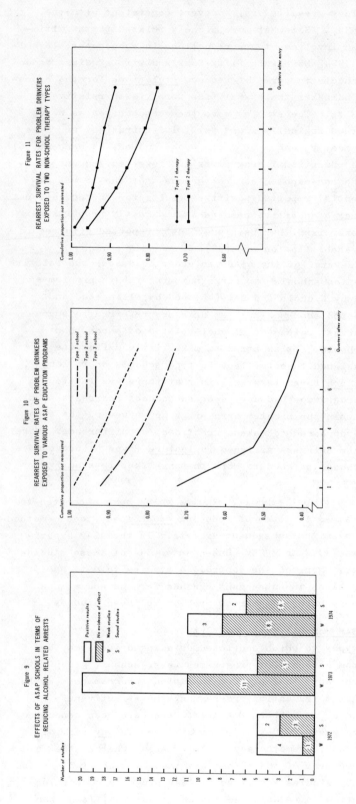

Figure 11

REARREST SURVIVAL RATES FOR PROBLEM DRINKERS
EXPOSED TO TWO NON-SCHOOL THERAPY TYPES

Cumulative proportion not rearrested

Quarters after entry

Type 1 therapy
Type 2 therapy

Figure 10

REARREST SURVIVAL RATES OF PROBLEM DRINKERS
EXPOSED TO VARIOUS ASAP EDUCATION PROGRAMS

Cumulative proportion not rearrested

Quarters after entry

Type 1 school
Type 2 school
Type 3 school

Figure 9

EFFECTS OF ASAP SCHOOLS IN TERMS OF
REDUCING ALCOHOL RELATED ARRESTS

Number of studies

Positive results
No evidence of effect
W   Weak studies
S   Sound studies

rehabilitation resulted in subsequently lower arrest rates for such persons. Nearly two-thirds of the 25 methodologically poor studies reported favorable results for the decision to refer drivers to rehabilitation programmes.

On a more specific note, there was one quite sophisticated study conducted in Los Angeles, California(41), which suggested that the use of disulfiram (chemotherapy) as a treatment component resulted in significantly fewer subsequent rearrests and/or crashes over at least a 6-month period than did the use of no rehabilitation at all. There are other indications in the alcohol rehabilitation literature that the use of disulfiram may be an important aid to any <u>problem</u> drinker referral programme. This California study also suggested positive results for the use of Alcoholics Anonymous as a referral option.

Again, on an overall rehabilitation basis using data from several projects, it appeared that social drinkers assigned to rehabilitation (most of them were assigned to educational programmes) had fewer subsequent alcohol-related rearrests than had those not assigned to rehabilitation. As Figure 11 points out, however, this was not the case for problem drinkers. Within the problem drinker class, those referred to more comprehensive, personalized (type 1) programmes had fewer rearrests than those assigned to less comprehensive (type 2) programmes(38).

In addition to the Canadian, Alberta Impaired Driver Program Mentioned earlier, efforts to rehabilitate the drinking driver were made in Germany(43), based on U.S. experience. Four group discussions of 2 hours each were held, based on group dynamics principles. In addition, the costs of drinking/driving convictions as well as suggestions for the treatment of drinking drivers were solicited.

Discussion of evaluation results

Although there are suggestions that generalized rehabilitation and possibly educational programmes may be beneficial in terms of reducing subsequent violations, there is almost no hard evidence available to date to show that such programmes are having a measurable <u>crash reduction</u> impact. Effects in terms of reductions in alcohol problem areas which are not driving-related have not yet been determined but are presently being looked at(42).

Still, on the basis of the results already gained using driving related criteria, some trends are apparent. First off, it appears that persons diagnosed as non-problem (or social) drinkers are less likely to be rearrested for drunk driving than are persons diagnosed as problem drinkers. This is a relatively stable finding in the ASAP experience and shows up in the Malfetti and Simon(34) study as well. More specifically, profile analyses suggest that convicted drinking drivers who have lower BACs at time of arrest, fewer prior convictions for drinking related offences, larger incomes and white collar jobs have a lower initial probability of being rearrested than do drinking drivers with converse characteristics. In addition to these lower initial rearrest probabilities, there is some evidence from the ASAP programme level analyses to suggest that social drinkers may be somewhat more responsive to treatment than are their problem drinker counterparts and that the type of treatment to which social drinkers are exposed (i.e., lecture versus interactive or extensive versus short-term) matters little. Thus, it can be hypothesized that the most economically efficient programmes should be suitable for social drinkers. These probably would constitute short-term, didactic, educational programmes. This hypothesis should now receive greater evaluation attention.

For persons diagnosed as problem drinkers, there is little evidence that rehabilitation programmes, overall, are having any substantial effect on improving their rearrest or crash records (at least not in the measurable short-term). More specific analyses, however, suggest that diagnosed problem drinkers exposed to interactive (rather than lecture) type schools and more personal yet intensive therapies have significantly fewer alcohol related rearrests than those referred to lecture-oriented or shorter programmes. In addition,

there are some indications from the general alcohol rehabilitation literature that programme characteristics such as length and intensity may be more important than theoretical
orientation(43).

For problem drinkers, there is also some evidence to suggest that the use of the
drug disulfiram (chemotherapy) may aid rehabilitation by facilitating the maintenance of
sobriety while the treatment process is getting underway.

It should be mentioned that studies of non-driving related alcohol rehabilitation
programmes have more often reported more favourable results than have drinking driver
studies. It is unclear as to whether this is due to lesser concern over experimental
rigour, or to the use of non-driving related criteria (e.g., job status, health, etc.)
which may be more sensitive to change than are driving related criteria, or both. Drinking driver programmes in the United States are now beginning to use these life change
criteria (in addition to crashes and violations) to evaluate programme effectiveness(42).
The employment of such criteria should also contribute to a more useful assessment of
programme characteristics which are most suitable for various client types. What is clear
is that a much more rigorous evaluation coupled with systematic re-development efforts
must be undertaken if this area is to become an acceptably effective countermeasure in
the traffic safety network. Such programmes probably cannot reasonably be expected to
result in dramatic crash reductions (at least in the short-term) since they deal only
with known offenders who, in turn, contribute to only a small proportion of the total
crashes in any one year. However, if such programmes can be shown to result in significant reductions in any socially relevant problems due to drinking (as well as in small,
but significant, crash reductions), such programmes can be cost-effective and worth continuing. On the other hand, if no such socially relevant improvements can be demonstrated,
the case for court referral programmes will become difficult to support. Again, it appears
that, to become effective, this programme area will have to undergo a rigorous period of
systematic evaluation and re-development efforts.

V.3 Supporting Countermeasures

While major efforts to counter the problem of alcohol have been centered on legislative action, public education and rehabilitation programmes, a number of other countermeasure possibilities exist which can be viewed as supportive of an overall programme.
These measures range from indirect legislative action such as restricting driving and
drinking age, mechanical deterrents to prevent impaired drivers from starting a vehicle,
chemical controls of impairment, to programmes designed to provide alternative forms of
transportation for drinking-drivers. The problem, state-of-the-art and potential effectiveness of some of these countermeasures are examined in the following sections.

V.3.1 Indirect legislative measures

In addition to legislating against impaired driving (see chapter V.1), there are
also laws which can indirectly influence drinking and driving. Among these are regulations
which restrict drinking age, driving age and the selling of alcoholic beverages.

Restricting drinking age

Limiting the use of alcohol and/or drugs among the younger age groups is one of the
most widely applied control procedures in use. The effectiveness of this control has been
examined in a number of jurisdictions which have recently changed the legal drinking age.
Whitehead et al.(44) compared the number of collisions experienced by young male drivers
in London, Ontario before and after the legal drinking age had been reduced from 21 years
of age to 18 years of age. By comparing the three year period before and after the change

with the two year period following the change, it was found that the number of alcohol-related accidents increased for both the 16-17 and 18-20 year old groups as compared with the 24 year old control group. A shortcoming of this study, however, was that the definition of alcohol involvement was based on police assessment. The data is therefore suspect since the police could have been influenced by the implementation of the lower drinking levels themselves, rather than by a real change in actual drinking drivers' behaviour. It is possible, therefore, that the change in the number of alcohol-related collisions may be related to a change in the frequency with which the police reported alcohol in accidents involving young drivers. Zylman(45) discussed this selectivity process and suggested that if there are more accidents caused by alcohol, the total number of accidents should increase. This statement would tend to support the conclusion that lowering the age limit in Ontario did adversely affect the accident profile since the total number of accidents among the 18-20 year old increased as compared to the 24 year olds in the Whitehead study.

Douglas, Filkins and Clark(46) studied the effect of lowering the drinking age in Michigan, Maine, and Vermont. Michigan and Vermont lowered the drinking age from 21 to 18 on 31st December, 1971 and Maine lowered the drinking age from 20 to 18 in June, 1972. As control states they used Pennsylvania and Texas, both having long-term 21 years drinking age, and New York and Louisiana having long-term 18 years drinking age.

In addition to alcohol-related crashes as defined by the police investigation, they generated other measures for the importance of alcohol in crashes. The main one was the frequency of single-vehicle crashes between 9 p.m. and 6 a.m. where the vehicle had a male driver.

In Michigan, both alcohol-involved accidents and single-vehicle accidents increased significantly for the 18-20 year group while there was no increase for the 21-45 year group. In Maine there was an increase for the 18-20 group and not for the 21-45 group. The increase was not significant but the authors believe that a longer after-period would have made it so. Neither in Vermont nor in any of the control states was there any increase in alcohol-related crashes for 18-20 year olds except in Pennsylvania where the older group accident experience increased as well.

The authors concluded that lowering the legal-drinking age led to an increase in alcohol-related accidents in Michigan and Maine but not in Vermont.

Williams, et al.(47) studied the involvement of drivers in fatal crashes in two American states - Michigan and Wisconsin - and the province of Ontario in Canada where the legal drinking age had been reduced to 18. The accident involvement was compared with three states respectively contiguous to them (Indiana, Illinois and Minnesota) in which the legal drinking age remained 21 during the period studied.

The study was based on fatal crashes in the three years preceding the change and the fatal crashes the year the law went into effect, for the age groups 15 to 17 and 18 to 20. In addition to the total number of fatal crashes, night-time crashes and single-vehicle crashes were studied separately.

Compared with the "control" states there was no significant effect on the number of fatal accidents. There was, however, an effect on the number of night-time crashes. The number of single-vehicle accidents did not change significantly, but when the 18-20 year group was analysed separately, there was a significant increase in single-vehicle accidents relative to states where the legal drinking age had not been reduced. The authors conclude that reducing the legal drinking age will have an effect in increasing the number of fatal accidents caused by alcohol.

The best indicator of any effect on alcohol-related crashes would be the frequency of drivers in crashes with a positive BAC. Unfortunately neither of these studies have data for the true frequency of alcohol in accidents. In Wisconsin, however, there is a programme for mandatory blood testing of traffic fatalities. For practical reasons tests are not performed in every case, but about 75 percent of driver fatalities are tested. This had made it possible to compare the frequency of blood alcohol in dead drivers before and after the legal drinking age was lowered(48). There was no significant change in the frequency of a BAC greater than 50. In the 18-20 year group the percentage increased from 56.8 to 57.7 from 1971 to 1972 and further to 62.2 in 1973 but this was still lower than what had been the case in 1969 and 1970.

The first three studies described found an increase in alcohol-related accidents for young drivers following a reduction in drinking age to 18 years; the fourth study does not find such an effect. The actual BAC is obviously a better criterion for alcohol-related accidents than police reports and this seems to favour the last study. But contrary to what was the case in Michigan and Ontario, in Wisconsin beer was legally available to 18 year olds before the reductions in legal drinking age. The change in legislation may therefore have caused merely a change in choice of beverage and less of an increase in drinking. For this reason the negative result does not invalidate the results of the other three studies. In conclusion there seems to be a slight increase in young driver accidents due to alcohol when alcohol is made more easily accessible by reducing the legal drinking age. The increase is however too small to legitimate restrictions in sale of alcoholic beverages to the age group 18 to 20. As Voas(49) points out, the total prohibition of teenagers from drinking can only partially deal with the problem since the largest number of night-time drivers (i.e. most serious drinking-driving period) fall in the 21 to 25 year old age group.

Restricting driving age

Since the effectiveness of changing the legal age at which a person can drink is of questionable value as a countermeasure, an alternative would be to change the age at which a driving licence can be obtained. Consideration must be given, however, to the fact that most young people learn to drink at the same time that they are learning to drive. The implication for traffic safety, therefore, is that these two processes should be separated so as not to occur simultaneously. Thus it has been suggested that with drinking ages being lowered, even lower age limits might be permitted for initiation of driving in order to have greater opportunity for learning driving skills prior to the initiation of drinking(49). However, evidence indicates that immaturity is a contributing factor in accidents among 16 year olds. Lowering the driving age further, would probably produce more problems that it would resolve.

Alternatively, the driving age could be increased, even though this might result in a reduction in accidents which are attributed to young drivers, plus the added advantages of fuel economy and reduced congestion on the road.

Time restriction on driving

One of the technologically feasible countermeasures which could be used for convicted impaired drivers is to restrict their driving to daylight-working hours. There are currently available tachographs used primarily by the trucking industry for monitoring speed and hours of driving. These devices could be installed in a convicted impaired driver's vehicle to monitor his driving speeds and hours of travel. Regular inspection of the graph would have to be a necessary condition for maintaining one's licence. In addition, the driver would have to be restricted to driving specific vehicles. This would also mean the vehicle could not be used by other drivers during the restricted hours unless a sophisticated driver identification module such as finger print identifier was added.

Impounding vehicles

One possible countermeasure against drinking driving is to impound the vehicle of
the convicted DWI offender. This measure, by itself, would probably lead to an increase
in used car sales or car rentals by suspended drivers. A further step to ensure the
effectiveness of this countermeasure would require the purchaser of any vehicle to present
a valid driver's licence. This in turn would require the issuance of some form of identification for non-drivers (i.e. the handicapped) so they could purchase vehicles.

These measures do not solve the problem of a suspended driver with an impounded car
getting a friend or relative to loan or purchase a vehicle. Confiscation of the vehicle
driven by a DWI suspended driver would probably reduce this problem but would also result
in the suspended driver having a friend purchase a very inexpensive vehicle where the
economic loss from confiscation would be low.

In summary the impounding of vehicles as a countermeasure has intuitive appeal but in
implementation a number of extensions in powers would be necessary to make the law work.

V.3.2 Mechanical deterrents

Vehicle interlocks

A variety of in-vehicle alcohol interlock systems has been proposed to prevent the
drinking-driver from starting his car. One type requires the driver to successfully complete a performance task before the vehicle will start. An example, is the General Motors
Phystester. When the ignition is switched on a series of five digits appears for several
seconds on a miniature display panel. The driver must then punch the same sequence of
digits on a push-button key board before the car will start. Failure to respond correctly
in three times with different series of digits renders the car starter inoperative for
about half an hour. The Bosch Company in Germany has also developed equipment which
requires the driver to input specific combinations of answers into a key board, following
the presentation of various signs and figures. At present, however, the device is not
differentiating impaired drivers from unimpaired drivers. Many impaired drivers are able
to pass the test while some sober individuals (especially older drivers) are failing the
test.

Honda has designed a second type of device which cuts the ignition starter circuit
if it detects the presence of alcohol in the car. It is not reported whether a drunk
passenger however, would immobilize the car for a sober driver[50].

Continuous monitoring

An in-vehicle one time test may not be sufficiently sensitive to changes in driver
performance due to alcohol. Another type of device which has been proposed would conti-
nually monitor driver performance (i.e. stearing wheel reversals, rate of brake application, etc.) and when an individual exceeds pre-set limits the device could activate either
a system to shut down the vehicle (i.e. a warning light that the vehicle ignition will shut
off in some pre-determined period) or activate a warning system to the surrounding traffic
(i.e. a set of blinker lights). Each driver would require to have an individual code on
board so the computer could compare current driving to previous driving performance.

On road performance test

Roadblocks or random stopping of drivers to test for the presence of alcohol is an
extremely inefficient use of police time because of the low frequency of impaired drivers
in the driving population. If there was a pre-screening performance test which drivers
could perform while travelling that could be monitored by the police, those that failed
the test could be stopped by the police and given a breath test. This would increase the
efficiency of the police in identifying impaired drivers and also vastly increase the

number of drivers whose performance would be assessed. This, in turn, would hopefully result in decreased impaired driving as the likelihood of arrest increased. Such a performance measure has not been developed and basic research on differences in driver's performance while impaired is needed.

Chemical controls (sober pills)

Since alcohol is a drug which produces impairment the question arises as to whether there are other drugs which can counteract the impairing effect. For such a "sober pill" to be an effective countermeasure, it would have to be relatively inexpensive, fast acting, have no detrimental side effect and reduce impairment by at least 40 mg%.

Basically, three types of sober pills have been examined. The first type is designed to assist the body to metabolize alcohol more rapidly. This approach seems least promising since the drug affects the overall metabolism of the body. The second type is designed to reduce or block the effect of alcohol on the central nervous system. Investigations are underway at present to determine the efficiency of this approach. The final type, which appears to be the most feasible, limits the absorbtion by the body of alcohol from the stomach and intestines.

At present, however, there is no drug which can safely counteract all the impairing effects of alcohol.

V.3.3 Incentive measures

Reduced insurance premiums

One incentive scheme which seems attractive is the provision of reduced insurance premiums for drivers who agree not to drive after drinking (abstainers).

One of the current conditions of this type of insurance is that the insured certify that he never drinks. This limits the incentive to a very small segment of the population. Hurst(51) has found that the accident rate when driving sober is significantly higher among individuals who report drinking less than once per year than among individuals who report drinking daily. If this relationship extends to abstainers, this selectivity of infrequent drinkers having higher accident rates may explain why insurance rates for abstainers are not lower than other classes of individuals.

There has never been an evaluation of the effectiveness of this incentive scheme but any country with such a scheme could, in a roadside survey of drinking driving, ask questions about the type of insurance the driver holds and determine if those holding abstainers insurance are in fact under-represented in the drinking driver group proportionate to their driving.

An alternative incentive scheme for drinkers would be insurance upon the pledge never to drive after drinking. A device similar to a breathalyzer could be developed to be installed in the vehicle. This device would monitor the air in the vehicle and record any detection of alcohol. A positive reading on the device in the case of an accident or on the yearly inspection for renewal of the insurance would invalidate first party coverage or the possibility of renewal. Three problems are immediately apparent with this proposal. First a driver could not drive an impaired friend home when the driver had not been drinking - a restriction many individuals may be willing to make. Secondly the device would have to be sensitive enough to detect alcohol when all the windows were open and finally the device would have to differentiate between ethyl alcohol and all other volatile substances.

Driver violation review

A variety of programmes exist in which the driving record of an individual results in a review of his driving privilege. These range from ASAP - AIDP type programmes which are of questionable success (see Chapter V.3) through driver interview programmes where a driver with an accumulated number of violations comes in to have his record reviewed, to warning letters being sent out.

The effectiveness of the interview programmes has never been evaluated. Warning letter programmes on the other hand have been evaluated with mixed findings. McBride and Peck(52) evaluated 9 different warning letters varying on degree of threat and intimacy that were sent to law violators who had accumulated 3 of 4 points for removal of licensing privileges. In turns of accidents and violations they found warning letters in general resulted in fewer accidents and violations while low threat letters were the best, and degree of personalization of the letter (referral to specific violation) made no difference.

Kaestner and Spight(53) found drivers, eligible for a suspension who were instead issued a one month prohibition licence had significantly fewer accidents during a one-year follow up period than did a comparable group-eligible for suspension but not suspended. Suspended drivers, drivers receiving warning letters or drivers required to take a Defensive Driving course did not have significantly different accident rates as compared with the control group.

Ben David et al.(54) on the other hand, found that sending threatening letters from a volunteer agency on observed violations had no effect on a future occurrence of the same violation (failure to come to a complete stop).

The effectiveness of the threat varied a great deal in the two studies. In the McBride and Peek(9) study, the drivers who received the Department of Motor Vehicles threatening letter had only one more violation before their licence could be legally re-moved. In the Ben David et al.(54) study, the drivers were randomly observed and the threat was for a voluntary organization to report a violation - not to remove the licence.

In summary then, threatening letters where the threat is backed by implied force has been demonstrated to reduce traffic violations. Whether this would also be true for al-cohol related offences remains to be tested.

V.3.4 Identifying corrected DWIs

Special licence plates

Part of the problem with DWI convictions is the anonymity of the conviction. If the potential for public embarrassment was present then a great number of persons may reconsider the utility of driving after drinking. Special licence plates which could publically identify the convicted DWI offender would achieve this objective. The offence could be identified by either a set of letters or numbers (i.e. DWI-937) for convicted drivers. This would be feasible in jurisdictions where the licence remains with the owner rather than the vehicle. The problem with this proposal is that a DWI driver could sell his vehicle to a friend or relative for a nominal sum and the unconvicted owner could then obtain the ordinary licence plates. To overcome this problem, the DWI convicted driver when reinstated would have to be restricted to driving specific vehicles suitably identi-fied.

Posting driver's licence

Another way to publically identify the DWI offender would be to require each driver to display his driver licence while he is driving. Different licences could be colour coded for different offences and suspended drivers would be easily identifiable. The licence would have to be easily portable, but identifiable from a passing vehicle or a sidewalk observer and located in a convenient place for easy posting. A pocket on the lower left hand corner of the windshield seems to be the obvious place.

REFERENCES

1. Hurst, P.M., Epidemiological Aspects of Alcohol in Driver Crashes and Citations. In M.W. Perrine (Ed.) Alcohol, Drugs and Driving. United States Dept. of Transportation, NHSTA. Technical Report, DOT HS 255-2-489, 1973.

2. Noordzij, P.C., The Introduction of a Statutory BAC Limit of 50 mg/100 ml and its Effect on Drinking and Driving Habits and Traffic Accidents. Institute for Road Safety Research, SWOV, Netherlands, 1976.

3. Wilde, C.J.S., In Transport Canada. Alcohol and Highway Safety. A Review in Quest of Remedies. Ottawa, 1974.

4. L'Hoste, J., Quelques résultats de recherches menées en France à propos de l'imprégnation éthylique des conducteurs. In proceedings of the Conference on Medical, Human and Related Factors Causing Traffic Accidents, Including Alcohol and Drugs. Montreal, Quebec, May 30-31, 1972.

5. Buikhuizen, W., Strafmat en recidivisme (Size of Penalty and Recidivism). In W. Buikhuizen (Ed.) Alcohol en verkeer. (Alcohol and Traffic) Boom en Zoon, Meppel, Netherlands, 1968.

6. Steenhuis, D.W., Een onderzoek naar het generaal-preventief effect van de strafmaat bij rijden onder invloed. Delikt en Delinkwent 5: 566-582, Nov. 9, 1975.

7. Sabey, B.E. and Codling, P.J., Alcohol and Road Accidents in Great Britain. Paper presented at the 6th International Conference on Alcohol, Drugs and Traffic Safety Toronto, Canada, 1974.

8. Carr, B., Goldberg, H., Farbar, C.M.L., The Breathalizer Legislation: An Inferential Evaluation. Transport Canada, Ottawa, 1973.

9. Biecheler, M.B. and al., Alcoolémie des conducteurs et accidents de la route. ONSER Cahiers d'études, 32, May, 1974.

10. Birrell, J.H.W., The Compulsory Breathalizer .05 % Legislation in Victoria. In Israelstam, S. and Lambert, S. (Eds.), 1975.

11. Borkenstein, R.F., Problems of Enforcement, Adjudication, and Sanctioning. Paper presented at the 6th International Conference on Alcohol, Drugs and Traffic Safety. Toronto, 1974.

12. Beitel, G.A., Sharp, M.C. and Glauz, W.D., Probability of Arrest while Driving under the Influence of Alcohol. Journal of Studies of Alcohol. Vol. 36, N°. 1.

13. Borkenstein, R.F., Crowther, R.F., Shumate, R.P., Ziel, W.B. and Zylman, R., The Role of the Drinking Driver in Traffic Accidents. Indiana University. February, 1964.

14. Anon. Statens Offentliga Utredningar. Trafiknykterhetsbrott. Statens offentliga ututredning. Stockholm, Sweden, 1970.

15. Ross, H.L., The Scandinavian Myth: The Effectiveness of Drinking and Driving Legislation in Sweden and Norway. The Journal of Legal Studies. Vol. IV (2), June, 1975.

16. Klette, H., Politics and Drunken Driving - The Swedish Experience. Paper presented at the 7th International Conference on Alcohol, Drugs and Traffic Safety, Melbourne, Australia, January 23-28, 1977.

17. Mäki, M., Linnoila, M. and Alha, A., Drinking and Driving in Helsinki. Accident Analysis and Prevention. (in press).

18. Bø, O., Screening av alkoholbelastningen blånt bilfører i normal trafikk. Institute of Transport Economy, Oslo, Norway, 1972.

19. Laural, H. and Jones, Unpublished report on Swedish roadside survey. Caroline Institute, Stockholm, Sweden.

20. Ross, H.L., Law, Science and Accidents: The British Road Safety Act of 1967. Journal of Legal Studies., 2, 1 - 78, 1972.

21. Anon. Drinking and Driving. Report of the Departmental Committee, Department of the Environment, HMSO, London, 1976.

22. Anon. Evaluation of the Alcohol Safety Action Programmes. United States Department of Transportation, Washington, D.C., 1976. (in press)

23. OECD Road Research, Road Safety Campaigns: Design and Evaluation. Prepared by G.J.S. Wilde with the assistance of J. L'Hoste, D., Sheppard and G. Wind, Paris, 1971

24. NHTSA, The Use of Mass Media for Highway Safety. DOT-HS-801-209, United States Department of Transportation, Washington, D.C., 1974.

25. Barmack, J.E. and Payne, D.E., The Lackland Accident Countermeasure Experiment. Highway Research Board Proceedings, 40, 513-522, 1961.

26. Sheppard, D., The 1967 Drink and Driving Campaign: A Survey among Drivers. Road Research Laboratory, Report LR 230, Crowthorne, Berkshire, England, 1968.

27. Newby, R.F., Casualty Reductions in Great Britain Following the Road Safety Act of 1967. OECD Symposium on Countermeasures to Driver Behaviour Under the Influence of Alcohol and Drugs, British Medical Association, London, September, 1971.

28. Ross, H.L., The Effectiveness of Drinking-and-Driving Laws in Sweden and Great Britain. Proceedings of the 6th International Conference on Alcohol, Drugs and Traffic Safety. Addiction Research Foundation, pp 663-678, Toronto, 1974.

29. Farmer, P.J., The Edmonton Study: A Pilot Project to Demonstrate the Effectiveness of a Public Information Campaign on the Subject of Drinking and Driving. Proceedings of the 6th International Conference on Alcohol, Drugs, and Traffic Safety, pp 831-843. Addiction Research Foundation, Toronto, 1974.

30. Pierce, J., Heiatt, D., Goodstadt, M., Lonero, L., Cunliffe, A., and Pang, H., Experimental Evaluation of a Community-Based Campaign Against Drinking and Driving. Proceedings of the 6th International Conference on Alcohol, Drugs and Traffic Safety, pp 869-879. Addiction Research Foundation, Toronto, 1974.

31. L'Hoste, J.L., Effectiveness of Campaigns. Paper provided to the OECD Research Group S14. Paris, 1976.

32. Stewart, E.I. and Malfetti, J.L., Rehabilitation of the Drunken Driver: A Corrective Course in Phoenix, Arizona for Persons Driving Under the Influence of Alcohol, Teachers College Press, Columbia University, New York, 1970.

33. Crabb, D., Gettys, T.R., Malfetti, J.L. and Stewart, E.L., Development and Preliminary Tryout of Evaluation Measures for the Phoenix Driving-While-Intoxicated Re-education Programme, Prepared for PPG Industries Foundation, Arizona State University, Tempe, Arizona, 1971.

34. Malfetti, J.L., and Simon, K.J., A Comparison of Changes in Knowledge and Attitude Between Problem Drinkers and Non-problem Drinkers Following a Re-education Programme. Proceedings of the 6th International Conference on Alcohol, Drugs and Traffic Safety. pp 737-748. Addiction Research Foundation, Toronto, 1974.

35. Zelhart, P.F., The Alberta Impaired Drivers Programme: Final Report, Phase I., University of Alberta, Department of Psychology, Edmonton, 1973.

36. Blumenthal M. and Ross H.L., Judicial Discretion in Drinking-Driving Cases: An Empirical Study of Influences and Consequences. Proceedings of the 6th International Conference on Alcohol, Drugs and Traffic Safety, pp 755-762. Addiction Research Foundation, Toronto, 1974.

37. Newman, J.R., McEachern, A.W. and Kirby, S., Drinking Drivers and their Traffic Records. University of Southern California, United States Department of Transportation, NHTSA, Contract DOT-HS-101-2-45, Washington, D.C., 1974.

38. Ellingstad, V.S. and Springer, T.J., Programme Level Evaluation of ASAP Diagnosis, Referral and Rehabilitation Efforts: Vol. III - Analysis of ASAP Rehabilitation Countermeasure Effectiveness, University of South Dakota, United States Department of Transportation, NHTSA Report DOT-HS-802-044 (available from National Technical Information Service, Springfield, Virginia 22161), September, 1976.

39. Smart, R.G., The Evaluation of Alcoholism Treatment Programmes, 17(1):41-51, Addictions, 1970.

40. Nichols, J.L. and Reis, R.E., One Model for the Evaluation of ASAP Rehabilitation Efforts. Proceedings of the 6th International Conference on Alcohol, Drugs and Traffic Safety. pp 893-926. Addiction Research Foundation, Toronto, 1974.

41. Ellingstad, V.E., 1975 Interim Assessment of Alcohol Rehabilitation Efforts, University of South Dakota, United States Department of Transportation, Contract DOT-HS-191-3-759, Washington, D.C., 1976.(a)

42. Ellingstad, V.S., Programme Level Evaluation of ASAP Diagnosis, Referral and Rehabilitation Efforts: Vol. IV - Development of the Short Term Rehabilitation (STR) Study, University of South Dakota, United States Department of Transportation, NHTSA Report DOT-HS-802-045 (available from National Technical Information Service, Springfield, Virginia 22161), September, 1976. (b)

43. Ruggels, W.L., Armor, D.J., Polich, J.M., Mothershead, A., and Stephen, M., A Follow-up Study of Clients at Selected Alcoholism Treatment Centers Founded by the NIAAA. National Institute on Alcohol Abuse and Alcoholism, United States Department of Health, Education and Welfare. Rockvill, Maryland, May, 1975.

44. Whitehead, P.C., Craig, J., Langford, N., McArthur, C., Stanton, B., and Terrence, R.G., Collisions Behaviour of Young Drivers: Impact of the Change in Majority. Journal of Studies on Alcohol, 36, 1208-1223, 1975.

45. Zylman, R., Fatal Crashes among Michigan Youth Following Reduction of Legal Drinking Age. Q. Journal for Studies in Alcohol, 35, 283-286, 1974.

46. Douglas, R.L., Filkins, L.P., and Clark, F.A., The Effect of Lower Legal Drinking Ages on Youth Crash Involvement. Highway Safety Research Institute, Ann Arbor, 1974.

47. Williams, Allan, F., Rich, R.F., Zador, P.L. and Robertson, L.S., The Legal Minimum Drinking Age and Fatal Motor Vehicle Crashes. Journal of Legal Studies, 4, 219-237, 1975.

48. Noar, L.M. and Nashold, R.D., Teenage Driver Fatalities Following Reduction in the Legal Drinking Age. Journal of Safety Research V. 7, pp 74-79, 1975.

49. Voas, R., Alcohol, Drugs and Young Drivers. United States DOT NHSTA, United States Department of Transportation, Washington, D.C., 1974.

50. Raymond, A.E., A Review of Alcohol in Relation to Road Safety Department of Transport (Australia), Report NR/3 - June, 1973.

51. Hurst, P.M., Epidemiologic Aspects of Alcohol in Driver Crashes and Citations. Journal of Safety Research, 5, 130-148, 1973.

52. McBride, R.S. and Peck, R.C., Modifying Negligent Driving Behaviour through Warning Letters. Accident Analysis and Prevention, 2, 147-174, 1970.

53. Kaestner, N. and Speight, L., Successful Alternatives to License Suspension. The Defensive Driving Course and the Probationary License. Journal of Safety Research V. 7, 2, pp 56-66, 1975.

54. Ben David, G., Levine, I., Haliva, Y. and Tel-Nir, N., The Influence of Personal Communication on the Driving Behaviour of Private Motorists in Israel. Accident Analysis and Prevention, 4, 269-301, 1972.

55. Ministerio dei lavori pubblici. Manuale sulle campagne di siuerezza stradale. Allegato IV: Conferenza Roma: 13, 14, 15 Ottobre 1971, Resoconto. Rome 1976.

56. OECD Road Research. Manual on Road Safety Campaigns. Drafted by P. Prigogine in co-operation with J. L'Hoste, M. Roche, D. Sheppard and G.G. Wind. Paris, September 1975.

57. Labadie, M.J. and L'Hoste, J., Influence sociale et sécurité routière. Réalisation d'une campagne expérimentale d'incitation au port de la ceinture de sécurité, C.E. ONSER, Arcueil, April 1978.

VI

CONCLUSIONS

VI.1 Introduction

Traffic accidents are a major cause of injury and death in industrialized countries, and it is widely recognized that <u>alcohol and drug</u> impairment are two major variables contributing to such accidents. Between one third and one half of fatal accidents to adults involve drivers with measurable alcohol and/or drug presence. In view of the high social acceptability of beverage alcohol in industrialized societies, and the increasing use of drugs both of prescribed and sold over the counter, the various forms of impairment of driving abilities caused by alcohol alone, by drugs alone, or by interactions of drugs and alcohol, are of great social concern.

Countermeasures against the <u>alcohol impaired driver</u> have been launched by many countries. Because of the shortage of sound scientific data, it has often not been possible to determine whether the countermeasures have been effective in reducing the incidence of driving after drinking; nevertheless some degree of success has been demonstrated for a variety of countermeasures, usually used in combination, in a number of countries. The recent availability of scientific methodologies to assess blood-alcohol levels from a breath sample has made it easier for law enforcement agencies to detect the alcohol impaired driver. Proposed legislative changes in some countries to permit broader application of breath analysis by police could potentially lead to an increase in drinking driving detection rates. An increase in alcohol-impaired detection rates is likely to occasion an increase among the motoring public of the subjective probability of being apprehended. Punitive approaches have had only limited value in eliminating hazardous driving behaviour. Similarly, the re-educational programmes which have been evaluated, have demonstrated a disappointing rate of recidivism.

To date impairment of driving abilities by <u>drugs</u> has not been adequately researched. There is reason to believe, however, that a wide variety of mood-altering drugs, pain relievers, anesthetics and others, which have adverse effects that can impair vision and eye-hand coordination, or which induce bodily discomfort, may be hazardous to driving behaviour.

Methodology for the detection of drugs in body fluids is complex and often impractical in terms of road safety, particularly if contemplated as a large-scale endeavour. Additionally, because of tolerance, there are few reliable data which directly relate drug concentrations in blood or urine to specific impairment of functions that are of paramount importance for safe driving.

A number of possible forms of countermeasures for both alcohol and drugs may be contemplated. Some are legislative in nature, using concomitant strict law enforcement continued over long periods of time, others may involve several forms of education aimed at both the learning and experienced driver. Some may be introduced in driving schools as a preventive measure while modified education courses may be employed as mandatory remedial measures for those already convicted of an impaired driving offence. Prior to primary licensing, or before the reinstatement of a driving licence for persons who have a chronic drug or alcohol problem, intensive treatment and rehabilitative measures may well have to be devised.

VI.2 Blood Alcohol Levels and Driving

Alcohol is involved in a high proportion of motor vehicle accidents. Of serious concern is the problem drinker or dependent user of alcohol, who persists in driving despite impairing high blood alcohol concentrations to which he has only partially adapted his whole social behaviour. Such drivers are over-represented in statistics in several countries with regard to fatal accidents. The blood alcohol concentration of these drivers is often twice that which is legally designated as the level of impairment.

Another problem is the adult drinker who is not necessarily dependent on alcohol but who consumes excessive amounts even on occasions when he has to drive. Such drivers sometimes lack tolerance to a moderate BAC, and in some instances may be impaired even at levels which are below the legal limit set by government.

The young driver is of special concern. He is often learning to drive and learning to drink at the same time, and has little or no tolerance of even relatively low blood alcohol concentrations. This type of driver is especially likely to be involved in nighttime crashes. It should be pointed out that an increasing number of young are using alcohol excessively and in many countries the phenomenon of increasing numbers of young dependent or problem drinkers is causing understandable concern.

Different countermeasures need to be formulated for these differing groups. Simple apprehension, a fine, a reprimand, or a minimum form of re-education is sufficient for some persons. For the problem drinker however, punitive measures alone are unlikely to provide any lasting benefit. Treatment of the drinking problem is the most appropriate remedial action. For all impaired drivers, the risk of apprehension as contrasted to the chance of escaping detection on the road must be sufficiently great if apprehension is to be a meaningful reality in terms of deterrence.

For the average person, subjected to a variety of tests in laboratory and driving experiments, a degree of impairment can be demonstrated at blood alcohol concentrations as low as 50 mg%. The addition of any psychoactive substance to even low blood alcohol concentration, may result in unexpected and severe degrees of impairment.

Statistics from both Europe and North America regarding risk of traffic accidents in relation to blood alcohol concentrations suggest that the level at which an appreciable rise in risk occurs depends on tolerance and drinking patterns. Nevertheless, some principles related to different levels have emerged. Between 50 and 80 mg% the risk curve begins to rise. Above 80 mg% the risk of accident involvement increases appreciably for the majority of drinking drivers. For more experienced drinkers and/or drivers the level may be higher, but beyond 100 mg% present evidence suggests that _all_ drinking drivers are impaired to an extent that their accident risk is definitely increased. More important, at the low level of 50 mg%, inexperienced drinkers and/or drivers (which by implication includes many young persons) are at greater risk than average. The level chosen for enactment of legislation has to be determined in each country by considering both social and scientific factors.

It has been demonstrated that _pedestrians_ with blood alcohol concentrations at or above the level of legal impairment for drivers, are not uncommonly responsible for vehicle-pedestrian accidents. For impaired _pedestrians_ the risk of accident involvement increases rapidly above 120 mg%.

VI.3 Extent and Characteristics of the Drinking-Driver Problem

Accident proneness studies which have measured the risk of accidents as a function of both alcohol use and driving, have demonstrated a number of variable personal profile factors. These include age, sex, marital status, education and occupation. The most important characteristics relate to maleness and age.

The place of the automobile as a perceived requisite for comfortable living in developed countries has resulted in an almost universal desire for a driving licence and, where possible, vehicle ownership at an early adult age. This fact, coupled with the ready availability of alcohol to this same age group, has led to an overrepresentation of young persons in alcohol-related road accidents.

Considerable variation exists between countries with regard to the legal driving age. In some countries driving is permitted prior to the age of legal drinking, while the converse is true for others. No data are presently available to demonstrate the superiority of one system over the other. In like manner, it has not been established that formal pre-licence driving instruction results in a lower incidence of subsequent accident involvement. This does not preclude the possibility that the inclusion of meaningful information concerning the deleterious effects of alcohol on driver behaviour within a formal driving school curriculum, and its reinforcement during the licensing examination, would not improve the situation.

Standard descriptive terms for the population at risk of alcohol related accidents are simplistic. Nevertheless, a number of invariable physiological factors are of paramount importance with regard to impairment. The concentration of alcohol in the blood is determined by factors that influence absorption, including the duration of time taken for ingestion, the dilution of the alcohol, the presence and the type of food in the stomach, and the type of beverage consumed. Distribution after absorption and the excretion rate are fixed by metabolic pathways, which are not significantly different from person to person. No specific method or substance is available which can increase the metabolic breakdown of alcohol or rapidly induce sobriety in an intoxicated person.

Research in some selected areas of alcohol impairment of driving skills is still required. There is a continuing lack of understanding of the underlying mechanisms causing impairment of driving proficiency, and gaps in our present knowledge of alcohol effects in some real-world driving situations. The nature and extent of physiological and behavioural tolerance to alcohol and the nature of dependence on alcohol are understood only in a fragmentary way. Research until now has been largely directed towards investigation of the effects of high blood alcohol concentrations; levels below legal limits have provoked little interest. It seems especially important to investigate the effect of small amounts of alcohol especially with relation to long-term monotonous driving, and driver fatigue. Impairment by low levels of alcohol may be even more relevant for motor cyclists and snowmobile operators than for those driving automobiles.

There are two special areas of concern. There exist forms of psychological and physical dependence or addiction to alcohol, which lead to compulsive use of the substance even during periods when driving is essential. By definition, the state of dependence lessens the ability of the individual to exercise a wise freedom of choice whether to drink or abstain. An accident victim who has ingested considerable quantities of alcohol is at increased risk of death if he sustains a head injury, suffers from shock, or needs an anaesthetic. This suggests a need for formulation of medical and surgical regimens specifically designed to manage these casualties.

A number of conclusions can be reached with regard to the dimensions of the drinking-driver problem, and its national characteristics:

- Roadside surveys conducted on a continuing basis will establish a national base of alcohol prevalence in the driving population in each country.
- So that results will be comparable, all countries instituting a road-side alcohol survey would be cooperating best by following OECD recommendations for road-side survey methodology.
- In order to evaluate the extent of involvement of alcohol in fatal traffic accidents, medical-legal autopsies of all fatally injured drivers, adult pedestrians, and other road users can easily include the alcohol content of the blood. These data may then be compiled for the purpose of constructing reliable national profiles of BAC distribution for all road users.
- In some countries legislation may have to be secured to permit examination of blood for its alcohol content in all drivers and pedestrians admitted to medical institutions after traffic accidents.
- Similarly when blood samples are drawn for medical reasons from victims of road accidents and this information is available from medical records, legislation may have to be secured to allow this information to be compiled for the purpose of research, without causing prejudice to the victim.
- In order to help determine whether or not a driver at risk is a problem drinker or a social drinker, full information can be obtained for drivers involved in fatal or injury accidents and convicted drivers with respect to the following primary variables:
  (a) driving experience
  (b) drinking experience
  (c) previous traffic offences and criminal records.
- Legislation may have to be secured to permit routine involvement by the police in breath testing of all drivers involved in any injury accident to which police are summoned.

VI.4 Drugs and Driving Behaviour: Background

There exist few, if any, comprehensive international data with regard to drug-induced impairment of driving skills. Consequently several subsequent sections are based on findings that require tests of validity and international corroboration.

There have been few attempts to relate the use of drugs to the occurrence of traffic accidents. Nevertheless those few which are available have established a variety of behaviours related to driving which are influenced by a number of psychoactive drugs. These include diminished sense of balance and eye muscle movement and coordination, eye-hand coordination, and visual tracking abilities.

There have been no determined efforts to associate the use of psychoactive drugs (excluding alcohol) with specific driving errors or with specific responsibility for accidents. In addition, psychoactive drugs are generally used by persons who are emotionally upset. It must be recognized that anxiety and similar emotional problems are in themselves hazardous in terms of driving ability, and it is unclear whether or not persons taking correctly prescribed psychoactive drugs are not more safe under the effect of the drugs than they would be in an unmedicated state.

Although a number of qualitative effects of drugs have been described, it thus far has not been possible to be quantitatively precise about the concentrations of drugs in body fluids with reference to respective degrees of impairment. This is partially due to inadequate instrumentation along with a lack of sufficiently sophisticated pharmacological techniques.

Some drugs affect more than one part of the brain and thus produce complicated mixtures of depression and stimulation. As a result any simple classification of drugs is imprecise. Indeed psychoactive substances in the past have been categorized for purposes of expediency of control, rather than on the basis of their pharmacological action. Drugs may have different effects in different doses; this is particularly evident for the sedative-hypnotic group of drugs which in low doses are mildly calming, but in larger doses are sleep inducers. For purposes of this report, drugs which effect the central nervous system are classified into a few convenient groups. Cannabis has been separated out in order to discuss its unique properties.

VI.5 Extent and Characteristics of the Problem of Drugs and Driving

It is not possible to compare directly drug consumption rates by the driving population between countries in view of: varying availability of certain drugs; differences in costs for the same drug between countries; differences in medical prescribing patterns; and different scheduling of drugs which has led to varying degrees of voluntary and mandatory restrictions from one country to another.

Nonetheless, there is a need for reliable national statistics for all drugs that are likely to pose a hazard for driving, or which can affect pedestrian safety in traffic. Corrective actions are difficult to implement or even envisage in the fields of public and professional education, unless reliable data have demonstrated specific areas of concern. In some cases, acquisition of drug data may require legislative change, or drug rescheduling may be necessary to ensure availability of adequate records. In view of the fact that many drugs sold over the counter now contain active psychoactive ingredients, records for these would seem as necessary as those for prescription drugs. These data would be additional to records already kept nationally for purposes of reporting to the International Narcotics Control Board.

While sales figures and information derived from prescriptions are valuable in assessing drug availability, of greater importance are statistics of actual use of drugs by the driving population. This will require special compilation techniques.

In addition to the monitoring of sales and the uses of drugs, it is encouraging to note interest in national statistics regarding motor vehicle accidents and fatalities connected with drugs. It is indeed logical that surveys be continued internationally by medico-legal experts who can include the results of toxicological examinations of the bodies of those who have been victims of driving collisions. Medico-legal information is virtually complete, because large amounts of not only blood and urine, but tissues such as liver, can be studied and analyzed for drugs, drug interactions, and interactions between metabolites of drugs. This remains however an area that is very incompletely researched.

Profiles of drugs found in the bodies of fatally injured drivers can provide information about the drug using habits of some drivers, but not all drivers on the road. Meaningful data will require statistics obtained from fatally injured drivers in conjunction with knowledge of drug use in the general driving population. Together this will provide an estimate of the driving population at risk from drugs.

There continues to be a need for coordinated information, storage, and retrieval of data relating to drugs and driving skills, which can be made available to all countries. It is recognised that there exists inadequate organisation and no centralisation of existing world literature concerning methodology in this field. A better system of analysis and review of existing data is needed. Increased manpower and extra funding above that already available will be necessary to handle new emerging data. It is suggested that there is a requirement for an annotated review of existing drug measurement methodologies that will take into account all involved costs. It would appear desirable to organise these activities on an international basis to include as many countries as possible.

Accumulation and analysis of national data concerning drugs and road accidents poses both scientific and financial questions of priority and practicability. For example, in terms of drug measurements, there is still a lack of basic knowledge of the metabolism and the body dispositions of many behaviour modifying drugs. For the constraints imposed by scientific demands for accuracy, legal requirements, and significance to the actual traffic situation, present technology may well be inadequate. Costs of upgrading facilities and the training of technicians as well as purchase of equipment, will be considerable. It should be noted that in a poly-drug user the total number of drugs and metabolites present in the body at any one time may exceed 100, and that present methodology, sophisticated though it may be, cannot handle this kind of situation on a large-scale basis.

It is clear nevertheless that advances in technology for the detection of drugs and their metabolites are important areas for future research. It also is clear that basic pharmacological and toxicological research will have to advance <u>by themselves</u>, before necessary developments in analytical methodology become useful to those who are primarily interested in highway safety and drug effects. For this reason no specific recommendation regarding the establishment of research and analytical methodology for drug detection can be made at this time. Despite this fact, the subject has great significance.

The non-medical use of drugs (or drug abuse) especially by younger persons in OECD countries poses additional problems. Traffic accidents in some countries are responsible for a considerable number of deaths among drug addicts. The motivations for drug use of the stimulant, sedative-hypnotic, narcotic, euphoriant or hallucinogenic types are still unclear, and because of this preventive programmes have so far been relatively inefficient. At the present time multiple drug use is the rule rather than the exception. This further complicates the behavioural changes which are engendered. In North America there has been a steady change from stimulants to sedative-euphoriant drugs such as cannabis, and use of this particular drug is increasing without any apparent decrease in the use of alcohol. The widespread phenomenon of deliberately altered states of consciousness by drugs is likely to continue in the next decade, and this may have a profound effect on driving safety, not only for drivers who are using drugs, but also the occupants of other vehicles and pedestrians.

While a certain amount of drug abuse is international in origin and scope, and there is considerable shipment of drugs from one country to another, domestic sources of drugs account for a large amount. Cannabis, which in former times was not grown in temperate climates, is now thriving as far north as the Canadian Prairies. The same can be said of mushrooms containing psylocybin. A wide variety of natural and cultivated plants containing psychoactive substances can affect driving behaviour during the time period of use, and possibly for many hours thereafter.

<u>Experimental studies however remain unclear in defining what relationships exist between drug effects, test performance, driver performance, and traffic crash causation.</u> Present experimental evidence has to conclude that a simple predictive measure of drug effects on human performance which is important in driving has not yet been obtained.

There are problems in the interpretation of studies which have employed acute dosages in non-drug habituated persons. This is due to the fact that drug effects may largely disappear by a process of tolerance after even short periods of time. In addition, many chronic studies that have been carried out involve persons who are using the drugs in a therapeutic manner. Under these circumstances it may be presumed that the drug is being

used by a patient who requires it, and its therapeutic action may therefore be reflected
in improved behavioural performance. In contrast, the same drug taken by normal subjects
may adversely affect behavioural performance. Ethical constraints prevent administering
a drug chronically to subjects for whom it is not therapeutically indicated. Another
concern regarding experimental drug studies relates to the fact that drugs under varying
conditions can have very different effects. Sleep deprivation and emotional strain for
example, may significantly affect drug responses. This is probably of no small importance
in regard to driving skills.

Because reliable data about the actual effects of drugs on driving behaviour are
almost unknown in any detail, it can be concluded that the main thrust of action in this
area must involve further research study. The following are suggested as relevant:

- Since the extent of drug involvement in traffic accidents is not extensively
  documented, it is necessary to devise valid research studies to investigate the
  extent and nature of drug use among drivers and pedestrians involved in fatal
  and non-fatal traffic accidents with controls from the general driving population.
- Verified drug histories could be obtained from all persons admitted to medical
  institutions who are suffering from the results of traffic accidents; body fluid
  analysis could be carried out in adequately equipped laboratories to confirm, at
  least in a qualitative manner, the presence or absence of drugs that may have
  played some part in the causation of the accident.
- Legislation may have to be secured on a national basis to permit the acquisition
  of the body fluids and tissues for the purposes of evaluating the presence of
  drugs in fatally-injured drivers.
- Post-mortem analysis of body fluids and tissues could be carried out in countries
  where facilities are available (and the law permits) for complex quantitative
  studies of drugs, their metabolites, and drug interactions.
- Continual surveillance and monitoring of mood-altering drug consumption by the
  driving population could be established within all countries. Information on
  sales, and therefore availability, of drugs to the driving population are likely
  to provide preliminary information that suggests hazard.

VI.6 Known Effects of Drugs on Driving Abilities

Common minor analgesics and antipyretics have no significant effect on driving
performance. On the other hand, anesthetic agents including injectable substances and
inhalational gases in addition to premedication, can prove hazardous for many hours or
even one or more days. Even local anesthetics may on absorption create central nervous
system stimulation and minor changes in driving behaviour.

Data are conflicting with regard to the amphetamines and amphetamine-derived drugs
which are used as anorexiants and mild stimulants. A recent study of professional drivers
has confirmed a deleterious effect of amphetamine use on long distance trips.

Anti-depressant drugs after the first few days or weeks of administration, usually do
not cause drowsiness and cannot be shown to have significant effects on driving performance.
On the other hand, these same drugs increase alcohol induced impairment of psychomotor
responses.

A wide variety of drugs used as antihistamines, antinauseants, and antidizziness
agents provide mixed pictures of impairment. Some antihistamines cause decrements of
alertness and responsiveness, while others fail to demonstrate this effect. Most antihistamines decrease psychomotor performance and this is of special significance because
of the fact that some drugs in this class are used by people who suffer from travel sick-

ness. Other drugs within this class may significantly impair eye-hand coordination.

Major antipsychotic drugs and tranquilizers may affect alertness. Particular importance is attached to the combination of benzodiazepines and alcohol. Drugs such as chlorpromazine produce impairment of driving performance after a delayed onset, and meprobamate and barbiturates produce moderate to intense impairment.

Drugs used in the treatment of coronary artery disease appear to be safe, as do mild psychostimulants such as caffeine and nicotine. Drugs used as antispasmodics produce some degree of drowsiness and perceptual disorders can be noted in some persons; combination of these drugs with alcohol is deleterious. Atropine is especially long-lasting in its effects.

Drugs used to treat glaucoma (increased intraocular pressure) such as pilocarpine, produce maximal effects on visual acuity, on accomodation, and in refraction. The most significant change is decrease in visual acuity for distance perception.

A wide variety of illicit psychoactive agents including cannabis, can lead to a variety of disfunctions. Speedometer errors are effected because of a distorted sense of speed and distorted time perception. One study carried out in Canada included downtown driving in traffic by persons using marijuana. This demonstrated a definite detrimental effect on driving skills and performance. To be stressed, however, is the fact that cannabis induced effects are not uniform. The combination of alcohol with cannabis is especially hazardous for driving.

Sedative hypnotic drugs including barbiturate and non-barbiturate sedatives, demonstrate significant impairment of psychomotor function that can last many hours. Indeed the effect of one of these drugs taken late at night, may still be present in the early morning hours. For example with hypnotic doses of phenobarbital and nitrazepam there is a hangover effect 12 hours after the administration of the drug, accompanied by psychological impairment and electrophysiological changes. Of significance in this area is the fact that normal fatigue is drastically enhanced after use of the drug methaqualone.

Codeine present in many mixtures and used as an antitussive agent in man has been studied under simulated driving condition and found to be capable of increasing accident frequency. Codeine given in combination with alcohol apparently causes negligence and some serious steering errors.

VI.7 Methodologies of Detection of Impairment

One of the major problems that is associated with the assessment of the effect of drugs and alcohol on driving behaviour, is that the various components of the driving task per se have not been well delineated. In recent years, however, there have been a number of tests developed that can measure some aspects of human performance as influenced by alcohol. Several have been developed to examine human behaviour with special reference to basic mental processes. Others have examined braking behaviour and dynamic visual acuity. While some of these tests have little relevance to real-world activity, a study of bus drivers has demonstrated a degree of correlation between the results of the laboratory testing and accident rates.

In studies of some psychotropic drugs limited efforts have been made to develop tests that are directly related to driving, or to simulate sub-tasks that are involved. While some of these efforts have been encouraging, the results have been inconclusive.

Technology exists to measure accurately deviant driving behaviour during nighttime by means of unobtrusive electronic devices. Utilisation by police of such apparatus can provide precise and reliable indices of suspicion. Utility of modern equipment such as this will be especially useful if roadside breath testing is to be established on a discretionary basis. Although equipment of this type is not uniformly available, an increasing number of moderately priced devices are expected to be marketed in the near future.

Direct driver observation or "within vehicle approaches" have removed some of the artificiality of the laboratory situation. Notwithstanding, actual highway operation (even with dual control vehicles) appears to present significant risks, and this is particularly true if evidence indicates that the drug under study is likely to affect adversely a person's behavioural patterns. This kind of study may thus be legally and morally unacceptable. Because of this, projects of this kind should not be undertaken without a rigorous examination of both ethical and legal problems.

Driving simulators are attractive technical devices, but all possess severe limitations as valid measurement instruments. The most severe criticism has been the inability to create in the artificial atmosphere of the laboratory the real life stresses of on-the-road driving.

A multitude of procedures involving performance tests have been devised in attempts to measure and evaluate performance related to driving. Some have focused on measurements of decision-making ability, others have examined vigilance and attention, some involved psychomotor components and some were aimed directly on psychomotor skill measurements that require both physical and mental coordination.

The basic problem in the utilization of the tests, and the difficulties of interpretation of the results, relate to a lack of actual evidence that the tests themselves, and the results of the tests, are related to driver impairment, or to the causation of highway accidents.

Thus, although systems exists for the detection and measurement of effects of both drugs and alcohol, they are of doubtful validity in regard to driving behaviour. Indeed a clear definition of the driving task in clear empirical terms will greatly facilitate the development of valid testing systems.

VI.8 Epidemiological Research

In addition to the paucity of hard data concerning the actual effects of drugs and drugs-plus-alcohol and driving, the majority of reports are difficult to extrapolate to the driving population in general. Moreover, methods employed in several studies have raised questions about the overall validity of the data and therefore the conclusions that have been drawn from them.

While a great deal of emphasis has been placed on the value of data collected from road-side surveys, this information does not in fact provide a definitive assessment of the drinking-driving problem in a given community. For example, the knowledge that 5 percent of the driving population at any given time are legally impaired, is a measure of the effectiveness of a previous campaign. It does not provide any information as to which drinking-driver is most likely to be involved in a fatal or injury accident. For this assessment, information on the BAC distribution of fatally injured and other accident involved drivers is required, as well as a BAC distribution of whatever fraction of the driving population is impaired. Analysis of this type of data provides a method for calculation of impairment risk factors related to the dependent variable (BAC) and age-related factors for assessment of total impairment risk factors.

A new goal of epidemiological research in the area of impaired driving is to define the role that drugs play in traffic accident causation. While some studies have dealt with this by selecting a sample of drivers from the crash population, and from the general driving population, and objectively determining drug presence, the number of studies in this category is extremely limited. More commonly, researchers have attempted to obtain data on drug use by indirect means such as questionnaires, or by retrospective studies using driving records with other drivers. Lack of rigorous control over the methodology of the collection of data has resulted in a number of both false positives and false negatives, both of which reduce validity.

In the area of drug detection, the very complexity of the apparatus which is available makes it virtually impossible to test for all potential drugs. Thus studies invariably limit their analytical testing to a selected number. This means that negative results, or reports that drugs are not present, are valid only for that limited number of drugs. Other drugs, not tested for, may or may not be present in this sample population. This is especially important for many psychoactive drugs where a metabolite may be more active than the parent compound. Many studies that have been reported have made no provision for testing for metabolites. Thus negative findings cannot be presumed to be conclusive in any sense. Conversely, some drugs remain in the body for inordinate periods of time and may be picked up in trace amounts many days after ingestion when all psychoactive effects have completely disappeared.

The analysis of data, their interpretation, and the conclusions drawn not infrequently leave much to be desired in view of many kinds of bias which may be ignored in the ultimate presentation of results. Problems always arise when inappropriate statistical procedures are utilised to examine data.

A number of specific conclusions have been reached with regard to methodologies of detection of driving impairment, and epidemiological studies:

1. As epidemiological research methodologies are now well established, surveys of the effect of alcohol and drugs and driving behaviour cannot be undertaken with hope of success unless there have been rigorous examination of design, appropriate controls, and agreement on the methodology of analysis of data.

2. Research is necessary in the area of definition of the components of the actual driving task in conjunction with development of a battery of behavioural tests for alcohol and drug induced driving impairments.

3. Legislation should be secured to permit research under controlled and safe conditions on the effects of alcohol and drugs on driving performance (in real car driving situations in a test circuit or in real traffic).

4. As a number of therapeutic agents unrelated to psychoactive drugs influence the metabolic processes in the liver which deal with alcohol, the effect of all drugs that can modify alcohol metabolism should be studied in both men and women.

5. Road-side breath testing is the substantive method of estimating blood alcohol content as this relates to driving behaviour.

6. Because drinking patterns (type of beverage, speed of ingestion, relationship to food, etc.) influence BAC and therefore driving behaviour, the effects of varying types of drinking behaviour within a national culture could be monitored with a view toward correlating this information with accident rates after drinking.

7. Considerable biomedical and behavioural research should be encouraged in order to further the basic knowledge regarding physiological and behavioural tolerance to alcohol at low and high concentrations, at various time periods between absorption and late post-toxic periods, all effects being measured with regard to concomitant factors such as monotony and driver fatigue.

8. In view of the facts that driving to work early in the morning after considerable ingestion of alcohol is not infrequent, and traffic conditions are often at their worst during early morning rush hours, the effects of a hangover on driving behaviour should be examined.

9. In order to estimate the extent of drug use in the driving population, it will
   be necessary to consider the advisability of limited, well-controlled road-side
   surveys of individuals by collection of information from body fluids.

10. Specific methodology using blood tissue and urine samples will have to be developed
    to establish the presence and concentration of all pharmacologically active forms
    of psychoactive drugs suspected or known to impair driving abilities.

11. As illness, especially if accompanied by discomfort, may in itself have a rela-
    tionship to driving behaviour, the additional effect of medication to relieve
    discomfort should be studied to establish the interelationships between illnesses,
    drugs and driving behaviour.

VI.9 Legislative Countermeasures

Legal restrictions which make it an offence for a driver to operate a vehicle while
impaired constitute the most common countermeasure in use. The form and method of implementation of the legal restrictions varies from country to country. Several types of
legislation can be identified based on various definitions of alcohol impairment.

In some countries impairment is assessed by means of observation or clinical examination; chemical tests are not required and consequently no reference is made to BAC
levels. In other countries impairment is determined by chemical tests but without specific
BAC levels. A third type of assessment is used by countries in which the law simply
states that it is an offence to drive when BAC is above a specified level. The legal
limit varies from 50 mg% to 150 mg% and in some countries several standards are employed
as a method of weighting the seriousness of the offence. In the absence of comparable
data it is difficult to establish which type of law is most effective in influencing
drinking driving behaviour.

Provisions for enforcing the BAC restrictions also vary from country to country.
For example in some there is no penalty for refusing to submit to a chemical test for
alcohol while in others a refusal carries the same penalty as a conviction for being
impaired. In addition, some laws allow road-side screening tests to assist police who must
otherwise make a decision to apprehend or not on the basis of observation alone. The use
of routine road-side breath testing by police to increase detection rates of legal impairment is a very recent innovation.

When evaluating the effectiveness of legislation, the following must be considered:
the types of penalties imposed, whether the penalty is effective as a general deterrence
in restricting the driving of vehicles after alcohol has been consumed, and whether the
penalty acts as a special deterrence in changing the behaviour of a convicted offender.
In evaluating the effectiveness of penalties imposed as general deterrence, it is difficult
to distinguish between the effectiveness of enforcement and of legislation _per se_. In
addition new legislation is usually accompanied by public education programmes which may
increase the understanding of drivers to the dangers associated with alcohol impairment.

Most research in this area has been designed to evaluate the effectiveness of new
and usually increasingly severe legislation. The following critical observations have
been made:

   (i)   new legislation affects the moderate drinker more than the heavy drinker;
   (ii) changes that do occur in drinking driving behaviour are of short term duration;
   (iii) the special deterrent effects of penalties do not reduce the seriousness of the
         drinking driving problem relative to the convicted offender.

A critical factor may be that the new legislation is sometimes not in accordance with the public's own notion of justice. The public may not accept laws stipulating strong penalties for behaviour which is common, and which therefore is not sufficiently deviant to be considered immoral.

The third observation above casts doubt on the effectiveness of penalties as a special deterrence in reducing the drinking-driving problem. This may be due to the fact that more severe penalties are usually reserved for the problem drinker, for whom the penalty is basically ineffective in resolving his drinking problem. The failure may also be attributed to the fact that, because offenders are often convicted months after the offence, the perception of the seriousness of the offence often diminishes.

In the realisation that only a small percentage of the driving population is convicted of drinking driving offences, it seems unlikely that the penalizing of offenders in it-self will greatly reduce the magnitude of the overall drinking-driving problem, unless the detection rates are greatly improved.

It is possible that the deterrent effect of legislation may lie only in the driver's subjective evaluation of his chances of being detected, charged and convicted. There is, however, little information to suggest how apprehension might be increased or for that matter maintained at that level usually experienced at the introduction of new legislation.

To improve the process of policy making in this regard, the following factors are suggested as worthy of consideration.

(i)   the effect that increases or decreases in the legal BAC level have on drinking-driving behaviour;

(ii) the effect that increased enforcement has on drinking-driving behaviour;

(iii) the effects of observational versus chemical tests upon the subjective evalua-tion of risk;

(iv) possibilities for improving detection methodology.

In evaluating these areas, consideration should be given to the social milieu within which the laws must be applied and hence to the ways in which legislative countermeasures are related to the individual social and legal norms of each country. Consequently, the question arises as to whether laws effective in one country can be applied to other coun-tries with the same hope of success.

A considerable number of legislative and non-legislative responses to the impaired driver problem could be quoted. The following represents a sampling of opinion, consider-ations, options, and alternatives from multi-national sampling.

- In the belief that general deterrence can be an effective countermeasure, it will be necessary to ensure adequate funding and training of law enforcement personnel to permit high rates of apprehension of impaired drivers.

- The results of scientific research clearly demonstrate impairment with as low a BAC as 50 mg% with increasing degrees of impairment above this level; it is clearly inconsistent with road safety objectives to accept legal levels above 80 mg%.

- In view of the fact that impairment may not be due solely to alcohol but rather be the result of drugs (alone) or drugs and alcohol combined, it is logical that drivers who are impaired but whose BAC is below the legal level for alcohol impairment should be required to submit to blood or urine analysis for drugs.

- For convicted impaired drivers whose problem is basically alcohol or drug <u>dependence</u>, mandatory submission to an appropriate treatment programme needs to be effected without delay: the licence to drive needs to be revoked until this treatment is successfully completed.
- Countermeasures requiring identification of high-risk drivers should take into account that epidemiological evidence indicates that a combination of darkness, age, and alcohol are interactive in the cause of road accidents.
- It would appear desirable that the OECD countries work cooperatively to establish a programme in which a centralized well-equipped testing laboratory would gather data on a number of drugs which have been identified as those most likely to contribute to driving errors.
- For a variety of drugs which may impair driving ability, easily readable prescription package inserts could well bear a cautionary statement to the effect that "this drug may seriously impair fitness to drive a motor vehicle and may increase the effects of alcohol".
- Physicians, medical students, and pharmacists need to be better informed about the adverse effects of drugs and especially the adverse effects on driving behaviour. As some forms of advertising of alcoholic beverages are likely to continue in OECD countries, it is highly desirable that codes of advertising practice for beverage alcohol specifically proscribe messages or visual presentations that in any way combine alcohol consumption and driving.
- Consideration could well be given to the establishment of a lower legal blood alcohol concentration (BAC) for young and new drivers (for example 50 mg%) with graduation to the standard BAC after a probationary period of driving; the same strategy may well be appropriate to motorcyclists who are impaired at relatively low levels.
- Successful countermeasures in one country may not work well in another country. To attempt to explain the reasons that underly the lack of reproducibility of countermeasure success between countries, it will be necessary to take into consideration a number of national characteristics such as police self-perception with respect to the enforcement of drinking-driving regulations, public perception of the role of police in enforcing drinking-driving legislation, and the public's attitude to driving-while-impaired convictions.
- In order to identify target groups more precisely and to help define suitable countermeasures against the promotion of alcohol in society, it is judged appropriate that government agencies responsible for road safety interact directly with the beverage alcohol industries that are operative within national boundaries.
- In view of the fact that dark adaptation can be impaired by blood alcohol concentration of more than 80 mg%, it is highly desirable that public education programmes warn drivers who already have dark adaptation problems, that alcohol ingestion may greatly contribute to the risk of night-time accidents.
- It is necessary to develop ways of raising the level of awareness of the highly undesirable social consequences of being detected, charged, and convicted of impaired driving.
- As one means of diverting some cases of impaired driving from the courts, especially when the impairment is slight and no property, or personal injuries result, warning letters containing specific information about the violation, and specifying clearly all expectations for the future, are worth considering; the actual effects need to be critically analysed and evaluated.

- Because a high proportion of persons receiving prescribed psychoactive drugs are drivers, it seems advisable that prior to the marketing of a new drug, the effects of the proposed agent on driving skills be assessed by means of a well-conducted clinical trial.

- In view of the substantive improvements in breathalizer equipment during recent years, and the steadily increasing technical acceptability of the method by which breath analysis is extrapolated to a blood alcohol concentration (BAC), it is now clear that use of the breathalyzer, both of the type utilised at the roadside and the larger non-portable type used in police stations, ought to be recognised as the definitive and preferred method by which legal impairment by alcohol is assessed.

VI.10 Public, Formal Education and Rehabilitation Programmes

While it would appear logical to include in the curriculum of all driving schools a considerable amount of information concerning the effects of drugs and alcohol on driving behaviour and responses, it is only very recently that they have been introduced and integrated into driver education programmes; to date none has been evaluated.

In an attempt to re-educate previously convicted drinking drivers, a number of rehabilitative programmes have been initiated in a few countries. So far, these have been informational in content rather than educational. They have stressed the physiological effects of alcohol, the psychological effects of excessive alcohol use, and the legal consequences of drinking and driving.

The fact that very few programmes have been assessed and evaluated suggests that the programmes are activity-oriented rather than result-oriented. Evaluative studies which have been attempted have often been equivocal in design. The criteria that have been employed so far in the evaluation of the effectiveness of alcohol re-education programmes for convicted drivers have been increased knowledge levels, improved attitudes towards drinking and driving, reduction in alcohol-related violation rates and, much less frequently, subsequent incidence of crash involvement among persons exposed to rehabilitative programmes.

Studies which have attempted to assess the effectiveness of driving schools in reducing the incidence and prevalence of crashes have suffered from considerable bias. About one fourth of the studies are perhaps acceptable in terms of suitable controls. One of the well-controlled studies of the effects of driver re-education programmes has reported no statistically significant reduction in subsequent crashes.

A variety of other rehabilitative programmes has been employed in a number of countries. These have included group therapy, individual psychotherapy, and, for chronic alcohol problems, the use of the drug disulfiram. In some instances in-patient programmes are mandatory prior to long-term out-patient follow-up. Of the relatively small number of studies that can be evaluated, only about 30 percent are considered to have been methodologically sound. About 40 percent of these relatively sound studies have suggested that the social and legal decision to send a person to mandatory rehabilitation is appropriate. Specifically, the use of disulfiram chemotherapy as a treatment component for chronic alcohol problems has resulted in significantly fewer re-arrests over a six month period as compared to no rehabilitation at all. It is entirely possible that effective non-drug rehabilitative programmes could accomplish the same end point; this, however, has still to be demonstrated.

Because there is little evidence that rehabilitative programmes are having a measurable impact on subsequent crash incidence, studies are required to determine what programme characteristics are most appropriate for specific clients. For example, social drinkers who are much more responsive to treatment require very little in the way of "rehabilitation" other than a few lectures and possibly some group interaction.

On the other hand, for problem drinkers, there is little evidence that present pro-grammes have any long-lasting effect. For some of these people, a period of separation from their usual milieu, followed by relatively long out-patient therapy, are important components of true rehabilitation. Use of the drug disulfiram may well be the indicated form of therapy to improve the results of rehabilitation for this group of convicted drivers.

A number of countries have introduced lower insurance premiums for abstainer drivers. These include Denmark, the Netherlands, Norway, Sweden, Switzerland, and both the United States and Canada. The reductions, however, are small except in the Netherlands and Sweden, where a 10 percent reduction is available to those who can, in some way, demonstrate that they do not use alcohol, and presumably also abstain from other mood-altering drugs. It is doubtful whether or not this amount of reduced premium will have any effect on the actual incidence of impaired driving.

A few conclusions may be drawn at this time. The fact that there are not more only indicates the paucity of critical evaluative research and therefore valid data.

- Because lessons learned in youth are often those retained longest in life, and in turn, are those which mould general behaviour and attitudes, it is obviously desirable that unbiased and objective information concerning the hazards of alcohol and drugs with relationship to driving be imparted to young people within the national education system.
- Public education which is aimed at both young people and adults must raise the level of understanding of the impairment occasioned by both alcohol and drugs, and define clearly the meaning of degrees of impairment with regard to road safety and accident risk in a manner which is relevant to each individual.
- In addition to punitive measures, such as fines and removal of driver licences for given periods of time, an appropriate re-education course should be required for all persons whose problem is deemed to be excessive alcohol intake, whether or not there is a factor of dependence.
- Rehabilitative programmes have to be designed to meet the varying needs of the different kinds of persons who are convicted of impaired driving. Special emphasis must be given to problem drinkers and drug addicts of any kind.

VI.11 Recommendations

1. Based on the fact that existing evidence indicates that alcohol is a major contributor to the cause of traffic accidents, whereas such evidence is not yet available for drugs, and based on the fact that countries are progressively developing more effective drinking-driving countermeasure programmes,
   - it is recommended that the major countermeasure activities continue to be focused on efforts to resolve the alcohol problem in traffic safety.

2. To this end,
   - it is recommended that all nations should adopt a scientific epidemiological research programme to assess and monitor the drinking-driving problem which includes:
     - (i) conducting roadside voluntary breath test surveys of a random sample of drivers in accordance with the established OECD specifications;

(ii)   chemically testing for the presence of alcohol in all vehicle occupants
        and adult pedestrians killed in crashes, and

(iii) chemically testing for the presence of alcohol in all accident victims
        admitted to a sample of hospital emergency wards.

3.   In order to identify countermeasure programmes which are most effective in resolving
     the drinking-driving problem,

- it is strongly recommended that all countermeasure efforts should be subjected to rigorous evaluation procedures whereby no such programme would
  be implemented without acceptable evaluation planning and whereby the programmes would continue only if they are found to produce positive results
  or if such programmes are significantly changed following a finding of
  negative results. Such a procedure would provide for cumulative positive
  effects to be documented over a period of time.

4.   Based on research findings which indicate that alcohol impairment can occur at
     levels at least as low as 50 mg%, that between 50 and 80 mg% the accident risk begins
     to rise, that above 80 mg% the risk of accident involvement increases appreciably
     and that beyond 100 mg% all drinking drivers are impaired with a definitely increased
     accident risk,

- it is recommended that road safety legislation in OECD Member countries be
  adapted in conformity with these findings. In fixing however, the maximum
  permissible BAC level in each country, both social and scientific factors
  must be considered.

5.   In order to effectively utilise legislative measures to reduce the drinking-driving
     problem,

- it is recommended that efforts be taken to create a deterrence by increasing
  the driver's perception of the risks of being apprehended. To achieve this,
  consideration should be given to the adoption of an enforcement programme
  that includes the following components:

    I.   A provision permitting the use of a chemical (breath) test to determine
         driver BAC.

    II. A provision making it lawful for police officer to demand a breath
         test at the roadside of any driver suspected of drinking or any driver
         involved in a crash or moving violation.

6.   In order to increase motivation and introduce a positive therapeutic atmosphere for
     problem drinkers convicted for impaired driving,

- it is recommended that legislation be secured to permit the courts to
  utilise the option of referring offenders to multi-modality treatment
  programmes within which the effectiveness of varying rehabilitation and
  punitive alternatives can be evaluated.

7.   Since the involvement of drugs in traffic accidents has not been adequately resear-
     ched or documented in any country,
              - it is recommended that valid research studies be designed to investigate
                the extent and nature of drug use among drivers and pedestrians involved
                in fatal and non-fatal traffic accidents with the appropriate control groups
                selected from the general driving population. THE MOST URGENT NEED IN THIS
                AREA IS THE DEVELOPMENT OF MORE SENSITIVE AND PRACTICAL ASSAY TECHNIQUES.

8.   Given the large number of psychoactive drugs which are known to interact deleter-
     iously with alcohol relative to driving-related behaviours,
              - it is recommended that efforts be made to increase the level of public aware-
                ness of the dangers by:

              I.   Providing relevant and adequate information within prescription package
                    inserts,

              II.   Encouraging doctors and pharmacists to advise and caution clients of
                    the dangers to driving posed when psychoactive drugs are ingested with
                    alcohol.

9.   The issues related to alcohol, drugs and traffic safety are so important and the
     technology of the field is changing so rapidly that there is a need for a continuous
     exchange of information, and whereas existing programmes are not coordinated inter-
     nationally,
              - it is recommended to coordinate and ensure implementation of the conclusions
                and recommendations put forward.

ANNEX A

RECOMMENDATION ON ROADSIDE SURVEYS

The following is an amended version of the research methodology included in the 1972 report by the OECD initiated group of experts entitled "Roadside Surveys of Drinking-Driving Behaviour: A Review of the Literature and a Recommended Methodology". This report has appeared in several publications, for instance "Alcohol and Highway Safety: A Review of the Literature and a Recommended Methodology. CTS-16-74. Road Safety Transport Canada. Ottawa, Ontario. In addition, the reader is advised to consult a paper by Arthur C. Wolfe, Senior Research Associate, Highway Safety Research Institute, University of Michigan, Ann Arbor, Michigan, "Sampling and Nonresponse Weights in a Roadside Survey" which is a useful document to achieve uniformity in the procedures employed in sampling drivers. This document can be obtained free of charge by writing to the OECD Road Research Secretariat.

RESEARCH METHODOLOGY

Biological Specimen

The biological specimen of choice for the determination of alcohol concentration is breath. Blood, tissue, or urine samples may be gathered in addition, but are not acceptable as substitutes for breath samples.

Results of breath alcohol analysis shall be reported in terms of BAC, based on milligrams of alcohol per 210 litres of deep-lung air. The standard unit of reporting will be milligram percent (mg%). Using this system 0.10% BAC w/v or $1,00^0/00/w/v$ shall be reported as 100 mg%.

Breath Testing Device

The breath specimen analyzed shall be expired deep-lung air. This is any phase of the breath that follows the first .5 litre of an exhalation. Determination of the BAC shall be based on the ratio between alcohol present in the blood and whole deep-lung air, using either a known volume or a continuous flow system. Indirect determination of the BAC by quantitative breath alcohol analysis shall be based upon the following ratio: 2.1 litres of expired deep-lung air contain the same quantity of alcohol as one millilitre of blood.

Loss of alcohol (from the breath specimen) through condensation shall be prevented by maintaining the breath specimen at a temperature sufficiently above body temperature, or by other satisfactory means.

In the analysis of vapours of known alcohol concentration over the range corresponding to BACs of 50 to 300, the instrument must be capable under field conditions of determining the BAC equivalent of the true value to within $\pm$ 10% of the true value.

When vapours of known alcohol concentration over the range corresponding to BACs of

50 to 150 are analysed under laboratory conditions, the results of a minimum of 50 consecutive determinations at any one concentration must have a standard deviation (sigma) not greater than 3. When vapours of known alcohol concentrations over the range corresponding to BACs of 150 to 300 are analysed under laboratory conditions, the standard deviation (sigma) of a minimum of 50 consecutive determinations at any one concentration must not exceed 2% of the expected value.

The instrument must be capable of performing a blank analysis on ambient air, free of alcohol, that yields an apparent BAC of no more than 10.

Instruments which singly or in combination collect a deep-lung air sample and temporarily store the specimen or its contained alcohol for subsequent analysis (remote sampling devices), shall meet all stated performance requirements. Such instruments shall be designed so that the result obtained is independent of barometric pressure or designed so that the result obtained is correctable for barometric pressure change if such correction is necessary.

A means must be employed to ensure that the subject has not ingested alcohol for at least ten minutes prior to collection of the breath specimen. The following alternatives are suggested:

(a) Collect the specimen at the end of the interviews. This will allow about five minutes of continuous observation during which the subject must not drink either an alcoholic or non-alcoholic beverage, or eat food. He should not smoke for at least one minute before the sample is collected.

(b) If the result is positive and the subject assures that he has had no alcoholic beverage for at least twenty minutes, the answer can be accepted.

(c) If the subject affirms that he has consumed an alcoholic beverage within the last twenty minutes, a second test should be administered after allowing an additional five minutes. The second test should be recorded. This step should rarely be necessary.

(d) If the answer is negative, the result can be accepted without question.

The testing procedure will include the analysis of a suitable reference or control sample such as air equilibrated with a reference solution of known alcohol content at a known temperature, the result of which must agree with a 100 BAC reference sample within the limits of $\pm$ BAC. Frequency of such monitoring of accuracy shall be dependent on the stability of the method employed.

Time

Samples must be gathered during the time period extending from 2200 to 0300 hrs.

Day

For the purpose of international comparison, samples must be gathered on Friday and Saturday nights.

Month

As to the time of year, it was decided to merely require sampling to be done either during the spring, the autumn, or both. Winter and summer were eliminated because of a desire to reduce variation due to tourists and to climatic extremes. To all intents and purposes, by "spring" is meant March, April, May and by "fall" is meant September, October, November.

Year

Sampling will be done on a yearly basis whenever possible.

Vehicles

It was agreed to sample all motorised vehicles (cars, trucks, motorcycles, mopeds, etc.) except:

commercial vehicles - trucks with three or more axles and taxis. (Note - most small trucks are used as passenger vehicles at night.)

All passenger vehicles should be sampled, regardless of nationality of the registration.

It was further decided that the vehicle type should be recorded for each sample. In this way, it will be possible to select a sub-group such as automobiles for further consideration at some future date.

Sample Selection

It was agreed that, in order to be able to properly evaluate a shift at the upper end of the BAC distribution, it is necessary to see what is happening to the rest of the distribution as well. It was deemed essential to gather complete information on both the drinking driver and the non-drinking driver who are selected for the survey.

Samples will be selected on a time-interval basis. The length of this interval will be equal to the total processing time for each subject (i.e., if the interview team can handle one person every five minutes, then a driver will be selected from the traffic stream every five minutes).

Vehicle Flow

It was felt that some measure of vehicle flow past each survey site would be necessary. The delegates decided that a simple measure of total traffic flow (only counting those vehicles which are travelling in the same direction as those vehicles which are selected for the survey) would be sufficient, and that a breakdown by vehicle type would not be required.

Time Limit

It was agreed that, if possible, a maximum time of two hours should be spent at any one site. If a longer period of time is necessary for practical reasons in some countries, then only the data from the first two hours should be considered as part of the data for the international study. If this is the case, it should be ensured that the first two hours of testing fall within the 2200 to 0300 hrs, core segment.

Site Location

It was agreed, after much discussion, that site locations would be chosen on a random basis rather than on a biased basis (i.e. selecting only prior crash locations). This means that the sites for the roadside survey must not be chosen because of their nearness to drinking locations, poor accident history, etc.

Sample Size

The number of drivers tested must be large enough to ensure that a sample of at least 100 drinking drivers is obtained. If there is any doubt as to how many drivers need to be tested in order to obtain this number of drinking drivers, 2,000 drivers should be tested.

Number of Sites

Samples should be obtained from as many sites as possible, and no site should be visited more than one time. Since crews will spend a maximum of two hours at each site, the number of sites required is determined primarily by the total required sample size, and the number of survey personnel present at each site.

Survey Area

For the purpose of the international study of drinking-driving behaviour, only studies of entire countries will be allowed. This does not preclude the sampling of regions to be evaluated, but does prevent the submission of a multitude of minor studies of small and perhaps atypical areas of a country.

Subjects

As much of the data from as possible should be completed for: (1) Those drivers who participate in the survey; (2) Those drivers who refuse to participate in the survey; and (3) Those drivers who would have been selected to participate in the survey, but who were arrested by the police.

Survey Questionnaire

The following information should be obtained for each subject. All data which is to be used in the international study must be presented in this format.

Questionnaire

Note: All spaces must contain a number. Where appropriate, place "0" in blank space.

1. Country (each country will be given a number)

2. Site number

3. Subject number (start with "1" at each site)

4. Location (1 = City; 2 = Country)

5. Day of month

6. Month

7. Year (73, 74, etc.)

8. Day of week (1 = Sun; 2 = Mon; 3 = Tues; 4 = Wed; 5 = Thurs; 6 = Fri; 7 = Sat.)

□ □ 9. Hour of day (24-hour clock)

□ □ 10. Minute of hour

□ 11. Vehicle type (1 - Car; 2 = Truck; 3 = Motorcycle;
4 = Other)

□ 12. Sex of driver (1 = Male; 2 = Female; 3 = Undetermined)

□ 13. Number of passengers (9 = 9 or more)

□ 14. Will you use miles, or kilometres in this form?
(0 = miles; 1 = kilometres)

□ 15. 0 = Subject agrees to participate; 1 = Subject refuses to
participate; 2 = Subject removed from sample by polyce

□ 16. Where were you when you last entered your vehicle?
(0 = refusal; 1 = home; 2 = friend's house; 3 = work;
4 = restaurants; 5 = pub or bar; 6 = other)

□ 17. Where will you be when you next leave your vehicle?
(0 = refusal; 1 = home; 2 = friend's house; 3 = work;
4 = restaurant; 5 = pub or bar; 6 = other)

□ □ □ 18. How many miles (kilometres) do you estimate that you will have
driven from the time you last entered your vehicle until you
next leave your vehicle? (000 = refusal; 001 = 1 mile or less;
999 = 1,000 miles or more)

□ □ 19. How many hours of driving will this involve?

□ □ 20. Minutes involved? (00 = refusal)

□ 21 What is the purpose of this trip? (0 = refusal; 1 = local
recreation; 2 = long trip (touring); 3 = commercial;
4 = to an from work; 5 = other)

□ □ □ 22. How many thousand miles (kilometres) would you estimate that
you drive in an average year? (000 = refusal; 001 = 1,000
miles or less)

☐ 23. Do you have an amateur or a professional driving licence?
(0 = refusal; 1 = amateur; 2 = professional; 3 = none; 4 = other)

☐ ☐ 24. How old were you on your last birthday? (00 = refusal)

☐ 25. What is your occupation?

1 = Business	5 = Office	9 = Other
2 = Professional	6 = Farmer	0 = Refusal
3 = Student	7 = Labourer	
4 = Sales	8 = Tradesman	

☐ ☐ ☐ 26. Blood Alcohol Concentration (999 = refusal)

In addition to the preceding information, which must be provided for each subject, the following information is required for each site, and must be submitted in the format shown.

Site Data Card

Note: All spaces must contain a number. One card must be completed for each site.

☐ ☐ 1. Country

☐ ☐ ☐ 2. Site number

☐ ☐ 3. Temperature (°C) (0 = temperature above 0;
1 = temperature below 0)

☐ ☐ ☐ ☐ 4. Altitude (feet or metres)

☐ 5. Precipitation (0 = none; 1 = rain; 2 = snow; 3 = other)

☐ ☐ ☐ 6. Vehicle count (in direction sampled)

☐ 7 Have you used feet or metres to measure altitude?
(0 = feet; 1 = metres)

Survey Methodology

A report outlining the methodology employed should be submitted with the results. This report should outline how the survey was conducted, with particular attention given to any unusual experiences or procedures which resulted in deviation from the recommended methodology. The following specific points should be reported.

(1) Type of blood analyser employed.
(2) Time of survey: year, month, day of week, time of day.
(3) Time spent at each site.
(4) Number of urban and rural sites.
(5) Method of selecting sites.
(6) Type of information collected from drivers; and
(7) Weighting procedure.

Survey Results

The following information should be reported:

(1) Number of drivers stopped.
(2) Number of drivers refusing to provide samples.
(3) BAC results for total sample*; and
(4) BAC results for the following single variables:
- day of week
- time of day*
- vehicle type
- sex of driver
- number of passengers*
- point of entering vehicle
- point of leaving vehicle
- distance between point of entry and point of exit*
- time taken to drive between the entry and exit points*
- purpose of trip
- amount of annual driving*
- type of drivers licence
- age*
- occupation
- urban/rural

---

* Categories are presented hereunder.

Countries are encouraged to submit the BAC results for any additional information that may have been collected.

When reporting in tabular form, footnotes should be used to explain any observations that were knowingly biased or confounded by uncontrolled circumstances. For example, an observation may have been biased because inclement weather caused the cancellation of a number of sites sampled during a particular time period, or because only a few subjects were tested at a particular site. Attention should be drawn to these unusual situations.

Data Categorisation for Non-Discreet Variables

(1) BAC

The BAC results (mg%) shall be reported for the following categories:

(mg%)	(mg%)
0-19	100-119
20-49	120-149
50-79	150-249
80-99	250 +

Those drivers falling within the 0-19 mg% category will be defined as non-drinking drivers. A drinking driver is, therefore, anyone with a BAC of 20 mg% or greater.

(2) Time of day

BAC results for time of day in which drivers were sampled should be presented in one hour increments. Thus, for the survey period 2200 to 0300, the BAC results would be presented for:

2200-2300
2300-0000
0000-0100
0200-0300

(3) Number of passengers

0 - no passengers
1 - one passenger
2 + - two or more passengers

(4) Distance between point of entry and point of exit

Kilometres

0 - 4	31 - 80
5 - 8	81 - 160
9 - 15	161 +
16- 30	

(5) Trip duration

Minutes

0 - 5	46 - 60
6 - 15	61 - 90
16 - 30	91 - 120
31 - 45	121 +

(6) Amount of annual driving

Kilometres

Less than 1,000	16,000 - 31,000
1,000 - 5,000	32,000 - 47,000
6,000 - 10,000	48,000 and more
11,000 - 15,000	

(7) Age of driver

Provide results for each year of age from 16 to 21. Thereafter, utilize the following age categories.

25 - 29	50 - 59
30 - 34	60 - 69
35 - 39	70 +
40 - 49	

RECOMMENDATIONS FOR CONDUCTING ROADSIDE SURVEYS

Pilot Projects

Those countries which are intending to participate in the international study, and which have not yet conducted roadside surveys, should undertake small scale pilot projects first, in order to gain first-hand experience with roadside survey techniques. The experience of those countries which have conducted roadside surveys demonstrates the value of such pilot studies.

Publicity

It is highly advisable to have some sort of press release prior to conducting a roadside survey. The main purpose of this release will be to give the press an accurate picture of what is transpiring, and thus prevent distortion and possible public reaction which might develop in the absence of accurate information. The press release must not contain any information as to the time or the location of future roadside survey sites.

Police Involvement

In the case of voluntary surveys (as will be conducted by most countries) the police contact with the driver should be minimal. The survey should be introduced and explained to the driver by the trained survey personnel, and not by the police officers.

Additional Data

It is suggested that roadside surveys of drinking-driving behaviour will afford the opportunity of gathering other information on the driving population. Seat belt usage, for example, is one piece of interesting information which can also be gathered for virtually no extra cost. The gathering of any additional information must not interfere with the primary purpose of the survey.

Lighting

The survey site, and in particular the area around the person responsible for stopping and directing traffic, must be well illuminated. It is suggested that a minimum of two 1.5 kw quartz-iodine spotlights be employed. Flashing red lights of a type employed by the police have been found to be most helpful in alerting drivers and reducing the speed of approaching vehicles.

Signing

Motorists should be given adequate warning that there is a survey in progress, and that they may be required to stop. Speed in the immediate survey area should be controlled and reduced to a safe level.

Site Location

The survey site should be located so as to provide adequate site distance from both directions. Every effort should be made to ensure that adequate space is available for the survey vehicles as well as a number of subject vehicles. Whenever possible, site locations should be chosen which do not provide the motorists with an apportunity to turn off the road when they realize that a survey is ahead.

Maintenance

Consideration should be given to hiring a general-purpose repairman as part of the back-up crew. The usually tight scheduling of roadside surveys demands that equipment failures be dealt with almost immediately if a large number of subjects are not going to be missed.

Hospitality Items

The provision of hospitality items such as coffee, cookies, etc., is not recommended. Although these things do create an informal atmosphere, and help the subjects to relax, they also contribute to congestion in the interview area and greatly reduce crew efficiency. It might be worthwhile to have an extra thermos of coffee available for unusual situations (such as an impaired driver having to wait for alternate transportation to be arranged). Opinion is not unanimous on this point as some researchers feel that hospitality items can be of considerable assistance in obtaining driver co-operation.

Interviewers

Interviewers should wear some sort of clothing or device that identifies them as members of a research team (e.g. armband, or white lab coat). It has been found in some studies that female interviewers had less difficulty than male interviewers in obtaining subject participation.

Smoking

Smoking by the subjects must not be allowed in the period preceeding the taking of a breath sample. To this end "No Smoking" signs in the testing area would be most appropriate. Furthermore, interview and testing staff should not smoke while in the test area or while interviewing subjects. The purpose of this is to discourage smoking by subjects.

Rest Days

In any survey of longer than seven days duration, two days of rest must be afforded each of the survey personnel. This was found to be necessary not only because of the physical demands of the job (irregular hours, a lot of travel, etc.), but also because of the psychological stress of a situation that involves confrontation with the public under unusual circumstances.

It should also be mentioned that these rest days can also be utilized most efficiently for repairing equipment, obtaining needed supplies and parts, etc.

Preliminary Planning

Perhaps the most vulnerable part of this sort of survey is in the area of planning and negotiations. Sufficient time must be set aside to ensure that the support of all relevant agencies is fully obtained before the initiation of the survey. It is also suggested that a clear statement of the survey operation and methodology be prepared and circulated to all key people.

First-Aid

Because the survey crews will be out on the roads, often in rather remote areas, they should each be provided with a First-Aid kit. At least one crew member should be able to perform elementary first-aid. The purpose of the first-aid precaution is to provide emergency aid not only to crew members, but also to members of the driving population who may become involved in accidents at or near the survey site.

Training

The need for and importance of adequate staff training cannot be overemphasized. Interview staff must have prior experience not only in presenting the project to the public and encouraging participation, but also in completing the interview forms. Breath-testing staff must be thoroughly familiar with their equipment and should be able to undertake emergency repairs on the breath-testing devices.

Interviewer Observation

Several researchers feel that it is very worthwhile to have the interviewers make an initial estimate of whether or not the driver has been drinking. In the event that there is a large number of refusals, this procedure would perhaps provide valuable information as to the type of person who refuses to take part.

ANNEX B

ALCOHOL LEVEL MEASURING EQUIPMENT

<u>BREATH TESTING</u>

1. Introduction

For research purposes the blood alcohol content (BAC) as a measure of alcohol use has physiological as well as methodological and other practical advantages.

Laboratory and field studies have shown a relation between BAC and performance or accident risk. These findings justify in turn the use of BAC as an element in traffic safety countermeasures.

Compared to blood analysis there are practical advantages in breath testing. There are even some physiological considerations in favour of breath testing. On the other hand, all kinds of reasons are conceivable, leading to inaccurate results when breath testing is routinely used. Repeatedly, it has been shown that the correspondence between BAC from breath as against blood testing left much to be desired. Blood analysis, however, has been accepted for a long time.

A historical review and a description of the present state-of-the art is given by Dubowski (1975). Harger (1974) discusses in detail the blood breath comparison studies. Both articles show that further improvements are possible and to be expected in the future. The application of breath analysis is governed by requirements to be met by a measuring instrument in a certain situation, on the one hand, and the capabilities and limitations of existing apparatus, on the other hand. With the present technological state of affairs and experiences in most situations, a compromise will have to be made between requirements and possibilities. In seemingly similar situations such a compromise may lead to different outcomes. In Europe, for instance, the interest in the use of breath testing for police purposes is mostly restricted to chemical test tubes, whereas in North America better screening instruments are required and at the same time evidential breath testers are in use.

The aim of this contribution is to review the available instruments together with a rough evaluation and to present some general background information.

2. General Description

The design of a breath testing instrument is to a certain extent influenced by the chosen principle of analysis. Mainly chemical analysis (wet or dry) was used. Today, the following principles are in use: gas chromatography, infrared absorption, fuel-cell, catalytic burning and semi-conducting. Each of these principles have their own specificity, sensitivity, stability, constructional details, operation and maintenance requirements, etc. The further design of an instrument refers to a.o. sampling arrangements, presentation of results, built-in checks and automated operation, power supply.

Remaining problems centre around sampling arrangements and the transformation of breath alcohol content to BAC. Both issues are closely related. Earlier, it was assumed that a few seconds of blowing or the discard of ca. 500 cc of breath was a sufficient condition for obtaining a breath sample with constant alcohol content. Several studies have shown larger discard volumes to give more accurate BAC determination. Recent investigations by Jones et al. (1975) and Flores (1975) indicate that, in order to obtain a constant breath alcohol content, a fixed volume of air has to be rebreathed several times, or the breath has to be kept for some time. Jones et al. (1975) assume that, only under such conditions, a complete equilibration of alcohol between breath and blood as well as between breath and the mucus of the upper respiratory track is obtained.

The presently available instruments have various arrangements to obtain a sample of deep lung breath after a single expiration:

- operator observation (possibly aided by visual or audible indication of blowing pressure or volume);
- analysis of a total volume of mixed tidal and deep lung air (e.g. 1 l.);
- automatic sampling after discard of a fixed volume (of say 500 cc or 2.);
- automatic sampling after a fixed timeperiod of blowing with a minimal blowing pressure (corresponding with a minimal discard volume of 500 cc or 1 l.);
- operator monitoring of the rate of change of the alcohol concentration during exhalation.

Attempts to correct the results on the basis of a measurement of CO_2 content have been abandoned. Dubowski (1975) concludes that, on the average, the discard volume should be more than 2.5 l. and further suggests simultaneous temperature measurement, a suggestion that has also been made by Wright (1975).

The ratio between alcohol content in breath and blood that is widely used for calculating a BAC from breath analysis is 1:2100. This is a theoretical value which, with present breath sampling arrangements, leads on the average to BAC values that are too low.

3. Research Activities

Research in the field of breath analysis may cover different areas such as technical development work, basic physiological research or evaluation of available instruments. The latter area is of particular interest to prospective users. This in fact relates to a series of research activities:

- general inspection of the instrument. Only simple measurements have to be obtained. Various aspects to be covered include: operation and maintenance instructions, sampling arrangement (volume, time, pressure, temperature), presentation of results, power supply, size, weight, costs, possible failures (as far as can be inferred from the construction);
- research into precision of measurement over a range of BAC values, stability of calibration, influence of factors such as temperature, humidity, vibration, instability of the power supply, air pressure, etc.;
- Laboratory comparison of blood and breath tests with special interest in the effect of e.g. characteristics of test persons, blowing techniques;
- field comparison of blood and breath tests.

The list of aspects to be inspected or tested may be adjusted to the particulars of the instrument and the field of application.

When comparing blood and breath tests, a number of things have to be observed. Shortly after alcohol consumption, differences may arise from mouth-alcohol, belching or incomplete equilibration of alcohol over body parts. The time between blood and breath sampling should be as short as possible. Errors or variation of results in blood analysis are not necessarily excluded. Rather than a comparison with blood tests, the breath tests may be compared to carefully determined alcohol content of rebreathed air. The range of BAC values included in the study may influence the outcome of statistical calculations, thus giving a wrong impression in case the BAC range in actual use is quite different.

Remarkable differences can be found among studies with regard to statistical processing, presentation and interpretation of results.

Laboratory tests may closely simulate the actual operational situation with regard to conditions, test subjects and operator characteristics. However, only a field test will enable a complete evaluation of an instrument because unexpected instrument failures, factors affecting the results or other problems may arise.

Field tests of instruments for police purposes present a methodological problem if information is restricted to subjects who are suspected of drunken driving. Persons with positive BAC who are not suspected (possibly on the basis of a screening breath test) are not included in such a study. Moreover, the results of blood testing may have been corrected before comparing them with the results of the breath test.

The main purpose of a field investigation is the comparison of blood and breath testing. Once the results have proved to be satisfactory, attention may focus on the effectiveness of (countermeasure) activities where breath testing is applied.

In the United States, stringent requirements are drawn up in order to make it possible to stimulate the development of more accurate breath testing instruments. The National Highway Traffic Safety Administration examines the testers on the basis of these requirements.

However, when the analysers meet all the performance requirements in the laboratory in practice, some problems may occur with accuracy and technical reliability.

4. <u>Fields of Application</u>

Breath analysis is mainly in use for police and research purposes. For police purposes it is customary to differentiate between portable screening or qualitative devices on the one hand and evidential or quantitative devices on the other hand.

A relatively new special type of screening test is the passive breath tester. Remote collection devices form a subclass of quantitative devices. For research purposes, the performance requirements are roughly similar to those for evidential devices. A recent application is the breath self tester. These analysers, which are usually coin-operated and accessible to the public, are developed for use in commercial drinking establishments, etc. This concept raises some fundamental questions about the desired accuracy, reliability of results and to what an extent such a device should be "fool-proof".

Some attempts have been made to develop starter interlock systems which, installed as a part of an automobile ignition system, preclude operation by the intoxicated driver.

Requirements for breath testers are largely dictated by operational conditions, characteristics of test subjects and the kind of decision to be taken on the basis of test results.

Broadly speaking, operational conditions include:

- location of testing and such closely related factors as: temperature, humidity,

lighting, power supply, transport;
- qualifications of operators;
- number of tests to be performed during a certain time period;
- acceptable time and effort per test;
- available funds.

Possibly relevant characteristics of test subjects are: range of BAC values, physical condition which to a certain extent is indicated by age and sex, illness, physical handicaps or injuries, willingness of the test subjects to co-operate.

The kinds of decision to be taken on the basis of the test results may vary between:

- BAC definitely above a certain level (excepting a number of cases that go unnoticed);
- BAC definitely below a certain level (idem);
- BAC most certainly within a certain BAC range;
- most accurate determination of BAC.

It has been noted before, in the introduction, that requirements may have to be weakened because of the technological state of affairs, especially in situations where the need for easy and quick determination of BAC (or quick sampling) is urgent.

References

Bubowski, K.M., Recent Developments in Breath-alcohol Analysis. In: Israelstam, S. & Lambert, S. (Eds.), 1975.

Flores, A.L., Rebreathed Air as a Reference for Breath-Alcohol Testers. Interim report DOT-TSC-NHTSA-74-4. U.S. Dept. of Transportation, Washington, D.C., 1975.

Harger, R.N., Recently Published Analytical Methods for Determining Alcohol in Body Materials — Alcohol Countermeasures Literature Review. Report DOT HS-801 242. U.S. Dept. of Transportation, Washington, D.C., 1974.

Israelstam, S. & Lambert, S. (Eds.), Alcohol, Drugs and Traffic Safety. Proceedings of the Sixth International Conference on Alcohol, Drugs and Traffic Safety, Toronto, September, 8-13, 1974. Addiction Research Foundation of Ontario, Toronto, 1975.

Jones, A.W. et al., A Historical and Experimental Study of the Breath/Blood-Alcohol Ratio. In: Israelstam, S. & Lambert, S. (Eds.), 1975.

Wright, B.M., Jones, T.P., Jones, A.W., Breath-Alcohol Analysis and the Blood/Breath-Ratio. Med. Sci. Law, Vol. 15, N° 3, pp 205-210, 1975.

REVIEW OF CURRENT BREATH ANALYSING EQUIPMENT

In the appendix, a list is given of current breath-testing devices together with the relevant literature. Some characteristics of and results with the more prominent instruments of the screening and evidential type are reviewed below.

1. Screening Breath Testers

In respect of the screening breath testers, nowadays two basic designs are available and in use: disposable chemical test tubes and re-usable electromechanical devices. In evaluating these instruments, there are two important types of error which may occur:

- the false positive reading: the subject is accused of possessing a higher BAC than his actual blood alcohol concentration; and
- the false negative result when the subject possesses a higher actual BAC than the result of the test showed it to be.

(a) Disposable screening devices

The disposable chemical reagent screening devices are all similar in design and operation. Each comprises a small glass tube containing an alcohol sensitive reagent and a breath volume measurement device (either a rubber balloon, plastic bag or air pump). Two important studies in which chemical test tubes were tested are those of Goldberg and Bonnichsen (1970) and Prouty and O'Neill (1971).

- Goldberg and Bonnichsen studied .5 and .8°/oo Alcotest tubes with regard to various factors such as rate of breath flow, volume variations and sensitivity to substances other than ethylalcohol. The Alcotest has been used for many years by the police in a number of European countries. In general, there is a weak relation between the length of the discoloration and the BAC (r = .70). The percentages of false positive and false negative results depend on the interpretation of the length of the discoloration and the distribution of the actual BAC. In this case, there are hardly any false positives against a considerable number of false negatives.

- Prouty and O'Neill conducted a study on several devices such as Alcolyser, Sober-Meter, Kitagawa Drunk-O-Tester and Becton-Dickinson devices. With the exception of the Becton-Dickinson devices which showed a narrow range in which erroneous results were obtained, and the Kitagawa Drunk-O-Tester which produced a great number of false negatives and only a small number of false positive results, all other devices produced erroneous results in practically all ranges of BAC which were tested.

It can be concluded that, in theory, the sensitivity of the chemical test tubes is sufficient for a screening test. Improvements in the design of the tubes and the sampling system are expected to give better results.

(b) Re-usable electromechanical devices

Since the American Department of Transportation, some years ago, took the decision not to approve tube-type screening tests, research was carried out to develop a more accurate instrument type test on the basis of several stringent requirements. This resulted in a limited number of instruments meeting the required criteria.

The recently developed portable self-containing instruments operate with various alcohol sensors such as fuel-cells, catalytic burners, and semi-conductors.

The chemo-electric fuel-cell generates a measurable electric current from the catalytic oxidation of alcohol in the breath, which is directly proportional to the amount of alcohol.

The catalytic burner "burns" alcohol at a small catalytically active element. A change in temperature from this burning induces a change in resistance, which is proportional to the amount of alcohol.

The solid-state semi-conductor measures alcohol through the change in surface resistivity with the absorption of alcohol on a transition metal oxide sensor.

The equivalent BAC can be displayed on those instruments either by meter, light or digital readouts.

Fuel-cell instruments require frequent calibration because of a certain instability of the sensor. Some fuel-cell devices are developed in two modes: one for screening purposes and another for the quantitative measurement of the BAC.

The catalytic burner and semi-conductor types are less specific for the determination of alcohol.

With intensive use, all these instruments require frequent recharging.

b.1 Alcolmeter

The instrument known as Alcometer or Alco-Sensor is probably one of the most advanced fuel-cell devices and was originally developed as a simple pocket analyser. Later, several versions of this instrument were developed incorporating an improved sampling system and a different presentation of the results; in the meantime, the sensor itself was improved, resulting in a greater stability.

Harger (1974) indicates some studies in which the Alco-Sensor was evaluated. Jacobs and Goodson (unpublished) found in the BAC range of 1.12 - 1.32°/oo with four instruments 18 percent of false negative readings with only one instrument giving no false readings.

Bailey (unpublished) observed no Alco-Sensor readings of above 1°/oo where the actual BAC was .8°/oo or below. With blood-breath pairs where the BAC was close to 1.2°/oo, 10 percent of the Alco-Sensor readings was below 1°/oo. Presumably, in both studies, the instruments were calibrated on 1.0°/oo.

An analogue type of the Alcolmeter pocket screen test was tested in the setting of a roadside survey reported by Noordzij (1975). The regression formula for predicting the BAC from the breath test result was found to be y = .97 x + .22 with a correlation coefficient of .905 and a standard error of estimate of .16°/oo on 33 observations. Two Alcometer evidential M2 instruments were tested under the same circumstances in 1975 (unpublished).

b.2 Alcohol Screening Device

This fuel-cell instrument was developed under contract for the U.S. Department of Transportation/National Highway Traffic Safety Administration.

Harger (1974) presents the results provided by Harriot (unpublished) with the ASD. The results were compared with breath tests using the Gas Chromatograph Intoximeter GCI. 474 observations were made; 5 percent false positives were found in the BAC range .9 - 1.0°/oo and 37 percent false negatives in the range 1.0 - 1.1°/oo, with unit calibrated on 1.0°/oo. The ASD with digital readout was tested by Alha et al. (1975) and Noordzij (1975).

Alha et al. made their observations in cases of suspected drunken driving and found good results in comparing of blood and breath samples if the BAC was below 1.5°/oo. At higher levels, however, the ASD showed too low results in most cases.

The results of the field study made by Noordzij indicated that the measured BAC by breath was substantially lower over the whole range of actual BACs.

Further field tests with the ASD are underway in several American states.

b.3 A.L.E.R.T.

The Alcohol Level Evaluation Road Tester (A.L.E.R.T.) is a semi-conductor device provided with light-readout, indicating the zones PASS, WARN and FAIL.

Dubowski (1973) studied the A.L.E.R.T. during the elimination phase of four subjects reaching peak values of 2°/oo.

Sixty-eight tests were performed. In 27 of them, the BAC was below 0.8°/oo with no A.L.E.R.T. test above 1.0°/oo (FAIL) which means no false positives. Five tests were in the BAC range of 0.8 to 1.1°/oo, two of the A.L.E.R.T. readings were FAIL and WARN for the other three. For the remaining 36 tests the BAC was above 1.1°/oo with all A.L.E.R.T. readings FAIL.

A field test programme was carried out in Hennepin County Minnesota (1974). The results of this study indicate that the tested models functioned accurately and dependably. The A.L.E.R.T. unit was employed in 898 cases of suspected drunken driving. (Rosen et al., 1974.) Forty-eight percent of the tests resulted in a FAIL (units calibrated on 1.1°/oo, 33 percent in a WARN and 19 percent in a PASS. Of the FAIL cases, 81 percent were charged with DWI. 298 FAIL cases were submitted to an evidentiary test which resulted in 37 false positives, i.e. failing the screening test but passing the evidential test with a BAC reading less than 1°/oo. In a limited study, Picton (1977) concluded to a higher percentage of 24 false positive readings. He states that screening device results cannot be expected to coïncide with subsequent evidential tests especially when the actual BAC is near the level at which the screening device is set. A means of reducing the number of false positive readings is to calibrate on a higher level than the legal limit, so increasing the number of WARN responses.

2. Evidential Breath Testers

The U.S. Department of Transportation has drawn up a standard for evidential breath testing equipment.

The basic techniques for alcohol detection and quantification used in evidential breath testers are photometric colorimetry, infrared absorption photometry and gas chromatography. Among the electromechanical screening testers there are some which can be used for the quantitative determination of alcohol. At the Seventh International Conference on Alcohol, Drugs and Traffic Safety, Jones et al. (1977) reported about a new Alcolmeter evidential instrument. An improved fuel-cell was used, resulting in greater stability. This instrument is particularly effective for analysing blood, urine and saliva.

At the same conference, Forrester (1977) reported the development of another version using the same cell. This instrument is equipped with a complete programme for calibration control, air blank and three breath tests, together with a volume control for the breath sample. The results are printed out. Most of the evidential instruments need external power supply, either 12 Volts DC or connection to the mains.

(a) Breathalyser

The first widely known breath analyser was the Breathalyser model 900, incorporating colorimetric determination of a discoloration caused by the oxidising of alcohol in liquid chemicals. Harger (1974) reports 15 studies on its accuracy. In most of them the result obtained with the Breathalyser was lower than the actual BAC by averages ranging from about 8 to 15 percent, while erroneously high results were almost never given. The instrument has no automatic sampling control and is, therefore, most useful with co-operative subjects.

A recent adaptation of this model is the Breathalyser model 1000, which is almost fully automatic. The actual analytical procedure is essentially the same as that of the model 900. A complete test-run takes several minutes. A disadvantage of this type of instrument is the handling of the ampoules with aggressive chemicals.

Although as yet no detailed studies on the performance of the model 1000 are known, one would expect that precision and accuracy of this model are about the same as that of the model 900. Dubowski (1975) presents a series of twenty blood-breath comparisons on ten subjects. No statistical analysis was performed and no conclusions were drawn.

(b) Intoxilyzer

The Intoxilyzer is a compact infrared spectrophotometer. Harte (1971) describes the construction and operation of the Intoxilyzer and gives three scatter diagrams which relate the breath test results with those from simultaneously obtained blood samples, for three subjects and twelve blood-breath pairs. Harger (1974) estimates from these diagrams that the deviation between Intoxilyzer and blood analysis results ranges from + 2 percent to - 11 percent with an arithmetic mean of - 3.2 percent.

The Intoxilyzer normally operates with a fixed blowing time and a minimum blowing pressure, corresponding to a minimum discard volume of approximately 2 litres, in order to operate the instrument. For higher BACs, underestimation of the BAC can occur because of this. The study of Noordzij (1975) contains information on 96 subjects tested on the Intoxilyzer. In contrast to normal operation, each subject was asked to continue blowing until the operator observed the maximum BAC-reading. Particularly for high BACs the results were obtained with discard volumes up to 3 litres. The correlation coefficient of the breath test results and the subsequent blood analyses was .985, the linear regression formula $y = 1.16 x - .066$, the standard error of estimate .08°/oo. In this study the correlation coefficient of results of blood samples from both arms was .995 with a standard deviation of .05°/oo.

(c) Gas Chromatograph Intoximeter GCI

Gas chromatography is a well known but complex analytic technique for organic compounds. The latest model of the GC-Intoximeter, the GCI Mark IV would appear to be a very simple instrument.

An evaluation carried out by Schmutte et al. (1972) showed a breath-blood correlation of 45 percent within 5 percent accuracy and 77 percent within 15 percent accuracy, leaving 23 percent beyond. The estimated arithmetic mean of blood-breath deviation was - 4.4 percent.

Harger (1974) reports that later studies of Morales (1974) with an improved type showed 34 percent within 5 percent accuracy and 90 percent within 15 percent accuracy, which indicates that the GCI is capable of yielding a better estimation of the BAC than was found by Schmutte et al.

In a study of Brenn et al. (1975) the GCI averaged .013 g./100 ml. lower than a direct blood analysis with a standard deviation of .014. The range of errors was from - .068 to + .30 g./100 ml., with 91 percent of the results showing a GCI-result equal to, or less than, its corresponding BAC. Presumably the 206 subjects in this study were suspected drunken drivers. The GCI can also be used in combination with a field collection kit.

LIST OF BREATH TESTING DEVICES AND LITERATURE

NAME AND MANUFACTURER   **LITERATURE**

1. Screening Tests

Chemical type

Alcotest
(Dräger, Western Germany)

- Bjerver, K., Andréasson, R., & Bonnichsen, R. (1966). A Field Study of the Use of "Alcotest" in Sweden. In: Harger, R.N. (Ed.), 1966.
- Cremers, H.T.P. (1968). Alcotest blaaspijpjes. Algemeen Politieblad, 117 (1968), N° 26: 612-613.
- Day, M., Muir, G.G., & Watling, I. (1968). Evaluation of Alcotest RSO Reagent Tubes. Nature, 219 (1968): 1050-1052.
- Dubowski, K.M. (1975). Recent Developments in Breath-Alcohol Analysis. In: Israelstam, S., & Lambert, S. (Eds), 1975.
- Froentjes (1968). Het bewijs van alcoholgebruik. In: Buikhuisen, W. (Ed.), 1968. Alcohol onder Verkeer; een studie over het rijden onder invloed. Boom, Meppel, 1968. Goldberg, L. & Bonnichsen, R. (1970). Bestämming av noggranheten i Alcotest-metoden och vissa andra utandningsmethoder. In: Trafiknykterhetsbrott, Statens offentli offentliga utredningar SOU 1970:61.
- Harger, R.N. (Ed.), 1966. Alcohol and Traffic Safety. Proceedings of the Fourth International Conference on Alcohol and Traffic Safety, Bloomington, December 6-10 1965. Indiana University, Bloomington, Indiana.
- Havard, J.D.J. (Ed.), 1963. Alcohol and Traffic. Proceedings of 3rd International Conference on Alcohol and Road Traffic. London, September 3-7, 1962. B.M.A. 1963.
- Israelstam, S. & Lambert, S. (Eds), 1975. Alcohol, Drugs and Traffic Safety. Proceedings of the Sixth International Conference on Alcohol, Drugs and Traffic Safety, Toronto, Sept. 8-13, 1974. Addiction Research Foundation of Ontario, Toronto, 1975.
- Leithoff, H. & Weyrich, G., 1959. Praktische Erfahrungen mit dem atem alkohol-Prüfröhrchen "Alcotest". Archiv für Kriminologie 123 (1959), N° 5, 6.
- Lereboullet, I. & Leluc, R. (1963). Le dosage de l'alcohol dans l'air expiré - sa valeur. In: Havard, J.D.J. (Ed.), 1963.
- Prouty, R.W., & O'Neill, B. (1971). An Evaluation of some Qualitative Breath Screening Tests for Alcohol, Research Report, May, 1971. Insurance Institute for Highway Safety, Washington, D.C., 1971.

Alcolyser (Lion Laboratories, Breat Britain)	- Goldberg, L., & Bonnichsen, R. (1970). - Dubowski, K.M. (1975). - Prouty, R.W. & O'Neill, B. (1971).
Alcomille (Etzlinger, Switzerland)	- Goldberg, L., & Bonnichsen, R. (1970).
Alcolor/Promillor (VEB East Germany)	- No reference available.
Pluralcol (Medicor Hungary)	- Nagy, J. (undated). The medico-legal aspects of acute ethyl alcohol poisoning. From: Horphologiai és Igarsagügyi orvosi szemle (Review of Morphology and Forensic Medicine (undated).
Detalcol (Czechoslovakia)	- No reference available.
Becton-Dickinson devices (Becton-Dickinson U.S.A.)	- Prouty, R.W., & O'Neill, B. (1971).
Kitagawa Drunk - O - Tester (Komo Company, Japan)	- Prouty, R.W., & O'Neill, B. (1971).
Sober-Meter (Luckey Laboratories, U.S.A.)	- Prouty, R.W., & O'Neill, B. (1971).

Electromechanical type

Alcolmeter/Alco-Sensor (Lion Laboratories, Great Britain)	- Jones, T.P., & Williams, P.M. (1972). Evaluation of the Alcolyser FCD (fuel-cell detector) for Breath Alcohol Analysis. Paper presented at the Sixth International Meeting of Forensic Sciences, Edinburgh, September, 1972. - Jacobs, W.B., & Goodson, L.M. (unpubl.). Evaluation of the Intoximeter Fuel-Cells for Breath Alcohol Testing. Report of Midwest Research Institute, Kansas City, Mo, to Intoximeters Inc., 1975. - Harriot, W.F. (1973). Status Report on Portable Breath Testers. Transportation Systems Center, U.S. Dept. of Transportation, Cambridge, Massachusetts, 1973. - Bailey, D.J. (unpublished). Evaluation of the Production Type Intoximeter Fuel-cell Alco-Sensors for Breath Alcohol Testing. Report of a Study at the University of Wales to Intoximeters Inc., 1973. - Noordzij, P.N. (1975). Comparison of Blood and Breath Testing under Field Conditions. In: Israelstam, S., & Lambert, S. (Eds), 1975. - Harger, R.N. (1974). Recently published analytical methods for determining alcohol in body materials - Alcohol Countermeasures Literature Review. Report DOT

HS-801 242, U.S. Dept. of Transportation, Washington, D.C., 1974.

- Moulden, J.V., & Voas, R.B. (1975). Breath Measurement Instrumentation in the U.S. Report DOT HS-801 621, U.S. Dept. of Transportation, Washington, D.C., 1975.

Alcohol Screening Device (ASD), Road Side Breath Tester

- Harriot, W.F. (1975).
- Harger, R.N. (1974).
- Noordzij, P.N. (1975).
- Moulden, J.V. & Voas, R.B. (1975).
- Alha, A., Laiho, F. & linnoila, M. (1975). Blood Alcohol in Breath Determined by ASD and in Blood by Widmark and ADH Methods. A Comparative Study Blutalkohol 12 (1975), 360-364.

A.L.E.R.T. (Borg-Warner U.S.A.)

- Dubowski, R.M. (1973). Studies in Breath-Alcohol Analysis: Evaluation of the Borg-Warner Breath-Alcohol Screening Device (model J24-1000) with respect to the specifications of the National Highway Traffic Safety Administration procurement request of August 30, 1973. University of Oklahoma College of Medicine, Oklahoma, 1973.
- Rosen, S.D., et al. (1974). Evaluation of portable breath test devices for screening suspected drunken drivers by police in Hennepin County, Minnesota. Report DOT HS-801 161, U.S. Department of Transportation, Washington, D.C., 1974.
- Picton, W.R. (1977). An evaluation of the alcohol level evaluation roadside tester (ALERT) under laboratory and field conditions. Paper presented to the Seventh International Conference on Alcohol, Drugs and Traffic Safety, Melbourne, 1977.
- Moulden, J.V. & Voas, R.B. (1975).

Aldet (Czechoslovakia)

- No reference available

Alco-Limiter (Energetics Science Inc., U.S.A.)

- Noordzij, P.N. (1975).
- Leavitt, W. et al. (1972). Evaluation of Energetics Science Inc. Alco-Limiter. Report of Transportation Systems Center, U.S. Dept. of Transportation, Cambridge, Mass., 1972.

Alcohalt (U.S.A.)

- No reference provided.

Breath Alcohol Tester (U.S.A.)

- No reference provided.

2. Evidential Testers

Ethanographe (Etzlinger, Switzerland)

- Cremers, H.T.P. (1969). De aethanograaf of wel vertaald: de alcohol schrijver- Algemeen Politieblad, 118 (1969)

N° 19, 457-459.
- Noordzij, P.N. (1975).

Alcolinger Automatic
(Etzlinger, Switzerland)

- Bonte, W., Phillipp, J.H. & Berg, S. (1970). Ergebnisse
  der Atemalkoholbestimmung mit dem Alcolinger Automatic
  in der Resorptionsphase. Blutalkohol 7 (1970), N° 6,
  454-462.
- Mebs, D., Geotze-Stelner, C. & Gerchow, J. (1975). Die
  Atemalkoholbestimmung mit dem Alcolinger Automatic.
  Blutalkohol 12 (1975), N° 5, 315-318.
- Monnier, D., Etzlinger, L. & Mussano, F. (1969). New
  Apparatus for the Determination of Breath Alcohol:
  Alcolinger Automatic. Alkohol und Verkehrssicherheit
  1969, II, 27-31.
- Noordzij, P.N. (1975).

Kitagawa-Wright/Hermes
(Great Britain)

- Wright, B.M. (1963). Breath Alcohol Analysis. In:
  Havard, J.D.J. (Ed.), 1963
- Begg, T.B., Hill, I.D. & Nickolls, L.C. (1973). A Sta-
  tistically Planned Comparison of Blood and Breath Alco-
  hol Methods. In: Havard, J.D.J. (Ed.), 1963.
- Begg, T.B., Hill, I.D. & Nickolls, L.C. (1964). Breath-
  alyzer and Kitagawa-Wright Methods of Measuring Breath
  Alcohol. British Medical Journal 1 (1964), 9-15.
- Goldberg, L. & Bonnichsen, R. (1970).
- Noordzij, P.N. (1975).

Breathalyzer (U.S.A.)

- Harger, R.N. (1974).
- Howes, J.R., Hallett, R.A. & Lucas, D.M. (1967). A
  study of the Accuracy of the Breathalyzer as Operated
  by Police Personnel, Journal of Forensic Sciences 12
  (1967), 444-453.
- Roberts, D.L. & Fletcher, D.C. (1969). A Comparative
  Study of Blood Alcohol Testing Devices. Rocky Mountain
  Med. J. 66, (1969), 37-39.
- Preston, W.L.K. (1969). The validity of the Breathalyzer.
  Med. J. Australia, I (1969), 286-289.
- Milner, G. & Landauer, A.A. (1971). Breathalyzer Faults:
  Principles and Practice. Med. J. Australia I (1971),
  1280-1284.
- Landauer, A.A. & Milner, G. (1971). The Breathalyzer
  Test and True Blood Alcohol Level. The Australian Law
  Journal 45 (1971), 360-362.
- Noordzij, P.N. (1975).
- Moulden, J.V. & Voas, R.B. (1975).

Intoxilyzer (U.S.A.)

- Harte, R.A. (1971). An Instrument for the Determination
  of Ethanol in Breath in Law Enforcement Practice -
  Journal of Forensic Science, 16 (1971), 493-510.

- Noordzij, P.N. (1975).
- Moulden, J.V. & Voas, R.B. (1975).
- Harger, R.N. (1974).

Gaschromatograph Intoximeter   - Penton, J.R. & Forrester, H.R. (1970). A Gaschromato-
GCI
graph Breath Analysis System with Provisions for Storage
and Delayed Analysis of Samples. In: Proceedings of the
Fifth International Conference on Alcohol and Traffic
Safety, Freiburg, W. Germany, September 22-27, 1969.
Hans Ferdinand Schulz Verlag, Freiburg im Breisgau,
W. Germany, 1970.
- Schmutte, P. et al. (1972). Comparative Studies of
Blood Alcohol and Breath Alcohol Concentrations with Gas
Chromatographic Breath Test (Intoximeter). Blutalkohol
9 (1972), 392-399.
- Morales, D.R. (1972, 1974). Summary of Activities
Relating to Evaluation of Instruments and Related
Accessories for Breath Alcohol Analysis.
Clinical Chemistry Laboratory, California State, Dept.
of the Alth. Report 1: 1972, Report 2: 1974.
- Harger, R.N. (1974).
- Moulden, J.V. & Voas, R.B. (1975).
- Breen, M.H., Siler, K.F. & Pearce, D.S. (1975). A Com-
parison between the Gas Chromatograph Intoximeter and a
Direct Blood Analysis. In: Israelstam, S. & Lambert,
S. (Eds), 1975.

Alcolmeter (Lion Laboratories, - Noorzij, P.N. (1975).
Great Britain)
- Jones, T.P., Jones, A.W. & Williams, P.M. (1977). A New
Method for the Rapid Analysis of Ethanol in Breath, Blood,
Urine and Saliva using the Alcolmeter Evidential Instru-
ment. Paper presented at the Seventh International
Conference on Alcohol, Drugs and Traffic Safety, Melbourne,
January 23-28, 1977.

Adrian Infrarot-Absorptions   - Adrian, (1977): Ein neues Gerät zur Blutalkoholbestimmung
photometer
über die Messung der Atemalkoholkonzentration. In:
Kongressbericht Jahrestagung 1977 der Deutschen Gesells-
chaft für Verkehrsmedizin e.V. Heidelberg. Unfall- und
Sicherheitsforschung Strassenverkehr, BAST, Heft 10,
Köln, 1977.

3. Remote Sampling

Alcolyser (Lion Laboratories   - Jones, T.P. (1970). Breath Alcohol Analysis with the
Great Britain)
"Alcolyser ADC" (Alcohol sample collector). In: Proceedings of the Fifth International Conference on Alcohol
and Traffic Safety, Freiburg, W. Germany, September 22-27,
1969. Hans Ferdinand Schulz Verlag, Freiburg im Breisgau,
W. Germany, 1970.

Breath Alcohol Indium   – Hoday, J. (unpublished). Chairman, Canadian Special
Tube Encapsulation   Committee on Breath Testing. Unpublished report to M.R.
                              Forrester.
                            – Harger, R.N. (1974).
                            – Morales, D.R. (1974)

4. <u>Breath Self Testers</u>

Alco-Meter
(O-Eight Electronics Ltd,
Canada)

A.L.A.R.M. (Alcohol Level
Awareness Reporting Mechanism)
(CEB Industries Inc., U.S.A.)

LIST OF MEMBERS OF THE GROUP

CHAIRMAN: Mr. G.A. Smith, Canada

AUSTRIA: Dr. Edeltraud Klebel
Kuratorium für Verkehrssicherheit
1031 Wien III
Olzeltgass 3

BELGIUM: Mlle Van Butseele
Conseiller adjoint - Secrétariat Général,
Ministère des Communications
62, rue de la Loi
1040 Bruxelles

M. de Coster
Directeur du Fonds d'études et de
recherches pour la sécurité routière
1405, Chaussée de Haecht
1130 Bruxelles

Major Muller
Directeur des opérations en matière de
circulation
Etat-Major de Gendarmerie
47, Rue F.-Toussaint
1050 Bruxelles

Dr. Vanoverschelde
Institut d'Hygiène et Epidemiologie
14, Rue Juliette Wytsman
1050 Bruxelles

CANADA: Mr. Barry Bragg
Department of Transport
Place de Ville
Transport Canada Building
Ottawa, Ontario KLA ON5

Mr. B. Cox
Chief, Research Secretariat
Research Bureau
Non-medical Use of Drugs Directorate
Dept. of National Health and Welfare
365, Laurier Ave. W.,
Ottawa, Ontario, KLA 1B6

Mr. I.W.D. Henderson
Non-medical Use of Drugs Directorate
Dept. of National Health and Welfare
365, Laurier Ave. W.,
Ottawa, Ontario KLA 1B6

Dr. Irving Rootman
Chief
Epidemiological Research
Non-medical Use of Drugs Directorate
Health Protection Branch
365, Laurier Ave. W.,
Ottawa, Ontario KLA 1B6

Mr. G.A. Smith
Psychologist
Road and Motor Vehicle Traffic Safety Branch
Ministry of Transport
Place de Ville
Transport Canada Building
Ottawa, Ontario KLA ON5

DENMARK:	Professor J.B. Dalgaard Retsmedicinsk Institute Finsensgade 15 DK-8000 Arhus C
	Mr. P. Lilholt Head of Section, Road Safety Division Ministry of Justice Købmagergade 48 DK-1150 Copenhagen K
FINLAND:	Mr. Markku Linnoila Tarkk'ampujankatu 9 A 14 00120 Helsinki 12
FRANCE:	Mlle Anne Le Gall Chargée de Mission Direction des Routes et de la Circulation Routière Pièce 256 Ministère de l'Equipement 244, BD. St-Germain 75007 Paris
	M. Jean l'Hoste O.N.S.E.R. B.P. 28 Avenue du Général Malleret-Joinville 94 Arcueil
	Mlle N. Neyroud O.N.S.E.R. B.P. 28 Avenue du Général Malleret-Joinville 94 Arcueil
	M. Monseur O.N.S.E.R. B.P. 28 Avenue du Général Malleret-Joinville 94 Arcueil
GERMANY:	Direktor und Professor Dr. Kroj Bundesanstalt für Strassenwesen 5 Köln 51 Brühlerstrasse
	Professor Dr. Med. Peter V. Lundt Consultant Ministry of Transport Rudesheimer Strasse 8 D-1000 Berlin (West)
NETHERLANDS:	Mr. P. Noordzij S.W.OVV. Deernsstraat 1 Voorburg
NORWAY:	Mr. Peter Christensen Research Engineer Institute for Transport Economy Stasjonsveien 4 Oslo 3
SWEDEN:	Mr. Hans Laurell Researcher National Swedish Road and Traffic Research Institute Fack 58101 Linköping

SWITZERLAND: Herr Dr. Phil. V. Hobi
                       University Psychiatric Hospital
                       4025 Basle
                       Wilhelm Klein Strasse 27

                       Prof. Dr. P. Kielholz
                       University Psychiatric Hospital
                       4025 Basle
                       Wilhelm Klein Strasse 27

                       Pd. Dr. D. Ladewig
                       University Psychiatric Hospital
                       4025 Basle
                       Wilhelm Klein Strasse 27

UNITED KINGDOM: Miss B.E. Sabey
                       Transport and Road Research Laboratory
                       Crowthorne, Berks RG11 6AU

                       Dr. G. Cahal
                       Department of Health and Social Security
                       16-18 Gresse Street
                       London W1P 1BB

UNITED STATES: Professor Herbert Moskowitz, Ph.D.
                       Psychology Department
                       University of California
                       Los Angeles
                       California 90024

                       Mr. James L. Nichols
                       U.S. Department of Transportation
                       NATC Highway Traffic Safety
                       400 7th St. SW RM5319
                       Washington D.C. 20590

                       Professor M.W. Perrine
                       B.M. Alcohol Institute
                       London WC1V 6XX

                       Dr. Robert B. Voas
                       Chief, Demonstration Evaluation Division
                       National Highway Traffic Safety Administration
                       Washington D.C. 20590

EEC: Mr. E. Levi
                       Commission of the European Community
                       CCR
                       21020 Ispra

WHO: Dr. C.J. Romer, M.D.
                       Medical Officer
                       Development of Community Services
                       8 Scherfigsvej
                       DK-2100 Copenhagen

OECD
SECRETARIAT: Dr. W. Diewald
                       Mme E. Fruton
                       Mr. B. Horn

LIST OF PUBLICATIONS OF THE ROAD RESEARCH PROGRAMME

Road Safety

Alcohol and drugs (January 1968)
Pedestrian safety (October 1969)
Driver behaviour (June 1970)
Proceedings of the symposium on the use of statistical methods in the analysis of
 road accidents (September 1970)
Lighting, visibility and accidents (March 1971)
Research into road safety at junctions in urban areas (October 1971)
Road safety campaigns: design and evaluation (December 1971)
Speed limits outside built-up areas (August 1972)
Research on traffic law enforcement (April 1974)
Young driver accidents (March 1975)
Roadside obstacles (August 1975)
Manual on road safety campaigns (September 1975)
Polarized light for vehicle headlamps (December 1975)
Driver instruction (March 1976)
Adverse Weather, Reduced Visibility and Road Safety (August 1976)
Hazardous Road Locations: Identification and Countermeasures (September 1976)

Road Traffic and Urban Transport

Electronic aids for freeway operation (April 1971)
Area traffic control systems (February 1972)
Optimisation of bus operation in urban areas (May 1972)
Two lane rural roads: road design and traffic flow (July 1972)
Traffic operation at sites of temporary obstruction (February 1973)
Effects of traffic and roads on the environment in urban areas (July 1973)
Proceedings of the symposium on techniques of improving urban conditions by
 restraint of road traffic (September 1973)
Capacity of at-grade junctions (November 1974)
Proceedings of the symposium on roads and the urban environment (October 1975)
Urban traffic models: Possibilities for simplification (August 1974)
Research on traffic corridor control (November 1975)
Bus lanes and busway systems (April 1977)
Transport requirements for urban communities - planning for personal
 travel (December 1977)
Integrated urban traffic management (December 1977)
Energy problems and urban and suburban transport (December 1977)

Road Construction and Maintenance

Research on crash barriers (February 1969)
Motor vehicle corrosion and influence of de-icing chemicals (October 1969)
Winter damage to road pavements (May 1972)
Accelerated methods of life-testing pavements (May 1972)
Proceedings of the symposium on the quality control of road works (July 1972)
Waterproofing of concrete bridge decks (July 1972)
Optimisation of road alignment by the use of computers (July 1973)
Water in roads: prediction of moisture content in road subgrades (August 1973)
Maintenance of rural roads (August 1973)
Water in roads: methods for determining soil moisture content and pore water
 tension (December 1973)
Proceedings of the symposium on frost action on roads (October 1974)
Road marking and delineation (February 1975)
Resistance of flexible pavements to plastic deformation (June 1975)
Bridge inspection (July 1976)
Road strengthening (September 1976)
Proceedings of the symposium on geometric road design standards (May 1977)
Use of waste materials and by-products in road construction (September 1977)

OECD SALES AGENTS
DÉPOSITAIRES DES PUBLICATIONS DE L'OCDE

ARGENTINA — ARGENTINE
Carlos Hirsch S.R.L., Florida 165,
BUENOS-AIRES, Tel. 33-1787-2391 Y 30-7122

AUSTRALIA — AUSTRALIE
International B.C.N. Library Suppliers Pty Ltd.,
161 Sturt St., South MELBOURNE, Vic. 3205. Tel. 699-6388
P.O.Box 202, COLLAROY, NSW 2097. Tel. 982 4515

AUSTRIA — AUTRICHE
Gerold and Co., Graben 31, WIEN 1. Tel. 52.22.35

BELGIUM — BELGIQUE
Librairie des Sciences,
Coudenberg 76-78, B 1000 BRUXELLES 1. Tel. 512-05-60

BRAZIL — BRÉSIL
Mestre Jou S.A., Rua Guaipá 518,
Caixa Postal 24090, 05089 SAO PAULO 10. Tel. 261-1920
Rua Senador Dantas 19 s/205-6, RIO DE JANEIRO GB.
Tel. 232-07. 32

CANADA
Renouf Publishing Company Limited,
2182 St. Catherine Street West,
MONTREAL, Quebec H3H 1M7 Tel. (514) 937-3519

DENMARK — DANEMARK
Munksgaards Boghandel,
Nørregade 6, 1165 KØBENHAVN K. Tel. (01) 12 69 70

FINLAND — FINLANDE
Akateeminen Kirjakauppa
Keskuskatu 1, 00100 HELSINKI 10. Tel. 625.901

FRANCE
Bureau des Publications de l'OCDE,
2 rue André-Pascal, 75775 PARIS CEDEX 16. Tel. 524.81.67
Principal correspondant :
13602 AIX-EN-PROVENCE : Librairie de l'Université.
Tel. 26.18.08

GERMANY — ALLEMAGNE
Verlag Weltarchiv G.m.b.H.
D 2000 HAMBURG-36, Neuer Jungfernstieg 21.
Tel. 040-35-62-500

GREECE — GRÈCE
Librairie Kauffmann, 28 rue du Stade,
ATHÈNES 132. Tel. 322.21.60

HONG-KONG
Government Information Services,
Sales and Publications Office, Beaconsfield House, 1st floor,
Queen's Road, Central.   Tel. H-233191

ICELAND — ISLANDE
Snaebjörn Jónsson and Co., h.f.,
Hafnarstraeti 4 and 9, P.O.B. 1131, REYKJAVIK.
Tel. 13133/14281/11936

INDIA — INDE
Oxford Book and Stationery Co.:
NEW DELHI, Scindia House. Tel. 45896
CALCUTTA, 17 Park Street. Tel.240832

IRELAND - IRLANDE
Eason and Son, 40 Lower O'Connell Street,
P.O.B. 42, DUBLIN 1. Tel. 74 39 35

ISRAËL
Emanuel Brown: 35 Allenby Road, TEL AVIV. Tel. 51049/54082
also at:
9, Shlomzion Hamalka Street, JERUSALEM. Tel. 234807
48, Nahlath Benjamin Street, TEL AVIV. Tel. 53276

ITALY — ITALIE
Libreria Commissionaria Sansoni:
Via Lamarmora 45, 50121 FIRENZE. Tel. 579751
Via Bartolini 29, 20155 MILANO. Tel. 365083
Sub-depositari:
Editrice e Libreria Herder,
Piazza Montecitorio 120, 00 186 ROMA. Tel. 674628
Libreria Hoepli, Via Hoepli 5, 20121 MILANO. Tel. 865446
Libreria Lattes, Via Garibaldi 3, 10122 TORINO. Tel. 519274
La diffusione delle edizioni OCSE è inoltre assicurata dalle migliori
librerie nelle città più importanti.

JAPAN — JAPON
OECD Publications Center,
Akasaka Park Building, 2-3-4 Akasaka, Minato-ku,
TOKYO 107. Tel. 586-2016

KOREA - CORÉE
Pan Korea Book Corporation,
P.O.Box n° 101 Kwangwhamun, SÉOUL. Tel. 72-7369

LEBANON — LIBAN
Documenta Scientifica/Redico,
Edison Building, Bliss Street, P.O.Box 5641, BEIRUT.
Tel. 354429—344425

MEXICO & CENTRAL AMERICA
Centro de Publicaciones de Organismos Internacionales S.A.,
Av. Chapultepec 345, Apartado Postal 6-981
MEXICO 6, D.F. Tel. 533-45-09

THE NETHERLANDS — PAYS-BAS
Staatsuitgeverij
Chr. Plantijnstraat
'S-GRAVENHAGE. Tel. 070-814511
Voor bestillingen: Tel. 070-624551

NEW ZEALAND — NOUVELLE-ZÉLANDE
The Publications Manager,
Government Printing Office,
WELLINGTON: Mulgrave Street (Private Bag),
World Trade Centre, Cubacade, Cuba Street,
Rutherford House, Lambton Quay, Tel. 737-320
AUCKLAND: Rutland Street (P.O.Box 5344), Tel. 32.919
CHRISTCHURCH: 130 Oxford Tce (Private Bag), Tel. 50.331
HAMILTON: Barton Street (P.O.Box 857), Tel. 80.103
DUNEDIN: T & G Building, Princes Street (P.O.Box 1104),
Tel. 78.294

NORWAY — NORVÈGE
Johan Grundt Tanums Bokhandel,
Karl Johansgate 41/43, OSLO 1. Tel. 02-332980

PAKISTAN
Mirza Book Agency, 65 Shahrah Quaid-E-Azam, LAHORE 3.
Tel. 66839

PHILIPPINES
R.M. Garcia Publishing House, 903 Quezon Blvd. Ext.,
QUEZON CITY, P.O.Box 1860 — MANILA. Tel. 99.98.47

PORTUGAL
Livraria Portugal, Rua do Carmo 70-74, LISBOA 2. Tel. 360582/3

SPAIN — ESPAGNE
Mundi-Prensa Libros, S.A.
Castelló 37, Apartado 1223, MADRID-1. Tel. 275.46.55
Libreria Bastinos, Pelayo, 52, BARCELONA 1. Tel. 222.06.00

SWEDEN — SUÈDE
AB CE Fritzes Kungl Hovbokhandel,
Box 16 356, S 103 27 STH, Regeringsgatan 12,
DS STOCKHOLM. Tel. 08/23 89 00

SWITZERLAND — SUISSE
Librairie Payot, 6 rue Grenus, 1211 GENÈVE 11. Tel. 022-31.89.50

TAIWAN — FORMOSE
National Book Company,
84-5 Sing Sung Rd., Sec. 3, TAIPEI 107. Tel. 321.0698

UNITED KINGDOM — ROYAUME-UNI
H.M. Stationery Office, P.O.B. 569,
LONDON SEI 9 NH. Tel. 01-928-6977, Ext. 410
or
49 High Holborn, LONDON WC1V 6 HB (personal callers)
Branches at: EDINBURGH, BIRMINGHAM, BRISTOL,
MANCHESTER, CARDIFF, BELFAST.

UNITED STATES OF AMERICA
OECD Publications Center, Suite 1207, 1750 Pennsylvania Ave.,
N.W. WASHINGTON, D.C.20006. Tel.   (202)724-1857

VENEZUELA
Libreria del Este, Avda. F. Miranda 52, Edificio Galipán,
CARACAS 106. Tel. 32 23 01/33 26 04/33 24 73

YUGOSLAVIA — YOUGOSLAVIE
Jugoslovenska Knjiga, Terazije 27, P.O.B. 36, BEOGRAD.
Tel. 621-992

Les commandes provenant de pays où l'OCDE n'a pas encore désigné de dépositaire peuvent être adressées à :
OCDE, Bureau des Publications, 2 rue André-Pascal, 75775 PARIS CEDEX 16.
Orders and inquiries from countries where sales agents have not yet been appointed may be sent to:
OECD, Publications Office, 2 rue André-Pascal, 75775 PARIS CEDEX 16.